Young People's Guide to Classical Music

Young People's Guide to Classical Music

HELEN BAUER

AMADEUS PRESS

Amadeus Press
An Imprint of Hal Leonard Corporation | New York

Copyright © 2009 by Helen Bauer

Published in 2009 by Amadeus Press
An Imprint of Hal Leonard Corporation
7777 West Bluemound Road
Milwaukee, WI 53213

Trade Book Division Editorial Offices
19 West 21st Street, New York, NY 10010

Illustration credits can be found on pages 269–270, which constitute an extension of this copyright page.

Every reasonable effort has been made to contact copyright holders and secure permission. Any omissions brought to our attention will be remedied in future editions.

Printed in the United States of America
Book design by Kristina Rolander

Bauer, Helen, 1943-
   A guide to classical music for young people / Helen Bauer. -- 1st paperback ed.
        p. cm.
   Includes bibliographical references and index.
   ISBN 978-1-57467-181-0 (alk. paper)
   1. Music--Instruction and study. 2. Music--History and criticism. 3. Music appreciation. 4. Composers. I. Title.
   MT6.B259G8 2009
   780--dc22
                              2009043302

www.amadeuspress.com

To all young people who enjoy music,
with a special dedication to
two very talented young ladies:
Julia and Jeanie

Contents

Introduction

Perhaps you are just starting to learn how to play an instrument, have joined a band, an orchestra, or a chorus, or simply want to know more about the basics of music and its history. Classical music is a vast subject to be studied; people spend their entire lives examining how the sounds of a piece of music function together and why they were structured in that particular way by the composer. The words used by musicians express and define the many unique qualities found in music. The theory of music investigates the elements that create music and develops the ability to recognize, understand, and describe the fundamental materials and processes of music. Music history traces the beginnings and progress of musical ideas and innovations through the centuries.

While keeping in mind that all music is to be enjoyed and the study of music should not be a burden, I have written this manual in order to present the fundamental concepts of music and to explain classical music structure and design in a basic, uncomplicated manner. This book is intended as a guide to help you become acquainted with the common terms and expressions used in Western classical music, as well as some of the theory, historical trends, composers, and background that led to these developments.

It does take some intense concentration to distinguish one specific instrument playing in a large orchestra or to be able to detect the progression of chords as a composition modulates to another key. This skill is best left to people in the music professions or serious students of classical music and is not the concern of this guide. The more you know about a subject, though, the more you can appreciate its beauty and brilliance. When you are comfortable with the material that is presented in this book and wish to continue to further your knowledge, hopefully you will explore the marvelous field of music in greater depth.

The word "Opus" indicates a number assigned by the composer or a publisher to identify the chronological order of the composition or the publication of a musical work. Opus is often abbreviated Op. (plural: Opera, abbreviated Opp.). In the past, publishers did not always provide a dependable chronology of a composer's works. The word "Köchel" refers to Ludwig Ritter von Köchel (1800–1877), who catalogued Mozart's music. A K. or KV followed by a number when indicating one of Mozart's compositions signifies Köchel's catalog numbers for Mozart's works.

Acknowledgments

This book would not be possible without the assistance and input of many people. I am indebted to my teachers at the High School of Music and Art and Hunter College, who provided me with the ability to appreciate classical music in all of its dimensions. To my friend Mali Vishnevsky, a classical guitarist living in Israel, whose email encouragement was very helpful: *todah rabah*. Susan Silberman, my talented friend, supplied her support and graphic artwork. Also, I am grateful to Anne Devlin, my literary agent, who diligently promoted this book. Heartfelt thanks to John Cerullo and the staff at Amadeus Press, who made this all possible. Lastly, I would like to thank my personal computer guru and dearest friend, my husband, Edward Bauer.

1 The Development of Music

*After silence, that which comes nearest
to expressing the inexpressible is music.*

ALDOUS HUXLEY, ENGLISH WRITER (1894–1963)

Music is an art form that can lift you to great heights. It can awaken all of your senses and emotions. Music is one of the ways individuals communicate with each other. It is an outgrowth of the need for individual and group expression. Reacting to music is a natural response; all cultures, throughout time, have developed their own musical forms, melodies, rhythms, and instruments. The most natural form of music is song, which is created when spoken words are given musical tones for expression. People throughout history have created songs that reflect all of the things that are important in their lives. There are work songs, love songs, lullabies, folk songs, religious songs, patriotic songs, songs that tell a story, and songs that are used in times of sorrow. These songs can be found in every country.

Dance also requires an element of music: in order to dance there must be, at least, a rhythm that establishes the speed and nature of the movements. Dance is also a natural outgrowth of the need for expression. Throughout human history, people have used dance to express themselves, to celebrate an event, or as part of a religious ceremony. Rhythm and melody are the foundations of music.

Music in Ancient Civilizations

Most likely, the first musical instruments were parts of the human body—creating vocal sounds, clapping hands, slapping body parts, and stamping feet. A natural outgrowth of this would have been striking stones together or beating sticks on a log to create sounds. This gave rise to the addition of rattles, clappers, and crude drums, which improved the effect. Prehistoric societies fashioned instruments to produce music. In an article for the *National Geographic News* entitled "Stone Age Art Caves May Have Been Concert Halls," Ker Than reported that "instruments such as bone flutes and 'roarers'—bone and ivory instruments that whir rhythmically when spun—have been found in decorated caves."

Pictures of prehistoric instruments have been found on the walls of caves. In Slovenia, Ivan Turk, of the Slovenian Academy of Sciences, recently unearthed what he believes is a flute made by Neanderthal people from the bone of a cave bear about 50,000 years ago. Archeologists also have discovered flutes made of bone, reeds made of bamboo, horns made of bone and tusk, and drums made of stretched animal skins. Music had an important role in ancient civilizations; the myths and traditions of early people assumed that music had divine powers.

During the time of the pharaohs in ancient Egypt, music was considered an important element of any event, and a high value was placed on musicianship. From the wall paintings found in the pyramids and other forms of burial chambers we have learned that flutes, sistrums (a sort of rattle), tambourines, tambours (small drums), and lyres (hand-held harps) were commonly used in various religious ceremonies and during celebrations. Inscriptions of songs have been found in tombs. Some types of work were accompanied by music. Music was used in war as well: the Egyptian army marched to the sounds of the trumpet and drums.

Certain Egyptian gods were specifically associated with music: Hathor was the goddess of music, love, and beauty, and Bes was the god of music and dance. The god Osiris was credited with inventing the trumpet and therefore was frequently worshiped to the sound of trumpets. The Egyptians constructed their own harps that were played in the temples by the priests. There is a seven-foot-tall Egyptian harp on display at the New York Metropolitan Museum of Art.

The people of ancient Egypt also employed professional musicians: temple musicians were often assigned as the musicians of a particular god or goddess, the royal household contained musicians, and musicians were hired as entertainers at festivals and parties. Pythagoras (c. 582–507 BCE), a Greek mathematician who grew up in Egypt, created a musical theory based on relationships between musical notes that could be expressed in numerical ratios.

Music played a central role in the lives of the Greeks. It was an important feature of religious festivals and social events. Education in music was an important ingredient in the training of the upper class; both women and men of this privileged class were taught to play musical instruments. Amateur achievements in music were recognized as signs of refinement and good taste. The Greeks believed that music was a powerful tool and had an impact on people; they associated specific instruments with certain deities. They also devised a system of musical notation. Some fragments of the Greek method of notation have been found but very little has survived over the centuries.

Apollo holding a kithara

The Greeks enjoyed a wide range of musical instruments, but three were favored: the kithara, the aulos, and the lyre. The lyre was introduced by the Greeks. Some scholars believe that the name "guitar" was derived from the Greek *kithara*, also spelled *cithara*. The instrument was associated with the sun god, Apollo; it belonged to the lyre family and originally had four or more strings made of sinew or gut that were stretched from a holder at the base of the instrument over a flat bridge to the crossbar that joined the two side pieces. It had a hollow sounding box. A sling was wrapped around the left wrist to help keep the kithara in place, and the instrument rested on the performer's shoulder. A small flat tool, called a plectrum, was used to pluck the strings, and the player usually stood while performing. The kithara was used during religious festivals and concerts, and professional kithara performers often entered competitions as well. Sophocles, the Greek dramatist, was well-known as a kithara player.

Aulos player

The ancient Greek version of the pipe called the aulos (plural: auloi) had either a single or a double reed and only four or five finger holes, and most often two were played at the same time. This instrument was identified with Dionysus, the god of wine. The aulos was frequently employed to accompany lyric passages in the Greek tragedies. The Romans added more finger holes and metal bands, which allowed the aulos to be tuned and gave it a greater range. The aulos probably sounded something like the present-day oboe. The aulos was known by many different names; until the early Middle Ages it was the major wind instrument of the people of the Middle East and Europe.

Another ancient Greek instrument was the lyre, which was believed to have been invented by the god Apollo. The lyre was also popular in Egypt and Sumeria.

In Greece the lyre was the instrument of choice for amateur musicians. This stringed instrument was like a small harp; its hollow base was usually covered with animal hide. The arms, made of wood or horn, were attached to the base and connected at the top with a stick. Strings, usually made of animal sinew or gut, were stretched to reach from the base to the stick and could be played using a plectrum or plucked by the fingers. The number of strings varied from just three to as many as twelve.

The biblical King David playing a harp

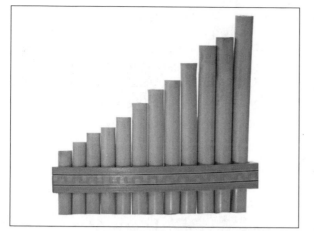

Panpipes

Panpipes or pan flutes, also called syrinx, were other instruments that the ancient Greeks believed had been invented by the gods. Panpipes were associated with the pastoral god Pan. These instruments were constructed of ten or more bamboo, reed, or cane tubes of the same or different lengths and arranged in a row that could be either straight or curved. The pipes were generally closed at the bottom and held together by a string or wax. When blown across the top, each pipe produced a different pitch. Pan flutes of various forms have been found in archaeological digs.

The Odeion, a covered amphitheater, was constructed in Athens, Greece, during the second half of the fifth century BCE—a sign of the importance of music and drama in Greek culture. This theater had seating for an audience of 1,400. The Greek theaters had excellent acoustic qualities, which allowed the words of the tragedies and comedies that were performed there to be heard clearly by the audiences.

Greek hydraulis

A Greek engineer named Ctesibius developed the first keyboard instrument: a water organ known as a hydraulis. The popular Greek hydraulis was quickly adopted by the Romans, who played it in theaters, at festivals, and in their amphitheaters. It became the favorite instrument of the Romans and of their emperors. Ancient references to the hydraulis and the remaining pictures of it indicate that the instrument was constructed in various types and sizes.

The ancient Hebrews also employed music in both religious and secular settings. Several instruments are mentioned in the Bible: the tambourine or timbrel; cymbals; the tof (a small drum); the ugab (a flute); the hasosra (a trumpet); the chalil (a pipe); the kinnor (a stringed instrument); the harp or lyre (which King David played); and the shofar (the horn of a ram or a goat). Exodus 15:20 states, "Miriam the Prophetess, the sister of Aaron, took the tambourine in her hand, and the women followed her with tambourines and cymbals." The biblical account of Jericho's destruction, found in Joshua 6:1–27, describes how the walls of Jericho were shattered when a shofar was blown as a call to battle.

Shofar

Music played an important role in the ancient Temple services; large numbers of musicians were employed in the greater Temple service, and the instruments they played were most likely the kinnor, the nevel (a big harp), the psaltery (another type of harp), and cymbals. Instrumental music was employed to celebrate festive occasions. A method of hand signals was developed to lead the chant during prayers. After the destruction of the Temple, these signals became the source for the development of a system of written musical notation, called *te'amim* in Hebrew or tropes in English, which uses symbolic representation calling for a specific sequence of notes that instruct the reader to apply a certain chant to the words during biblical readings.

Chinese music is as ancient as Chinese civilization. A 1999 article by Henry Fountain in the magazine *Nature* reported that archaeologists in China had discovered what is thought to be the oldest still-playable musical instrument: a 9,000-year-old flute carved from the wing bone of a crane. Over 5,000 years ago Chinese melodies were performed on hand-held bells, drums, tuned chimes, and flutes. Confucius, a great Chinese philosopher (551–479 BCE), observed that music is vital to maintaining order in the universe and in society. During the Zhou dynasty (about 1027–256 BCE) the sons of princes and noblemen considered the study of music an essential part of their schooling. The emperor Han Wudi, who reigned from 140 to 87 BCE and is considered to be one of the wisest of the Chinese emperors, created a music bureau called Yuefu to collect songs for ceremonial events.

Gregorian Chant

During the sixth century the Catholic Church began using what is known as Gregorian chant or plainsong. Gregorian chant was based upon the ancient prayers chanted during Jewish worship services in the Temple and in the synagogues. Plainsong also absorbed influences from the Greek and Syrian musical traditions. Employed in the Catholic liturgy (public religious worship), the simplest form of this chant is monophonic (a single vocal line), that is, a single melody without any type of harmonic accompaniment. Gregorian chant consists of a free-flowing melodic line that follows the words of the text; in effect, it is a form of musical speech.

Over the centuries different forms of chant began to develop in the various parts of Europe; these chants were composed and preserved in monasteries. Pope Gregory the Great, who was in office from 590 to 604, assembled the different forms of plainsong and then selected, revised, and ordered the various texts and chants. They were then recorded in a liturgical book called an antiphonary, which allowed Gregorian chant to be transmitted to other countries. Most Western European church liturgy was based on the work accomplished by Pope Gregory. Plainsong was unaccompanied since, in the early days of the church, instruments were not permitted to be used during worship services. Over hundreds of years the original melodies of Gregorian chant were altered and regular rhythms and harmonies were added, completely changing the sound and flavor of this music.

For centuries chants could only be transmitted orally or by a system of neumes, which were basic marks that could not indicate exact pitches or rhythms. An

Italian Benedictine monk, Guido d'Arezzo, observed that the lack of a system for writing down liturgical melodies had resulted in tremendous confusion. His theoretical work *Micrologus*, written between 1025 and 1033, explains his method of using a staff in order to clearly indicate the exact relationship between pitches. He also employed syllables as a device for singing musical pitches. This form of musical notation began to be used during the Middle Ages. Guido d'Arezzo's concepts of musical syllables and the basis of his system of a four-line staff were revolutionary steps in the development of music theory and notation.

Gregorian chant notation

The patterns of the melodies used in Gregorian chant were classified by modes. There are eight modes, which correspond to the white keys of a piano; they gradually evolved into our major and minor scales. Harmony developed during the early part of the Middle Ages, and modal harmony refers to the type of melody and harmony used at that time. Modal is often contrasted with tonal. Tonal music is based on the major/minor system and its harmonic structures, such as chords and key changes, create functional harmony (so called because each chord has a function or purpose), while modal music is not actually in a key and modal harmony is not functional.

Advances in Music

The church modes became the foundation of European art music. During the Romanesque period, from about 850 to 1150, polyphony arose. Polyphony is the ability to perform several musical lines together, and its development was due to the establishment of definite rhythmic patterns. This was the most vital development in the history of Western music because polyphony added depth to a musical work. Since music must be written so that the performers can know which pitches and rhythms are to be played, the evolution of the staff had a major role in this emergence. Composers were able to write down their scores. Now the minstrels and troubadours could harmonize their secular songs in the courts, and church choirs could add depth to their sound. A piece of written music could promptly be read by many musicians, and instruments could provide an accompaniment with harmony.

As the centuries passed, all of the advances in music led to what we can hear and enjoy today. Music was thrust out of the realm of the mystical and religious world into the secular. The function of music in society changed, and the ability to perform music became more universal. Improvements continued in the creation and refinement of instruments, the ability to transmit musical works, and the availability of music to the public.

Today technology has been able to create new methods of creating the sounds that we call music. Electronic equipment produces sounds using different tones and pitches. Electronic music is produced by electronic processing through an electronic instrument, a tape recorder, or a computer and involves the use of loudspeakers. One of the first electronic instruments was the theremin, invented by the Russian Léon Theremin in 1917. This instrument has no keyboard; instead, it translates hand movements into sounds.

Theremin

Moog control panel

In the mid-1960s Robert Moog introduced the first commercially available synthesizer. The introduction of the Moog synthesizer started an electronic music boom and revolutionized modern music; the synthesizer offered musicians a revolutionary new way to produce sound.

Musical Instrument Digital Interface, known as MIDI, is a protocol that allows electronic musical instruments, computers, and any other necessary equipment to communicate so that they can create music. Computers and cell phones can play MIDI files. Electronic musical instruments are now widely used in many styles of music. Many rock bands utilize synthesizers to create particular electronic sounds. Sometimes the electronic instruments are combined with conventional instruments while other composers use only electronic means to create their work. The development of new electronic musical instruments continues to be a highly active and interesting field of research.

2 Reading Music

Music expresses that which cannot be put into words and that which cannot remain silent.

VICTOR HUGO, FRENCH WRITER (1802–1885)

Music Notation: Staff, Clef, Key Signature, Tone, and Notes

Classical music has both a language and a culture. As different forms of classical music developed, the terms used to describe and communicate that culture increased and expanded. Learning about music requires an understanding of these words and phrases because they are used so often, either to describe something technical such as directions, tempos, or dynamics or in a discussion about music. Music notation is how music is expressed in writing; it presents a type of graph for the musician to follow. Learning how to read the symbols and notes that communicate the musical ideas is not difficult, but it is challenging.

Musical notation has developed over hundreds of years, and it is still expanding and increasing. Over time, the system of notation has been adapted to meet the requirements of composers and musicians; it continues to be adapted to the needs of modern musicians. It is not a perfect system; however, it is a practical and accurate method.

A staff

Treble clef

Bass clef

To understand how to read music we must begin with how it is presented on paper. Today, Western music is based on a five-line staff. A staff is the framework upon which the notes are written. There are five lines and four spaces on a staff. Each line and each space is associated with a note.

Each staff has a clef indicated at the beginning of a staff (plural: staves). The word "clef" comes from the Latin word *clavis*, which means "key." The clefs are a key to the musical code written on the staff. The clef states the pitch (highness or lowness of sound) of the notes. High sounds are written on a treble clef, also called a G clef because the G clef circles the second line of the staff, which is the note G above middle C. This clef is used by instruments of a higher range and by the right-hand part in piano music.

Low sounds are written on a bass clef; it is also known as the F clef because the two dots indicate that the fourth line is the note F below middle C. This clef is used by instruments of a lower range and by the left-hand part in piano music.

A staff that has the treble-clef line and the bass-clef line joined together is a grand staff.

Besides these two main clefs there is the alto clef, which is a type of C clef; however, it is rare to see a C clef in music today, except in music for certain instruments of middle range such as the trombone, viola, and cello. The C clef is movable: that is, the symbol for this clef establishes middle C on whichever staff line it is centered on.

Treble, alto, and bass are also types of singing voices. The clef indicated on a staff gives us a good idea whether the music was written for a high voice (treble), a medium voice (alto), or a low voice (bass).

For instruments that have no specific pitch, like percussion instruments, there is a neutral clef that does not indicate pitch. The number of lines can vary in a neutral clef, and each line may represent a specific percussion instrument within a set.

Grand staff

C clef

Neutral clef

Key of C major

Key of A major

Key of F major

The key signature tells the tone in which the music was written. The key signature is placed at the beginning of the staff. The key signature informs you which notes in the music will be sharp (♯) or flat (♭); it takes the place of indicating each note that is sharp or flat in the line of notation. When a sharp or flat appears in the key signature, all the notes on that line or space are sharp or flat. The key provides the guide for a particular piece of music; it controls and determines the tune and its harmonies. There are twelve major keys and twelve minor keys. For example, C major has no sharps or flats, A major has three sharps, F major has one flat, and so on.

Composers often change keys to create variety, drama, or tension in a piece of music; the tension can then be resolved by returning to the home or tonic key, or the basic key in which a piece of music is written. Passing from one key to another is called modulation. Music can also be transposed from one key to another. The pitch will differ, and so will the number of sharps and flats, when a tune is shifted into another key by transposition. Music is transposed in order to accommodate a voice that would be more comfortable in a lower or higher range than the one in which the piece is written, or to adjust a piece of music to suit a particular instrument's range.

Players of all instruments used in Western music read music in the same way. Middle C is called middle C no matter what instrument is being played, but middle C does not sound the same on all instruments; for that reason we transpose music for certain instruments and sometimes for voices. Most instruments are C instruments—that is, their middle Cs all sound the same—but others require transposing. Transposing means playing or singing music in a key other than the key written on the sheet music. Instruments that transpose are often referred to as being in a certain key, such as the B-flat (B♭) clarinet. The clarinetist seeing a C written on the score will play a note that sounds like a B♭. The clarinet is therefore called a B-flat instrument. Sometimes music is transposed to make it easier to read; for example, a piece written in a key with lots of sharps or flats is more difficult for a new musician than a piece written in a key with fewer sharps or flats. Most professional musicians can transpose music as they read it.

Music is made of tones, also called notes. A tone is a sound of specific and distinct pitch, quality, and duration. Music is an art that organizes tones into patterns. You can consider each tone as a sound step in a chain. We hear the tones in relationship to each other. A musical interval is the difference in pitch between two musical tones. The interval of a whole step, also called a whole tone, is made up of two half steps. Whole steps occur between the notes A and B, C and D, D and E, F and G, and G and A. The black keys on a piano keyboard are grouped together in alternating groups of two and three. The note C is the white note just to the left of each group of two black notes.

Middle C on a piano

Music is written in special symbols called notes. Each note has a special property that is its pitch or sound. Notes follow the alphabet as they ascend, starting from the letter A and going up to G, then reverse when they descend.

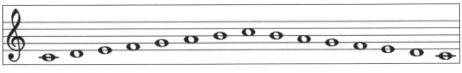

The C major scale

A half step, also known as a semitone, is a musical interval. It is the smallest interval notated and is played in most of the music that we hear. It corresponds to the interval sounded by striking two adjacent keys on a piano: either one white key and its neighboring black key, or two white keys where there is no intermediate black key. A piano keyboard does not have a black key between the notes B and C or between the notes E and F; therefore, the pitch interval between B and C, or between E and F, is a half step.

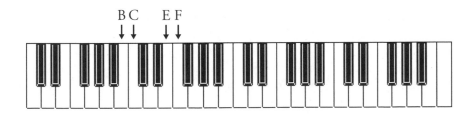

Melody, Motif, Theme, and Duration

When tones of different pitches are arranged together to form a pattern the result is called a melody. A song is an example of melody. A melody is a musical line; sometimes it is called a tune, a voice, an air, or a melodic line. Melody is a basic component of music. Often you may want to hum or whistle a melody that especially appeals to you.

A theme is a musical passage that states an idea; it is the melody or the subject of a musical work. A theme is often used to propel a work to drive forward. Often, a theme is the musical line that we remember and which appeals to us. A phrase is a small section of a composition containing a musical thought. It is a short musical idea.

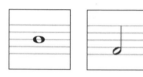

Whole note

Half note

Quarter note

Eighth note

Sixteenth note

Thirty-second note

Sixty-fourth note

Flagged note

A theme can be further broken down into a motif or motive. A motif is a melodic or rhythmic unit that acts as a major building block in the musical structure and is often repeated throughout a piece of music. A motif may be of any length but is usually fairly short. A musical composition may contain several motifs that are played with and against each other.

The length of time a note is sounded is called the duration. It is indicated by the way the note is written. There is a mathematical system for expressing the duration, or time value, of the notes relative to each other. Whole notes can be divided into half notes, quarter notes, eighth notes, and so on. One whole note equals 2 half notes, 4 quarter notes, 8 eighth notes, or 16 sixteenth notes. When a whole note receives 4 beats, a half note receives 2 beats, and a quarter note receives 1 beat. The quarter note may be divided into 2 eighth notes, and an eighth note may be divided into 2 sixteenths.

When you look at the notes you can see that all of them, except the whole note, have a stem and a head. Some have flags: eighth notes have one flag, sixteenth notes have two, thirty-second notes have three, and so on. Flags are attached to stems at the opposite end of the note head.

Consecutive notes with flags are often joined together by using beams, which are one or more lines at the top of the stem. The beams replace the

Beamed
notes

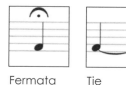

Dotted
note

Fermata

Tie

Slur lines

Staccato

Whole rest

Half rest

Quarter
rest

Eighth rest

Sixteenth
rest

10

Multiple-
measure
rest for ten
measures

individual flags of the notes—consecutive eighth notes are joined by one beam, consecutive sixteenth notes by two beams, and so on.

Dotted notes have a dot placed to the right of the note which indicates that the note is to be held for an additional duration equal to half of the duration of the (undotted) note. So a dotted half note, for example, would last as long as a half note plus a quarter note. If the whole note gets four beats, then the dotted half note gets three beats.

A fermata is a symbol indicating that the note, chord, or rest should be sustained beyond its note value for a time that is not determined mathematically, as with dotted notes, but is left up to the judgment of the performer.

When two melodies are written on the same staff, the stems for the notes in one melody are pointed up, and the stems for the notes in the other are pointed down.

A tie is a curved line that connects two notes of the same pitch. This indicates that the notes are to be played as a single note, with no break between them. Ties are the only way to show that a pitch should be held across a measure line.

A slur line indicates that the notes it covers are to be played without any separation.

A staccato mark indicates that a note is to be played short and separately, and that there is to be a brief silence between the notes. Staccato is normally indicated on each individual note by placing a small dot above or below the head of the note, on the opposite side from the stem.

A rest is a symbol placed on the staff to indicate that the musician is to be silent. Rests also have definite lengths. For each note there is an equivalent rest:

Dotted rests, like dotted notes, are held for an additional duration which is equal to half the duration of the rest. When you add up all of the time values of the notes and rests in a measure, these values equal the time signature.

Scales, Octaves, Accidentals, and Range

Notes are arranged in a series of tones called a scale. A scale is a progression of tones in a certain order; it is the set of the notes belonging to a key (the notes used in that piece of music). A scale begins on the tonic, which is the note from which the key gets its name.

There are major and minor scales. To find the rest of the notes in a major key, start at the tonic (the first note of a musical scale) and go up the series in the pattern whole step–whole step–half step–whole step–whole step–whole step–half step. This will take you to the tonic one octave higher than where you began and includes all of the notes in the key in that octave. Another way to think about the scale is to use the *do–re–mi–fa–sol–la–ti–do* pattern; these are the seven tones of the scale (eight if you count the *do* that completes the pattern.)

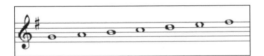

G major scale

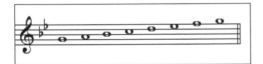

G minor scale

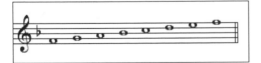

F major scale

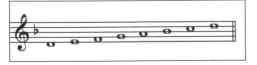

D minor scale

Minor scales have a sound that is different than major scales because they are based on a different pattern of intervals. Just as in major scales, starting the pattern on a different note will give you a different key signature—a different set of sharps or flats. To create a minor scale, start on the tonic note and go up the series using interval pattern whole step–half step–whole step–whole step–half step–whole step–whole step.

For every possible key signature, there are one major scale and one minor scale that use that same signature; we call those related scales. For example, F major and D minor are related scales since they share the same key signature of one flat (B-flat). The minor scale is the built on the sixth note of its relative major scale.

An octave

Sharp, flat, and natural

An octave is a group of eight notes arranged in a pattern of steps. Each step has a name: *do, re, mi, fa, sol, la, ti, do,* or C, D, E, F, G, A, B, C. These syllables, *do, re, mi,* and so on, are known as solfège or solfeggio syllables. From one G to the next G is a distance of eight notes, that is, an octave. Each note represents a pitch.

There are also half steps, which are indicted by a sharp symbol (♯) or a flat symbol (♭). A sharp raises the pitch by a half step, and a flat lowers the pitch by a half step. A symbol called a natural (♮) is used to cancel a flat or a sharp.

A piano keyboard demonstrates the arrangement of whole and half steps. The distance between two white keys is a whole step; the distance between a white key and the black key beside it is a half step. From one C we can play eight white keys up to and including the next C; these eight notes create an octave and the *do–re–mi–fa–sol–la–ti–do* scale.

The arrangement of whole steps and half steps on a keyboard

If the pitch of a note is to be altered in a certain key, a sign is placed before the note to indicate its new pitch. These sharps, flats, and naturals are referred to as accidentals. They are notes that are not in the key that most of the piece is written in and do not belong to the established key.

A chromatic scale contains notes that are each separated from one another by a half-step or semitones. This type of scale includes all the sharps and flats into which the octave is divided. There are twelve semitones, or half steps, to an octave in the chromatic scale.

Chromatic scale ascending and descending on C

Ledger lines are short lines placed above or below a staff to accommodate notes higher or lower than the range (limit) of the staff. A ledger line is a tool of music notation that indicates notes that lie outside the regular lines and spaces of the staff, and they follow the same musical alphabet pattern as the staff does. Although a

Ledger lines

piece could have an unlimited number of ledger lines, using more than four or five of these lines makes it difficult to read the notes, so their use is limited. Ledger lines can extend above or below the staff, no matter which clef is being used.

A repeat sign is the musical symbol that tells the player to repeat a passage in a composition. An open repeat sign is a heavier line followed by a fine line and two dots; this tells the musician the beginning of a part to be repeated; a close repeat sign is pointed in the opposite way and tells the musician that the section to be repeated has ended.

Repeat

Measures and Bar Lines

A measure, also called a bar, contains a specific amount of musical time. The notes written in the space between the lines create a measure. Measures or bars are separated by measure lines or bar lines. These lines, which are written as vertical lines at the end of each measure, divide music into groups of equal beats that go at a certain rate of speed. Single bar lines are used to separate music into bars (or measures); double bars with two fine lines are used to mark off sections within a piece; and double bars with a fine line followed by a heavier line mark the end of a movement or a work.

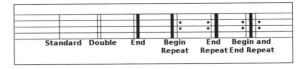

Standard	Double	End	Begin Repeat	End Repeat	Begin and End Repeat

Measures and bar lines

Rhythm, Time Signature, and Tempo

A melody is set to a beat. A beat is a rhythmic stress that gives a piece of music its pulse. Rhythm is the pattern of musical activity created by the combination of long and short, even and uneven sounds that convey a sense of movement. When we march, we move our feet in the pattern left, right, left, right. So a march would be considered to have a one-two beat. A waltz has three beats, with the accent on the first beat: *one*–two–three, *one*–two–three. Rap music may not have a melody, but it always contains a rhythm. Rhythm is an important part of music.

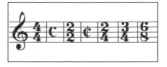

Examples of time signatures

A time signature on the staff tells how many beats are in a measure and which type of note gets one beat. The time signature is also called the meter. A measure or a bar contains a specific amount of musical time. The notes written in the space between the lines create a measure. The time signature is placed after the key signature at the beginning of the staff. There are two numbers, one above the other. The top number tells us how many beats there are in a measure, and the bottom number tells us what type of note equals one beat. In other words, the top number designates how many, and the bottom number designates which kind.

4/4 This time signature means that there are 4 beats in the measure, and a quarter note would get 1 beat, a half note would get 2 beats, and a whole note would be held for 4 beats.

3/4 This time signature means that there are 3 beats in each measure, and a quarter note would get 1 beat.

The symbol for common time is sometimes used in place of the 4/4 time signature.

The symbol below means cut time, for instance, 2/2 instead of 4/4; it is also called alla breve. This time signature means that there are two beats in each measure, and a half note gets one beat. It is often used in marches.

A metronome is an adjustable device used to indicate the beat by making a clicking sound or emitting a pulse of light. Metronome markings are written in beats per minute. Because it can be set to

Symbol for common time

Symbol for cut time

Metronome

a specific speed or tempo, the metronome is often used in practice to help the musician maintain a certain number of beats per minute. A metronome mark, also called metronome marking, is indicated at the start of a score and when there is any significant change of tempo. The music is marked as having a certain number of beats per minute, which tells the performer the duration of all note values within the score.

The beat has a speed called tempo; this is an important element of rhythm. A tempo sets the pace of the music; it can be fast, slow, or anything in between. "Tempo" (plural: tempi) means time in Italian. Many of the words used to describe tempo are written in Italian because most of the important composers of the seventeenth century, when tempo first began to be indicated in music, were Italian.

The Most Common Tempo Terms

accelerando (accel.): speed up

adagio: slowly

allegretto: lively

allegro: fast

andante: walking pace

a tempo (Tempo I): return to original tempo

con brio: with vigor

grave: very slow

largo: slowly and broadly

lento: moderately slow

moderato: moderate speed

molto: very

non troppo: not too much

poco: little

presto: very quickly

prestissimo: very, very quickly

ritardando (rit.): gradually slower

vivace: quick and lively

3 Harmony, Chords, and Tonality

Music produces a kind of pleasure which human nature cannot do without.

CONFUCIUS, CHINESE PHILOSOPHER (551–479 BCE)

The Role of Harmony and Chords

Usually the melodies we hear are performed with accompaniment either by a single instrument, a group of instruments, or a voice. There is typically a background that plays a supportive role in music. Harmony, the combining of notes, appeared in Western music about a thousand years ago. Western music—the kind that first developed in Western Europe, and the kind most of us listen to most of the time—employs harmony, which is created by two or more notes being sounded together. There are many kinds of harmony; however, all harmony is related to the structure and relationship of notes or chords to each other. Harmony—the movement and relationship of chords—adds depth to musical sounds.

When a guitarist accompanies a song or a pianist plays a melody with his right hand while his left hand plays blocks of notes, we recognize the music being produced by the guitar or by the left hand as having a supportive role. When the wrong note is sounded we are upset; the improper background sound breaks the agreement between the melody and the setting that accompanies it.

Three or more notes played simultaneously that have a harmonic relationship to each other create a chord. Chords contain intervals that are certain distances apart on the chromatic scale. Intervals are always made up of two notes; the differences in pitch between two notes of a chord are the intervals, which are all about the same size in a chord. Chords are built by combining intervals.

In tonal music the fundamental chord is called the triad, which is built on a given tone plus a major or minor third and a perfect fifth. For example, the C major triad contains the notes C, E, and G.

C major triad

Instruments playing different notes at the same time can create chords. Chords using three pitches are called trichords. Chords using four notes are known as tetrachords, those using five notes are called pentachords, and those using six notes are called hexachords.

Looking at the white keys on a piano, you can see that there are seven different notes.

Piano keyboard

By playing three or more of these notes at the same time, a musician can create a number of different chords. A chord, with the notes played all together, is considered a single unit, and each chord has a distinctive sound and mood. A chord progression is a series of chords performed in a certain order; they are usually associated with a scale, and the chords in the progression are based on that scale.

Chords are created by stacking thirds; that means that you add major or minor thirds to the lowest note of the chord—the root or bass note, which anchors the sound harmonically and determines the key.

All chords have certain characteristics: they contain a root note, the fundamental note of the chord, and an interval. In our example of a C major chord consisting of C, E, and G, C is the root note, E is the third, and G is the fifth (and also the third above E):

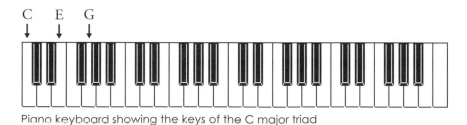
Piano keyboard showing the keys of the C major triad

This can be extended further by adding more thirds above the G: taking the example of the C major chord, adding a B (a third above G) creates a major seventh chord (Cmaj7 or CM7), so named because it is based on the C major scale.

B, the third above G

G, the fifth

E, the third

C, the root

C major
triad

A triad is a type of chord made up of a combination of three tones; it is the most common and most basic chord. For example, the triad C–E–G is built using the first, third, and fifth degrees of the *do–re–mi* scale, namely, *do–mi–sol*. Similar triads may be built using other degrees of the scale.

A triad can be major: root, major third, and perfect fifth. Or a triad can be minor: root, minor third, and perfect fifth. For example, if the root of the triad is D, the D minor triad would consist of the notes D, F, and A.

D minor
triad

A triad can have a normal fifth (also called a perfect fifth), an augmented fifth, or a diminished fifth. An augmented or sharp interval means one semitone or half step higher; a diminished or flat interval means one semitone or half step lower.

A chord can have a pleasant sound or it can sound dissonant. Dissonant sounds give the music a feeling of conflict, restlessness, or tension; it is the opposite of a consonant chord, which is a more pleasant arrangement of sounds to the listener. A dissonant chord creates tension, whereas a consonant chord resolves it.

Chord names are written in a type of shorthand that makes them immediately recognizable. For a simple major chord, the type is omitted, so C major would be written as C. For chords that are not a simple major chord, first the root note is indicated by an uppercase letter. Next a sharp or a flat would be placed next to the root if needed. Then the chord type is indicated. Using this kind of shorthand, a C minor chord would be represented as Cm: C is the root, and the third is E♭ instead of E because it is a minor chord. C aug. means C augmented; this contains C as the root note, E as the third, and G♯ as the augmented fifth.

An inverted chord has a note other than the root as the bass note. In an inverted chord the order of the notes in the chord has been changed. Triads in root position are the normal form; however, the C major triad can also be played in first inversion, as E–G–C:

C major
triad in first
inversion

or in second inversion, as G–C–E:

An arpeggio is a broken chord in which the notes are played in succession, rather than simultaneously.

C major
triad in
second
inversion

Arpeggio
notation

Musical Style: Keys, Modulation, and Chordal Relationships

Why does a composer choose to use one key over another for a piece of music? A composer typically hears the music in his or her mind in a certain key, and that influences the decision. The range of the instruments chosen to perform the piece and the mood of the music are also major reasons why a particular key seems to be the right one for a specific piece. In Western music, minor keys have a different sound and produce a different emotional feeling from major keys; minor intervals are usually heard as more sorrowful sounds, while major intervals are heard as having a more cheerful quality.

Sometimes a piece moves from one key to another; this is called modulation. Modulation introduces an element of variety to the music, changing the mood by changing the tonality. Interest is also added to the music by having the piece modulate from a major key to a minor key or vice versa. The contrast between the keys and the ability to move from one key to another is a basic element of musical structure. Modulation can be a brief interval in the piece or a complete change to another key. There are different types of modulation: direct modulation occurs when a key changes suddenly; common-chord modulation moves from the original key (that is, the beginning key) to a closely related key usually using a pivot chord (or common chord) that functions in both keys to lead directly into the modulation. Generally, a composer begins in a key and returns to that key to end the piece.

In 1728 a German composer and music theorist, Johann David Heinichen, developed a simple method to understand how chords are related to each other. He devised a circle of fifths to portray the relationship of the keys to each other in the chromatic scale. On this circle, as we move from keys with fewer sharps to those with more, we see that each key is a perfect fifth above the previous one. In addition, each key contains all the sharps of the previous key plus one more, and each sharp that is added is a fifth higher than the previous one. The key of C has no sharps.

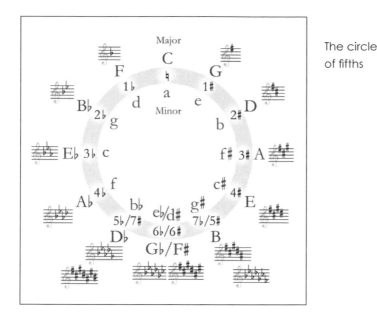

The circle
of fifths

Starting on any note on the outside of the circle and steadily moving by the musical interval of a perfect fifth, you will eventually land on the same note one octave higher.

The circle of fifths can also tell you how many sharps or flats are in a given key. The numbers on the inside of the circle tell how many sharps or flats would be in the key signature for a major scale built on that note. For example, a major scale built on E will have four sharps in its key signature. Keys that differ by only a single accidental, for example, D major (2 sharps) and F♯ minor (3 sharps) are referred to as closely related keys.

Another method of discovering key relationships by fifths is to look at a piano keyboard and, starting at any key, count seven keys (both black and white) to the right to get to the next note on the circle above—which is a perfect fifth. In other words, seven half steps from the first to the eighth key on a piano is also a perfect fifth.

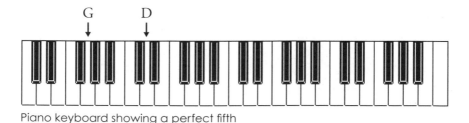

Piano keyboard showing a perfect fifth

Often composers will choose to change keys by modulating to the relative major (if the beginning key was minor) or relative minor key (if the beginning key was major). A relative minor (or major) is the key that has the same key signature as a major (or minor) key but has a different center. For example, G major and E minor both have a single sharp in their key signature, so we say that E minor is the relative minor of G major.

Tonality

In any musical system there must be a method of organizing tones into a relationship that makes musical sense. In Western music the tones are generated by the key center called a tonic, and the other tones are related to this tonic. A key is a group of related tones with a common center. Scales are based on a tonic. We can demonstrate this using solfeggio by starting on a tone and singing the syllables; we are not satisfied with the progression until we complete the entire line of the scale. When we listen to a piece in a specific key, the tonic is the element that functions as the fundamental point of attraction. If a work is written using the scale of G major, the key is G major. Chords and harmony help to define the tonality of the piece. Tonality is based on the sense of relationship to the central tone. In both the chromatic and the whole-tone scales, all of the intervals are the same—these scales have no tonal center. Therefore, no one note is any more or less important than the others.

4 Musical Structure

Music is the space between the notes.

CLAUDE DEBUSSY, COMPOSER (1862–1918)

Musical Form and Genre

It is often stated that music is the art of sound, but this definition does not allow us to understand how music works. Musical analysis is the attempt to understand how a work is constructed—how the composer has put a piece together. In order to be able to explore and understand this, we need to know the terms used in this type of evaluation.

The term "musical form" has two meanings; it may describe the genre (pronounced "ZHAN-ruh"), or the type of composition (such as a symphony), or it may describe the structure of a piece of music. Sometimes the term "form" in music refers to what is really genre, or the type of piece, such as a sonata, a symphony, an opera, and so on; and sometimes it refers to structure, such as ABA, binary, and so on. In this book the word "genre" will be used for the type of piece, and the word "form" or "structure" to refer to the way a composer organizes the sections of a piece. The musical form of a piece is a blueprint. Just as an architect plans a building, a composer plans his or her music. There are elements that are unique to each piece of music that the composer has used to make it distinctive and satisfying to the people who are hearing it. For example, composers may employ harmony, repetition, contrast, and variation to make their piece appealing and exciting. A composer takes a melodic idea as a basis for a piece and builds it into a theme or subject that is then developed and expanded into a larger work.

The structure of a musical work can be broken down into its parts. We can take a close look at how a piece is organized and draw a plan for its structure. Specific musical forms were popular at different times in music history. The forms reflected the function of the piece, its genre, which instruments were available, the objective of the composer, and the musical tastes of the time.

Basic forms are either binary or ternary. Binary form has two parts and is represented as AB: an initial section followed by a contrasting section. The two sections complement each other and are about the same in length of performance time (duration). The first section will begin in a specific key and then will usually modulate to a related key. The second section of the piece typically begins in the newly established key and eventually will return to the original key of the first section to end the work. Ternary form has three parts, ABA: an initial section followed by a contrasting section and then a return to the initial section. There are also more advanced forms that will be discussed in a later chapter on types of compositions.

Musical Styles

Over the centuries the style of music has changed. Styles that were popular during one era might go out of fashion in the next. Composers needed to make sure their audiences appreciated what they would be hearing. They had to be aware of the tastes, national culture, and beliefs of the society in which they lived, as well as any new developments in art and literature. Style is a way of presenting the thoughts of the composer to the audience. The forms that composers used and the devices they employed in their works were based on all these factors.

Musical Notation

The system of musical notation progressed over many centuries. The symbols used today to write down music arose from earlier attempts to communicate pitch and tempo. Notation has been adapted over time to meet musicians' needs. It offers directions that allow performers to read, understand, and play a work as the composer intended. Today's standard Western notation of music has been adopted by other musical cultures and altered to fit their requirements.

Performers add their own touches to written notations. A composer can indicate many aspects of the composition, yet the player has some leeway to add interpretation, feeling, timing, technique, and style. The performer makes the work come alive through his or her musicianship, understanding, and presentation of the music. No composition has only one single right way of performance; this variability makes playing or listening to a piece of music interesting and stimulating.

Articulation

accent: strike the note harder

fermata: hold the note longer (approximately twice its value)

glissando: glide from one note to the other

marcato: stressed, pronounced

legato: played smoothly together

staccato: play the note short and detached

sforzando: accent a single chord or note forcefully

tenuto: hold the note for its full value

Accent

Fermata

Glissando

Marcato

Legato

Staccato

Sforzando

Tenuto

Dynamic Notations

Written music has expressive effects that a composer can indicate through the use of dynamic notations. Music notation is the graphic representation of music. A composer writes many things on the score: the notes, the tempo, the key, and the dynamic notations.

Volume is the degree of loudness or softness with which a musical piece is to be played. Composers indicate their concept of the dynamics of a piece by writing expression marks, which are dynamic notations meant to inform the conductor or musician how the composer believes the music should be executed. Of course, the performers include their own preferences and interpretations when they play the piece. The range, limitations, and capabilities of the specific instruments selected to perform a piece of music also determine how a piece of music is to be expressed during a particular performance.

The Most Common Dynamic Notations

accelerando: louder and faster

al niente: fade to silence

crescendo: growing louder. To crescendo means to gradually get louder over a marked period of time. A crescendo marking can be expressed with two lines beginning from a point opening up into an angle. The length of the crescendo lines varies depending on how long the crescendo should last.

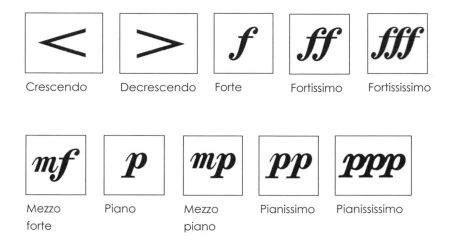

Crescendo   Decrescendo   Forte   Fortissimo   Fortissississimo

Mezzo   Piano   Mezzo   Pianissimo   Pianississimo
forte   piano

decrescendo or **diminuendo**: growing softer. The decrescendo or diminuendo has the opposite effect of the crescendo. To decrescendo or diminuendo means to gradually get softer over a marked period of time. It is marked by two lines that are angled and converge to a single point. The length of the lines shows how long the decrescendo should last.

forte: loud

fortissimo: very loud

fortississimo: as loud as possible

mezzo forte: moderately loud

piano: soft

mezzo piano: moderately soft (about half as soft as piano)

pianissimo: very soft

pianississimo: as soft as possible

Ornaments

grace note or **appoggiatura**: a very brief note played before another note

mordent: a note that is to be played in a single rapid alternation with the note above or below it

trill: the rapid alternation between two adjacent notes of a scale

turn: to play the note above the main note, the main note, the note below the main note, and then the main note again

Grace note

Mordent

Trill

Turn

5 Musical Terms

*Music, of all the arts, stands in a special region,
unlit by any star but its own, and utterly without
meaning ... except its own.*

LEONARD BERNSTEIN,
COMPOSER AND CONDUCTOR (1918–1990)

Why Musical Terms Are Written in Foreign Languages

Music always has had an important role in Italian culture. Italy was a major center for the development of classical music, especially in the Middle Ages and the Renaissance. The roots of classical music are firmly planted in the innovations of the sixteenth- and seventeenth-century Italian theorists, composers, and craftsmen of musical instruments.

Guido d'Arezzo, an Italian monk (995–1050), is known for his many contributions to musical notation and theory. As one of the first music theorists, his developments allowed early composers to begin recording their work on paper. He created a four-line staff and clefs. He also came up with a method of sight reading employing Latin syllables that eventually led to the use of solfeggio. His ideas were explained in his textbook *Micrologus*, written around the year 1030.

Italy provided many of the foundations of classical music tradition, so Italian was the language used for a great many musical terms, and they are still used today.

Many words that convey a musical concept or term were also passed down from French and German composers. Some English terms are also used now.

A Glossary of Commonly Used Musical Terms

a cappella: one or more vocalists without instrumental accompaniment

accent: the emphasis on a beat so that it is louder or longer than another in a measure

accompaniment: the support provided through harmony, rhythm or melody to the main theme in a piece of music

alto or **contralto**: the lowest female voice or an instrument in an alto range

arpeggio: a chord in which the notes are played one after the other rather than together

arrangement: a change in a musical piece; not in the same form as that in which it was originally composed

a tempo: return to the original tempo

atonal: music without a tonal center; all pitches are equally important

augmented: made larger; usually refers to the raising of the pitch of a major or perfect interval by one half step

ballad or **ballade**: a simple song that typically tells a story

baritone: a male singing voice whose range lies between that of a tenor and that of a bass; an instrument with a range between tenor and bass

bass: a male voice of low range

basso continuo: continuous bass

bel canto: beautiful singing; an elegant style of operatic singing

bridge: a transitional passage that connects two parts of a composition; also the part of a stringed instrument that holds the strings in place

cadence: a sequence of chords that leads to a close

cadenza: an elaborate melodic flourish or an extended solo passage usually performed toward the end of a piece

canon: a melody that is started by one voice and then repeated by another voice that starts after a short interval (also called a round)

Example of a canon: the beginning of the psalm motet *De profundis* by Josquin des Prez

chamber music: music intended for a smaller group using a limited number of instruments

chanson: French word meaning song

chant: an unaccompanied single melodic line; resembles the rhythm of speech

chromatic: a melody or harmony built from proceeding by half steps (semitones) on a musical scale. For example: C, C#, D, D#, etc.

chromatic scale: a type of scale that includes all twelve notes of the octave

Coda symbol

coda: the closing section of a composition or an added ending

coloratura: a soprano with a high range and the ability to perform trills and other complicated passages

concertmaster/concertmistress: the leader of the first violins of an orchestra by tradition; usually the assistant to the conductor

concert pitch: the tuning pitch for an orchestra or an ensemble

contralto: the lowest female singing voice

counterpoint or **contrapuntal**: the combination of two or more melodic lines played against one another simultaneously. Counterpoint combines two separate musical lines or melodies that interact at the same time. Think of the song "Row, Row, Row Your Boat," where one person starts and another joins in at a specific point; this is called a round and is an example of simple counterpoint.

countertenor: the highest male singing voice (above the tenor)

da capo (**D.C.**): return to the beginning

diatonic: the notes that naturally occur in a major or minor scale; the melody or harmony built from the seven tones of a major or minor scale

diminished: made smaller (usually referring to the lowering of the pitch of a minor or perfect interval by one half step)

discord or **dissonance**: notes or sounds that conflict with each other; the opposite of consonance

dominant: the fifth tone of a scale

double bar: a set of two vertical lines drawn on the staff to indicate the end of a section

downbeat: the first beat of a measure

duet or **duo**: a composition for two musicians

Double bar

dynamics: the loudness or softness of a musical work; the symbols used to represent the dynamic marks

embellishment: ornament added to music to make it more interesting

encore: French word meaning again; a piece of music played at the end of a recital due to the audience's request for more

ensemble: a musical performing group, such as a chorus, orchestra, or chamber group

etude: French word meaning a study or an exercise

falsetto: a high, light, artificial voice used by males to sing notes that are above their normal register

final bar: a set of two vertical lines, one thinner and one heavier, drawn on the staff to indicate the end of a work

finale: final; the last movement of a piece

form: the structure of a musical work

frequency: the rate of vibration of a string or column of air, which determines pitch

genre: the standard category or style of a work

Gregorian chant: unaccompanied, monophonic religious chant; also called **plainchant** or **plainsong**

homophonic: having a single melodic line with accompaniment

hymn: a song of praise

imitation: the repetition of a theme or a melody as presented in one part and then restated or answered in another part

improvisation: music that is created by the musician during a performance

intermezzo: a short movement separating the major sections of a long composition

modal: music that is based on modes other than major and minor

monophonic: a single-line melody without accompaniment

movement: a complete, self-contained section within a larger musical work

orchestration: the art of writing a score for the orchestra

ornamentation: the decoration of a melodic line with a note or notes to add interest

phrase: a musical unit; a short musical idea

pitch: the highness or lowness of a tone

polyphonic: two or more melodic lines combined

prelude: an instrumental work that is an introduction to a larger work

quartet: a composition calling for four instruments

quintet: a composition calling for five instruments

refrain: a part of a song that is repeated, often at the end of each verse

register: a part of the range of a composition, instrument, or voice

relative keys: the major and minor keys that share the same key signature

resolution: the conclusion of a musical idea

semitone: a half step in an octave; there are twelve semitones in a chromatic scale octave

sextet: a composition calling for six instruments

subject: the theme; the musical basis upon which any composition is constructed

suite: a series of unrelated and normally brief instrumental pieces, movements, or sections played as a group

symphonic poem or **tone poem**: an orchestral piece that conveys a story, creates a mood, or sets a scene

syncopation: a purposeful upsetting of the meter by changing the accent to a weak beat or offbeat

texture: refers to the structure of a composition; details how many parts or voices there are and how they interact

theme: the subject; the musical basis upon which a composition is constructed

tutti: all; for the entire ensemble, chorus, or orchestra

upbeat: the last beat of a measure which anticipates the first beat of the next measure (the downbeat)

variation: a change in the theme that makes it different but still recognizable

vibrato: a very slight vibration or fluctuation of the pitch of a note that intensifies the sound

virtuoso: a performer with great skill

6 Musical Genres and Forms

If music be the food of love, play on.

TWELFTH NIGHT (CA. 1601), BY WILLIAM SHAKESPEARE,
ENGLISH PLAYWRIGHT (1564–1616)

Musical genres have basic structures that define what they are and more or less correspond to a specific plan that outlines the requirements of that genre. These genres are not so rigid that they cannot be altered by the composer; however, they must roughly fit into the framework of that genre. No two symphonies are exactly alike; each one is the composer's response to writing a piece of music that is suited to a customary genre.

Musical genres fall into one of two categories. The first category, program music (a term invented by the Hungarian composer Franz Liszt), is instrumental music that conveys a mood, tells a story, or illustrates a picture. The "program" of a work is its story or subject. Beethoven's Sixth Symphony, the *Pastoral*, Op. 68, composed in 1808, suggests joyful images of country life and is considered the first example of this type of work. Nocturnes and symphonic poems are other examples of program music.

The second category is absolute music, which is considered pure music without a literary or dramatic context. Absolute music is always instrumental. It is the opposite of program music in that it does not depend upon setting up a scene or mood for its expressive content. Rather, members of the audience are expected to apply their own thoughts and emotions as they listen. The composers, of course, may communicate how they were feeling or what they were thinking when they created such pieces, but the listeners certainly can come to their own conclusions.

The Motet

During the early Renaissance a motet had a Latin text and was an unaccompanied polyphonic composition. Later, the meaning was expanded to include a type of choral work that was either religious or secular and was performed with or without accompaniment. Motets were written for religious or festive occasions. The word "motet" is derived from the French word *mot*, which means word. Originally the themes for this genre were taken from Gregorian chants or melodies. Using this thematic material, composers of motets varied the rhythms and embellished the melodies.

In the fifteenth century the musician Josquin des Prez (1450–1521) was an important figure in the Franco-Flemish school, which composed a certain style of polyphonic (two or more melodic lines combined) music. Known by his first name, Josquin was the most significant composer of the Renaissance; he wrote masses, motets, and secular songs in both French and Italian. Josquin created a style that involved having different vocal lines flow in a free and continuous imitation of each other. His compositions typically use four voices that join in contrapuntal harmony or respond to each other (usually in pairs). Josquin was one of the first composers who made the words an equal partner with the music. Although he worked for the church, he wrote both sacred and secular pieces. His motets are expressive and dramatic, taking complex contrapuntal themes to new altitudes. Josquin's *Memor esto verbi tui* (Remember your promise to your servant) is a motet for four voices that set a high standard for future composers. The motet is based on Psalm 119 and is a model of balance, contrast, and melodic imitation. Later composers who wrote pieces in this genre included Roland de Lassus, Johann Sebastian Bach, and Wolfgang Amadeus Mozart.

The Concerto

The concerto (plural: concerti or concertos) is a musical composition in which the interest is focused on a solo performance. Normally a concerto has three movements, or distinct and separate sections. The orchestra's job is to accompany and contrast with the soloist. This opposition of the soloist and the orchestra allows contrasting themes to be presented, developed, and restated.

Arcangelo Corelli (1653–1713) was an Italian virtuoso violinist who also composed instrumental music in a genre called the concerto grosso (grand concerto). This term is used only to define the baroque-period concerto established by Corelli in which the concertino (a small group of instruments) plays in contrast to a larger group called the ripieno. The differences in sound and color between the smaller group of instruments and the larger one created the contrast required for a piece to be called a concerto. The concertino group might consist of two violins and a cello, while the larger ripieno group was usually string instruments; sometimes a few woodwinds were added. Often a harpsichord provided harmonic support for both groups. The movements were usually in a fast–slow–fast arrangement, with the first and third sections typically in the home key and the second in a related key. The concerto grosso began in Italy but quickly spread to other European countries.

Using the basic concept of the concerto grosso, the baroque solo concerto developed at the same time. In the solo concerto, only one instrument plays against the ripieno. The Italian composer Antonio Vivaldi (1678–1741) created a repeating-passage formula called ritornello form in which a musical passage (the ritornello) returns throughout the piece. Although he wrote over 250 concertos, Vivaldi's *The Four Seasons* stands out as one of the most famous sets of baroque concertos. It was written as set of four works, each based on a sonnet about one of the seasons. Toward the end of the eighteenth century the solo concerto became the favored genre, and the concerto grosso disappeared.

In the classical era composers liked to alternate passages for the soloist and the orchestra and then have them join together at various points. The ritornello form evolved into the rondo form, in which the main theme is repeated and alternated with contrasting secondary themes. Wolfgang Amadeus Mozart (1756–1791) was an Austrian composer who brought the concerto to a higher level. His concertos also had three movements, but he replaced the ritornello and rondo forms with the newer sonata form. The sonata form is discussed later in this chapter.

Born in Hungary during the romantic era, Franz Liszt (1811–1886) was well-known all over Europe as a wonderful pianist. In nineteenth-century works the goal was to unite and bring together the various elements in a piece of music. Liszt organized the concerto by employing the same themes in all of the movements. He viewed the concerto as a showcase for virtuoso soloists. His Piano Concerto No. 1 in E-flat Major is a breakthrough in this approach: it is actually a single movement in which four contrasting sections are performed without a break between them. Altered but still recognizable basic themes reappear in each section; this is called cyclic form. The soloist and orchestra contrast with each other, but it is more like a conversation than a battle. Sometimes Liszt brought in unusual instruments; in the Piano Concerto No. 1 in E-flat Major he included a triangle. The awesome finale (climax) of this work forever changed the concerto; Liszt bound all of the themes together and brought the concerto to a close with an energetic march.

Some twentieth-century composers restored the concerto grosso genre. Béla Bartók (1881–1945) was born in Hungary and was greatly influenced by Hungarian folk songs and by earlier composers' works. Like most modern composers, he adapted the traditional forms and genres by transforming them into his own unique style. His concertos are filled with elements of folk music. His 1943 *Concerto for Orchestra* treats the orchestral instruments as the soloists. The composer discarded the traditional concerto formula: although he called the piece a concerto, it did not include the expected single soloist. Instead, he contrasted individual instruments in the orchestra with the entire orchestra so that every section of the orchestra received a turn in the spotlight.

The Fugue

The basis of the fugue is counterpoint, a term that comes from the Latin *punctus contra punctum* (note against note). A fugue combines two or more separate musical lines or melodies called voices that interact at the same time. The word "fugue" comes from the Latin word *fuga*, which means flight. The fugue is an exciting form that reached its peak during the baroque period. In a fugue, several independent voices present a theme that they each imitate and that flies back and forth between them. A fugue can be written for a group of instruments or as a solo; it can also be composed for singing voices.

Johann Sebastian Bach (1685–1750) was a great representative of the fugue form. He had an enormous influence on music in his own time and on future musicians. Bach, a German organist and composer, brought baroque music to the highest points it could reach. His fugues were brilliant and incorporated a variety of rhythms, rich themes, and a wide assortment of treatments. He was a genius of contrapuntal (counterpoint) development. Bach's *Art of the Fugue* is a textbook on fugue form; it contains fourteen fugues and four canons (a piece of music where one voice repeats the part of another), progressing from the simplest to the most difficult and complex counterpoint. Since each fugue in this manuscript employed the same D minor key and subject, Bach had to utilize many transformations of it to avoid boredom. He varied the theme by flipping it, shrinking it, enlarging it, mirroring it, merging it with other themes, doubling it, and turning it backward. This work was intended as a teaching tool, but it truly demonstrates Bach's thorough mastery of this complex musical form.

In a fugue a short opening motif or theme called the subject begins in one of the voices without accompaniment; the imitation of this subject by the next voice is called the answer. While the answer is being presented, the first voice continues with a countersubject or countertheme. The subject then appears in a third or a fourth voice while the other voices weave their counterthemes. The composer works the theme into all kinds of variations using different techniques—for example, he or she might invert the theme by turning it upside down or augment it by lengthening the note values.

Other techniques include the use of stretto, the double or triple fugue, the counterfugue, and the mirror fugue. Stretto is a particularly effective device used in fugues; it means that the subjects and answers overlap and crowd up on one another or that two subjects enter closely together. This technique intensifies and complicates the drama of the music, because the second voice enters before the first voice has completed presenting the subject. A double fugue contains two main themes and, of course, a triple fugue contains three. In a mirror fugue the second voice is a mirror image of the first voice; in other words, the entire piece is inverted.

The strict structure of any fugue is an alternation of the exposition (the first section, consisting of the presentation of the subject in all voices) with episodes (interludes). Fugues contain contrasts of key, and one purpose of the episodes is to bring about a modulation to a related key, which adds variety. Often the theme is presented in the home key and the answer is given in a contrasting key. Once the theme has appeared in each voice, the first exposition ends. However, the exposition may be repeated, and the voices may enter in a completely different order. When an exposition has concluded, the fugue continues alternating between exposition sections and episodes—interludes that are usually based upon some subject or countersubject from the exposition. The final statement of the subject is often made in a coda (conclusion).

As the fugue unfolds, the tension in the work mounts, and the listener has a sense of the themes maturing as the piece progresses. A fugue is a process of constant imitation of a theme and expansion on that theme while counterpoint supplies variety and adds interest. The fugue was a principal baroque form and was adapted in later periods, but at the end of the baroque era interest in this form faded as new musical styles came into favor.

The Minuet and Scherzo

Until the late eighteenth century a favorite dance in the courts of Europe was the minuet. The name was derived from the French *menuet*, meaning small or dainty. It was an elegant and stylish dance performed in large palace ballrooms; its graceful steps characterized the ideal of refinement in an aristocratic era. Most popular in the French court of Louis XIV, this dance was performed by one couple at a time. Written in 3/4 time, the minuet had a clear structure typically based on phrases of four to eight measures. The tempo of this dance ranges from rather moderate and dignified to relatively lively and spirited (some Italian minuets were composed in 3/8 or 6/8 time, making them faster than those written in the French fashion).

In the seventeenth century dances were typically presented in pairs and then the first was repeated after the second, so it became customary to have a combination of minuet–trio–minuet. A trio was an arrangement for three instruments that usually had a faster pace than the minuets. At the conclusion of the trio section the composer often simply wrote da capo or D.C., meaning "from the beginning." Some composers used this dance form in their operas and ballets; others closed the overtures to an opera with a minuet.

Following the French Revolution, this aristocratic type of dance was no longer in fashion; however, the minuet was carried over into other musical genres such as the sonata and the symphony. In the nineteenth century the minuet developed into the scherzo (the Italian word for joke; plural: scherzi), which, like the minuet, is in 3/4 time and in three-part form: scherzo–trio–scherzo. Yet the scherzo differs from the more elegant minuet in the sense that it contains sudden mood changes and a much livelier tempo. The scherzo is meant to be humorous and lighthearted (as the name suggests), but often composers used the name without any regard for its meaning. The scherzo replaced the minuet as the second or third movement in symphonies and sonatas. Beethoven essentially used the scherzo as an alternative to the minuet in his works. Later composers sometimes employed the scherzo not only as part of an extended work such as a symphony or sonata, but also as a separate, independent genre.

Lieder

The German word for song is lied (pronounced "leed"; plural: lieder). This type of art song was a product of the romantic era. Lieder were created through a combination of poetry and music in the early nineteenth century. This musical genre developed out of a literary movement that cultivated romantic and lyrical poetry. In the 1800s numerous poets in many countries wrote short, expressive verses that embraced a love of nature and gave voice to tender feelings. In 1798 the English poets William Wordsworth (1770–1850) and Samuel Taylor Coleridge (1772–1834) published *Lyrical Ballads*, which began the romantic literary movement in England.

At about the same time, two German poets, Johann Wolfgang von Goethe (1749–1832) and Heinrich Heine (1797–1856), gained recognition as important figures in the realm of German poetry. Their lyrical poems lent themselves to a union of words with music that displayed the sentiments of the romantic era. It was the words of these poets, set to music, that established the model for the art song. Lieder deeply touched the consciousness of the nineteenth century.

Franz Schubert (1797–1828), an Austrian composer, is especially remembered as the finest composer of German lieder. During his short life Schubert wrote over five hundred songs, each containing the romantic ideal of poetic expression. *Der Erlkönig* (The Elf King) is based on a poem by Goethe; it depicts a father on horseback carrying his sick child through a stormy night. Schubert's music is very dramatic; the piano accompaniment eerily imitates the beating of the horse's hoofs as the words tell the tragic tale. The interplay between the singer and the pianist, the sense of movement, and the haunting melody combine to make *Der Erlkönig* an outstanding example of this type of art song.

The romantic era featured large musical genres that had time to develop and expand on a musical idea. The shorter pieces, like the lied, had to be written more simply and in a much smaller framework. This led to the expansion of the genre by means of a cycle or series of smaller pieces that were bound together by a musical or literary idea. The cycle was employed by Schubert in his 1823 work *Die schöne Müllerin* (The Pretty Maid of the Mill), a series of twenty songs telling a love story about a young apprentice who falls in love with the daughter of the master of the mill.

The Nocturne and Other Lyrical Genres

The nocturne is a short, lyrical, free-form instrumental piece. It reached its fullest development in the nineteenth century. The word is derived from the French for "nocturnal" or "nighttime," and was initially composed for evening gatherings at parties called salons. Some nocturnes are labeled by the Italian name *notturno*. Composers often titled these works to evoke nighttime images: the nocturne from *A Midsummer Night's Dream* by Felix Mendelssohn is an example.

John Field (1782–1837), an Irish pianist and composer, was the first to label his works as nocturnes in 1814. These pieces were composed for the piano rather than for other instruments. Nocturnes are considered "character pieces" because they set up a mood or portray an image. Most often they are written as a single movement in an ABA structure that contrasts two moods; the first movement might be cheerful and the second gloomy, or the other way around. The ABA structure produces a balanced and symmetrical form.

A description of the nocturne would not be possible without mentioning the Polish composer and pianist Frédéric Chopin (1819–1849), who wrote a total of twenty-one nocturnes. The pure beauty of the melodies and the wide range of moods make these pieces timeless. Chopin's piano nocturnes require a high level of technical mastery, and the composer's originality of style revolutionized piano playing. These nocturnes are fabulous and deservedly famous; they are fascinating to hear.

Another short, lyrical genre is known as a rhapsody, from the Greek word *rhapsodia*, which refers to reciting poetry. This genre is another instrumental equivalent of a song, and the name is applied to pieces that were inspired by the romantic ideas of the nineteenth century. Like nocturnes, rhapsodies are character pieces. They typically follow an ABA structure and present two different and contrasting moods.

Other names given to these brief compositions that illuminate a mood or are classified as character pieces include the bagatelle, usually for piano; the caprice, a quick and lighthearted composition; the intermezzo, which means interlude; and the fantasia, which means fantasy or a flight of the imagination.

The Overture

The word "overture" comes from the French *ouverture*, which means opening. The overture serves as an introduction to an opera, an oratorio, a theatrical play, or a longer work. Until the seventeenth century and the development of opera, there was no specific genre called an overture.

Some overtures are performed independently in a concert hall because they have attained great popularity with audiences. A concert overture is a free-standing work specifically written for an orchestra in concert presentation. This type of overture is often classified as program music, since it evokes a picture or mood in mind of the listener. During the romantic period a one-movement orchestral concert piece based on a literary idea became popular. Because the source of the piece was literary, it was typically dramatic, descriptive, patriotic, or a character piece. Two examples are Pyotr Ilyich Tchaikovsky's *1812 Overture* and *Romeo and Juliet Fantasy-Overture*.

The Sonata

The term "sonata" comes from the Italian *suonare*, meaning "to sound." A sonata is a large instrumental work containing a cycle of contrasting movements. Originally, the term "sonata" was used simply to tell an instrumental piece apart from a vocal piece; therefore, concertos and several other genres were labeled sonatas. During the baroque era, sonatas developed into two types: the *sonata de chiesa* (church sonata), with its four movements in a slow–fast–slow–fast arrangement, and the *sonata da camera* (sonata for chamber ensemble), whose multiple movements were dance pieces. Later, in the eighteenth century the trio sonata became the predominant type of sonata genre. The trio sonata required two solo melody instruments and a basso continuo, which consisted of a harpsichord plus another stringed bass instrument such as a cello. So despite its name, the trio sonata was actually for four musicians: two who provided the basso continuo and two who performed two different melodic lines.

Just as the concerto grosso eventually fell out of favor and was replaced in the classical era by the solo concerto, the trio sonata died out and was replaced by the solo sonata, now called simply sonata. Around the same time, a three-section form developed called a sonata-allegro form (or sonata form). Based on a contrast between two closely related keys, it contains an exposition, a development, and a recapitulation, usually followed by a coda. (A four-part form was also becoming common in the classical period; however, the standard sonata form implies three sections.) In the exposition, the composer presents the movement's main contrasting themes, of which there are typically two: the first theme establishes the main key, and the second establishes the contrasting key. Between these themes there is a bridge, a transition that modulates from the first key to the second. Sometimes a third theme is present; once the themes are presented, a closing passage called a codetta (small coda) leads into the next section.

The development further explores the themes as the composer exposes and releases their possibilities. The themes are often broken up into motives and new patterns created to expand, propel forward, and refashion the musical material. The tension of the contrasting themes builds as the development comes back to the main key.

The recapitulation, which begins when the main key is reestablished, is the climax of the sonata-allegro form. In this section the themes are usually repeated in their original form; the tensions and contrasts become toned down and are drawn together. At the end of this section the coda, the final portion, which is made up of thematic material that was presented in the other sections, rounds out the movement. The sonata-allegro form was the most frequently used instrumental form in Western music from about 1760 to the early twentieth century, appearing not only in sonatas but also in symphonies and concertos.

Ludwig van Beethoven's Piano Sonata No. 8 in C Minor, Op. 13, was published in 1799 and is one of his most popular works. Beethoven (or his publisher) titled this work the *Pathétique*. It consists of three movements: the first is in sonata-allegro form, the second is a rondo, and the third movement is in sonata-rondo form. Beethoven opens the *Pathétique* with a grave (slow) tempo containing the main motif but quickly shifts to an allegro (fast) tempo. The second movement, labeled adagio cantabile (slowly and in a "singing" style), is a rondo, a form of composition in which the first section returns after the second section is played; then comes a third section, followed again by the first, and so on. The last movement is in sonata-rondo form. This form, like the sonata-allegro form, was developed by classical-era composers. Also like the sonata-allegro form, it depends for its structure on rich key contrasts and transitional patterns, but, like the rondo form, it has a main theme that generally alternates with one or more secondary themes. The rondo and sonata-rondo were popular forms in both eighteenth- and nineteenth-century music and appeared often in sonatas, concertos, and symphonies. Rondos were also written as independent, free-standing pieces.

The Symphony

A symphony is a large-scale piece in several movements for orchestra. The word comes from the Greek *sumphonia*, meaning harmonious. The (usually) four movements are typically written in a fast–slow–moderately fast–fast sequence. Of course, composers often break this pattern. The movements further contrast with each other by differences in mood and character, but they come together to form a powerful and important genre. A symphony is a prime example of absolute music.

The structure of the classical symphony was established in the middle of the eighteenth century; prior to that time the term "symphony" was used to describe a range of pieces that were parts of a larger work. This genre was crafted over time by several composers living in Germany, Austria, France, and Italy. Each composer created an innovation that was then adopted by others who shaped it to suit a piece they were working on. The changes to the form made by the baroque composers led to the full flowering of the symphony in the classical era.

By the 1760s the classical symphony had acquired four movements: the first is in sonata-allegro or sonata form, which then is followed by a slow movement. Next comes a minuet and trio; the final movement is commonly in rondo or sonata-rondo form. In the first movement, the exposition presents at least two themes, which contrast with each other; one theme might be lyric and the other highly rhythmic, with a bridge being employed as a transition from one theme to the next. After the codetta, the development section combines, blends, and separates the themes, creating drama and excitement. The recapitulation restates the themes first heard in the exposition, giving them new depth and significance. A coda usually ends the movement.

The second movement of a symphony is typically slow and lyrical. Composers have elected to use different forms for this movement, including the sonata-allegro form and the rondo form. In the symphony's early years, the third movement was a minuet and trio; in the late classical and romantic eras, though, this became a scherzo and trio. Sometimes these two movements are interchanged by a composer and the third movement is the slow one. The fourth movement or finale may be written to balance the first movement; in most romantic-era symphonies this movement was written using the sonata-allegro form.

As permanent orchestras became widespread in major cities, the symphony became the favorite choice of composers, conductors, and concertgoers. Wolfgang Amadeus Mozart's Symphony No. 40 in G Minor, K. 550, was composed in Vienna during the summer of 1788 and later revised to include clarinets. This symphony and Nos. 39 and 41, Mozart's last symphonies, were written over a period of about six weeks. Of his three last symphonies, the G Minor is the best known. During this time his wife was ill, and he was heavily in debt; in addition, his six-month-old daughter had died in June. It was probably one of the lowest points in his short life. It has been said that Mozart's troubles may be reflected in this symphony.

Originally scored for flute, two oboes, two bassoons, two horns, and strings, the G Minor Symphony is a good example of the inventiveness of Mozart's music. The first movement, in sonata-allegro form, begins with an intense allegro molto (very fast) opening. The G minor home key is established by the first theme, performed by the violins. A bridge leads to the contrasting key of B-flat major, which is the relative major of G minor. Woodwinds and strings enter to introduce the second theme, which contrasts further with the first in the sense that it is melodious and mild in comparison with the energetic and forceful first subject. The second movement, in E-flat, is a lyrical andante (moderate speed) in sonata-allegro form—an unusual choice for a work in this period. This section takes surprising turns as Mozart explores an assortment of chromatic (foreign to the given key) relationships, opposing the minor home key with the contrasting major key.

The third movement returns to G minor and is as dramatically tense as the first. The minuet is energetic instead of stately, and the trio, in G major, is calm, completely different in tone from the minuet. The woodwinds and strings perform alternately in the trio. This was innovative, because symphonies written during Mozart's time did not normally have the melody played by the woodwinds. The minuet is then repeated, giving the movement as a whole a balanced ternary structure.

The finale is written in eight-bar phrases, again in sonata-allegro form, marked allegro molto (very fast). The first theme in G minor is called a rocket theme because it launches upward with great force. The contrasting theme is in the related key of B-flat major. Mozart included an outstanding modulating passage in this movement, which is filled with instruments hurriedly imitating the motives in a complex and intricate manner. The strings and the woodwinds recapitulate the second theme, which shifts into the home key of G minor. This section achieves the peak of classical musical structure. An admirer of Mozart once wrote: "There are few things in art that are perfect. The G Minor Symphony is one of them."

The Symphonic Poem or Tone Poem

The symphony served the classical era's need for organization, clarity, naturalness, purity, and balance. The composers of that period created an expressive and dynamic style that allowed all of the orchestral instruments to participate in the interchange of themes. The symphony grew into the most important form of absolute music. During the romantic period composers sought a freer kind of orchestral music, a need that was met by the symphonic poem, a one-movement piece of program music for orchestra. It is also known as a tone poem. Franz Liszt is credited with being the first composer to use the term "symphonic poem," in 1848.

This one-movement genre has contrasting sections that inspire a mood, create an atmosphere, depict a scene, or develop a poetic idea. It is a flexible genre that matched the romantic spirit and the romantic composer's ideal of seeking to unite the creative spirit of the different arts. Ideas for symphonic poems were gathered from poets and artists that impressed and inspired the composers: the literary figures on which composers drew were often Goethe, Shakespeare, and Rousseau; the painters that motivated them included Michelangelo and Raphael. These compositions were also inspired by patriotic topics and the romantic era's love of nature. The symphonic poem became the most commonly composed type of program music in the nineteenth century.

Claude Debussy (1862–1918) was the most important French composer of the early twentieth century. His *Prélude à l'après-midi d'un faune* (Prelude to the Afternoon of a Faun) premiered in 1894. The composition is one of Debussy's most-loved pieces. It was inspired by a poem by Stéphane Mallarmé that tells about a mythical forest creature, half man and half goat, called a faun. Originally Debussy planned to write an orchestral work in three parts, of which this was to have been the first (this is why the title includes the word "prelude"), but he later revised this design to make it a stand-alone piece. The work was revolutionary and it had a profound effect on the next generation of composers; it was an entirely new kind of musical experience. It is frequently heard on concert programs, where the audience experiences it as a tone poem.

Prélude à l'après-midi d'un faune contains a world of bright sounds and pure colors. Debussy sets the scene by opening with a flute solo; the theme then passes from one instrument to the others in turn. Using the chromatic scale, the melody moves along in a pattern with a single continuous theme that establishes unity in the piece and depicts an image of the faun against a forest background. It is marked "très modéré—doux et expressif" (very moderate—soft and expressively). There are slow and dreamy glissandos (rapid ascents or descents of a scale) on the harp and a relaxed rhythm throughout the composition. The influence on Debussy of impressionist painters is evident as this fluid and dreamlike prelude unfolds.

Contemporary Music Genres and Forms

"Contemporary music" means any music being written in the present time—today generally considered to be from the mid-twentieth century onward. During the middle of the twentieth century, classical music branched out in many different directions. There are certain elements of style that label a piece as contemporary: rhythmic patterns, melodic structure, harmonies, textures, and orchestration. Although classical music has always been concerned with form and genre, modern composers have not just copied forms and genres from earlier periods; rather, they have selected the elements that they wished to keep and added their own fresh harmonies and rhythms in order to meet the modern demand for flexibility. Much of what has happened in the past and that which is happening in the present influences classical contemporary composers. Jazz, primitive music, machine music, folk music, non-Western music, newer concepts of tonality, and the preferences of present-day audiences have helped to determine the direction of contemporary music.

Rhythm has turned a corner from the former standard patterns; today composers utilize rhythms that are asymmetrical (unbalanced) and write measures containing odd numbers of beats. A piece might contain several meters, shifting from one rhythmic pattern to another within a bar. The bar line no longer must contain a certain beat; it may enclose a free and flexible rhythmic flow. Rhythms have become much more complex in contemporary music. The term "polyrhythm" is used to describe several independent rhythms sounding at the same time in a work. Innovative rhythmic structure is a major change in contemporary music.

Often contemporary music is accused of being unmelodious. Present-day composers have a different concept of what a melody should express. Dissonance (notes or sounds that conflict with each other), atonality (music that is not centered on a central key or scale), and serialism have expanded our thinking about melody. Serialism is an extension of the twelve-tone method that set of all the notes of the chromatic scale arranged in a certain order to form a tone row, which is the basis for the composition. Using this technique, no tone of the scale can be repeated until all the others have been sounded. Unusual and untraditional harmonies and tonal schemes thrive in contemporary music. Music, some contemporary composers believe, no longer must be harmonious, and they often create friction and tension with new dissonances that are not always resolved. It should be pointed out that the composition of tonal music still continues in the twenty-first century, but composers enjoy the freedom to explore new possibilities.

The Influence of Jazz

An important influence on contemporary classical music has been jazz, which originated in New Orleans, Louisiana, during the twentieth century. Jazz combines various elements of African, American, and European music. Classical musicians became aware of this truly American art form after World War I. Jazz began as dance music but soon grew into an independent genre.

The key features of jazz include improvisation (spontaneous composition), syncopation (stressing a beat that is usually not stressed), polyrhythms (two or more rhythms at the same time), and experimentation with methods of performing. Various types of jazz have emerged, each containing its own exotic sounds and styles. Classical composers were attracted to the inventiveness of jazz, which provided them with interesting material to explore. George Gershwin's *Rhapsody in Blue* and Aaron Copland's *Nocturne and Ukelele Serenade* are prime examples of the influence of jazz on modern classical composers.

Innovations in Modern Music

The rapid changes in society since the beginning of the twentieth century have been demonstrated in modern music. These innovations have led to novel harmonies, atypical rhythmic patterns, and attempts to make classical music "multicultural." The various styles that have appeared throughout the past hundred years have given music lovers additional material to listen to and decide whether or not it agrees with their tastes.

7 The Conductor

Technique is communication: the two words are synonymous in conductors.

LEONARD BERNSTEIN,
COMPOSER AND CONDUCTOR (1918–1990)

The Role of a Conductor

Although he does not play an instrument, the conductor is certainly one of the most important elements of an orchestral performance. His instrument is actually the entire orchestra, and it is his job to keep the musicians working together. The conductor sets the tempo of the music, beats out the time, and indicates when the various instruments are supposed to enter. He or she also gives shape and meaning to the written notes by indicating how a melody should be phrased and how the instruments are to be balanced against each other. There are no definite rules about how to conduct an orchestra or a band of musicians. Each conductor develops a personal style and decides on a definite interpretation of the music to be presented. It is the conductor who sets the mood of the music for the audience. He or she molds the musicians into a coordinated group and must be able to communicate to the orchestra his or her knowledge of the music and idea of how it should be performed.

The Conductor's Tools

The conductor, who stands on a podium (platform), often uses a baton (a wooden wand). Normally, the conductor's right hand sets the beat, while the left hand uses gestures that set the shape of the music, such as its loudness. His hand movements let individual musicians know it is their time to come into the composition (this is called cueing) so that the musicians can act together. Musicians must pay attention to the conductor so that they can be aware of their part in the group. Many orchestras invite guest conductors, which means that the musicians must constantly adapt to new styles and methods of conducting. Some conductors are very showy and use grand gestures, while others are very restrained and use slighter movements to indicate what they want.

The conductor's
score and baton

Orchestra musicians must also pay careful attention to the other musicians so that they can blend in with and support each other. During rehearsals the musicians learn how the conductor wants to present a piece and also how to balance the sound of the orchestra. Even though the musicians are well trained and skilled, they require rehearsal time to practice and perfect their performance. The word "concert" has several meanings, one of which is a public performance by two or more people. A concert hall is the place where concerts are performed.

A conductor uses a score, which shows what and when each instrument will be playing. The score is a blueprint of the work being performed by the orchestra; it is a written or printed piece of music with all the vocal and instrumental parts arranged on staves, one under the other. An orchestral score is a complicated device, and a conductor must know it thoroughly in order to be able to direct the orchestra through the performance. The word "score" can also mean the music itself, as in the score for a movie.

Score of Brandenburg Concerto No. 1 by J. S. Bach

The conductor

A score may contain rehearsal letters, which are large letters found on sheet music that allow a conductor to tell the orchestra where to start playing when he or she does not want to go all the way back to the beginning—for example, "Take it from letter G." Another method that is often used to facilitate following the score is called measure numbers (or bar numbers). There are several options for the placement of measure numbers: they may be located at regular intervals, for example, every five or ten measures; at the start of every line; above every measure; or at certain positions, like rehearsal letters. These numbers must be large enough to be readily seen by the conductor and the players.

8 The Orchestra, Orchestration, and Orchestral Instruments

It's easy to play any musical instrument: all you have to do is touch the right key at the right time and the instrument will play itself.

JOHANN SEBASTIAN BACH,
COMPOSER AND ORGANIST (1685–1750)

The human voice is an instrument in its own right; it generates sounds when air from the lungs makes the vocal cords vibrate. Tension on the vocal cords creates the tones. The human voice is the oldest and most popular of all instruments. It has been the model for many instruments, yet instruments can do many things that are not possible for the human voice.

As musical instruments were developed, they reflected the culture that created them; in turn, the music of a culture is always influenced by the instruments available to its musicians. Instruments can perform alone, in a small group such as a chamber music ensemble (two to nine instruments), or in larger groups of eighty or more such as a symphony orchestra or a philharmonic orchestra. The word "philharmonic" comes from the Greek word for music-loving, and "symphony" stems from the word for sounding together. A symphony orchestra performs symphonies, concertos, and other concert music and is typically seated on a stage. A philharmonic orchestra originally meant one that was associated with an opera house, but nowadays it is synonymous with the symphony orchestra.

A string orchestra might have many musicians but does not have any wind or percussion instruments. A smaller orchestra (forty players or fewer) is called a chamber orchestra. Orchestras that are used for a ballet or an opera are part of a theatrical performance and are seated in an orchestra pit, which is located in front of (and usually partly beneath) the stage.

The ancient Greeks used the word "orchestra" to describe a space in a Greek theater that was used by the actors, dancers, and singers to present a play, either a tragedy or a comedy. This theater was not in a building; instead, it was an open area with a space for the performers. Later on, seats were added for the audience, and the orchestra area was paved with a substance such as marble for the actors.

Ancient Greek theater

The Development of the Orchestra

In the late sixteenth century composers began writing music for instrumental groups, but until the seventeenth century the modern orchestra did not exist. Aristocratic courts sometimes maintained small ensembles for their own private entertainment; when a larger group was required, extra musicians were hired to perform with these ensembles. Thus, orchestras were gathered only when there was a need for them. The first instrumental groups that could truly be labeled orchestras were brought together in the 1600s for the Italian operas.

By the early part of the eighteenth century a normal symphony orchestra consisted of around twenty players. Later in that century this was expanded to about forty musicians; pairs of flutes, oboes, clarinets, and bassoons, French horns, and sometimes trombones were added. Keyboard instruments, which had been included in the past, were now removed. By the mid-nineteenth century a symphony orchestra customarily had sixty members.

Today we use the word "orchestra" to describe a large group of musicians playing instruments. A major, modern symphony orchestra, at full strength, contains about one hundred musicians playing anywhere from eighteen to twenty-five different kinds of instruments. Many factors contributed to the expanded size and shape of the modern orchestra.

Ludwig van Beethoven greatly influenced the current structure of the orchestra. His symphonies required an increase in the number of instruments to achieve the full richness of tone and orchestral effects that were called for in his scores; therefore, during his lifetime the number of musicians was increased to thirty or forty players. The legendary orchestra of Mannheim, Germany, also set the higher standards that led to the modernization of the orchestra. This orchestra demanded discipline from its members and introduced new musical techniques such as the use of the crescendo.

The percussion section has seen the most dramatic transformations. It has added a wide range of unusual, untuned instruments and many devices that provide special effects. By the nineteenth century many other instruments joined the orchestra, including the tuba, the harp, the English horn, the bass trombone, the contrabassoon, the bass clarinet, and the E-flat clarinet. Romantic composers required a much larger orchestra than previous composers did. Richard Wagner wrote scores that demanded even larger orchestras to obtain the combinations and effects that he required.

Each composer selects the orchestral combinations that suit the purpose of a particular musical work. An example is Tchaikovsky's *1812 Overture*, Op. 49: the composer punctuated the climax of this composition with cannon fire and a fierce ringing of bells. The *1812 Overture* was written to celebrate the seventieth anniversary of the Russian victory over Napoleon's armies. The tone of this orchestral work is very patriotic, and it is often heard in the United States during Independence Day celebrations. The cannon blasts are frequently performed on a bass drum, but modern technology has enabled orchestras to add an even more authentic sound to this musical climax.

The seating plan of an orchestra allows the instruments to combine and contrast. Each musician is seated within the section provided for his or her type of instrument. Similar instruments are seated near one another; for example, in the string section the violins and violas are placed close together. Each section functions as a unit. Softer instruments are placed in front, while the louder ones sit farther back. Other instruments are added on as they are needed—for instance, a work may call for a larger brass section, or two harps. Sometimes a piano is required for contemporary scores.

Because most orchestra members play while sitting down, a person's position in an orchestra is known as a chair. A musician occupying the first chair in a section is called the principal of that section. These principal musicians usually are selected as the orchestral soloists at a concert. The first-chair player of the first-violin section is known as the concertmaster or concertmistress and has certain assigned tasks. The concertmaster serves as a mediator between the conductor and the musicians; he or she also makes decisions about the technical details of violin playing, such as coordinating the bowing of the stringed instruments. Today orchestras frequently employ rotating seating plans for the string sections, and only the first two or three positions in each section are unchanging.

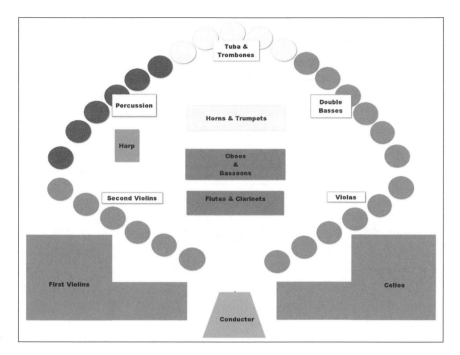

Seating plan of a modern orchestra

Orchestration

The right music played by the right instruments
at the right time in the right combination:
that's good orchestration.

LEONARD BERNSTEIN (1918–1990), COMPOSER AND CONDUCTOR

Renaissance and baroque composers did not orchestrate (arrange a composition for performance) their scores. Since who was to be a participant in a performance was dependent on who was available and the payment that was offered, the makeup of ensembles varied greatly. In fact, until well into the seventeenth century, composers did not usually specify which instrument had to be used for a particular part; as a result, any instrument that had the appropriate range could be employed.

Orchestration is the practice of writing down a piece of music for an orchestra or adapting music composed for another medium for the orchestra. It is an art. The composer must plan in great detail the music he or she envisions, deciding which instruments to include and which ones will present the themes while keeping in mind the capabilities of each instrument. The background or accompaniment must be decided, as well as the way the instruments will interplay with each other for harmony, balance, color, and contrast. Musical traditions and restrictions also enter into the composition process when the composer decides which genre or form to use. This shapes the design of the work.

Composers also have to know the capacities and limitations of each instrument. Every voice and instrument has a range, which is the distance from its lowest to its highest note, and a limit as to how loudly or softly it can sound. An instrument is also restricted by its technical peculiarities; for instance, it is fairly easy to perform rapid scales on a piano but much harder to do the same thing on a tuba.

Timbre (a French word that is pronounced "TAM-ber") is the word used to describe the quality of a sound. Every instrument has its own tone color and produces a mood or emotion that is unique to that instrument. The same tone will sound different depending on which instrument it is produced by. The same note on a violin sounds very different from that note played just as loudly and for the same length of time on a flute; that difference is the color of the sound.

Combinations of different instruments produce various mixtures of tone colors and textures. A composer has a choice of all of the available instruments, non-instrumental sounds, and human voices to use in his or her musical composition. Timbres can be contrasted, blended, harmonized, or used in some other fashion to create the effect the composer wishes to produce. Timbral combinations provide unique possibilities for music.

The Instruments of the Orchestra

The instruments of the orchestra belong to four main categories.

STRINGS

The string family is made up of violins (usually divided into firsts and seconds), violas (alto violins), cellos, and double basses. They are played by drawing a bow (a slightly curved wooden rod with horsehair stretched from one end to the other) across stretched strings pitched a fifth apart, or by plucking the strings. The bow is drawn up and down the strings of some stringed instruments to create sound. Violins, violas, cellos, and basses use bows. Harps and guitars are stringed instruments that do not use bows; instead, their strings are plucked.

WOODWINDS

The woodwinds include the flute, oboe, bassoon, and clarinet, and at times also the piccolo, English horn, and saxophone. Woodwinds are a remarkable family of instruments, for they differ widely in pitch and have quite distinct and easily identifiable tone colors. The tone is produced by a vibrating column of air within the pipe that has holes cut along its length. When one of these holes is closed (by stopping it with the finger or pressing down on a key), it changes the length of the column of air in the pipe.

The three branches of the woodwind family have different sources of sound according to the way they are blown. The piccolo and flute are played by blowing across a hole in the side of the pipe; the oboe, clarinet, bassoon, and English horn are played through a hole at the end of the instrument. Woodwinds belonging to this latter group are reed instruments (reeds are small pieces of cane). Vibrations begin when air is blown across the reed, or across two reeds. In the case of single-reed instruments (such as the various kinds of clarinet), a reed is clamped to a mouthpiece at the top of the instrument and vibrates against the mouthpiece when air is blown between the reed and the mouthpiece. For double-reed instruments (such as the oboe, English horn, and bassoon), two reeds are tied together. This double reed fits into a tube at the top of the instrument and vibrates when air is forced between the two reeds.

BRASS

Orchestral brass instruments are the trumpet, horn, trombone, and tuba. Sometimes other brass instruments such as the euphonium (a small tuba) are added to the brass section for certain musical works. Brass players control their instruments by means of valves and have to master embouchure (pronounced "OM-buh-shur"), the technique of placing the lips, lower facial muscles, and jaw to create notes of different pitch. The mouthpieces of these instruments are cup shaped, and as the player blows air into the tube he stretches his lips, which causes the column of air in the tube to vibrate. The slide or valves of the instrument, together with the variation in the pressure of the lips and breath, allow the player go from one pitch to another. Playing a brass instrument requires excellent muscular control.

PERCUSSION

Percussion instruments form a broad and highly varied family. They range from a simple striking of a block of wood, to the tambourine, which is both struck and shaken, to timpani (also called kettledrums). Even a piano can be played in a percussive rather than a melodic way. The only thing that percussion instruments have in common is that they are beaten, either with sticks, mechanical hammers, or bare hands; or are clashed together, like cymbals and castanets. The percussion section of an orchestra highlights the rhythm and adds excitement to the timbre. There are two categories of percussion instruments in an orchestra: those instruments with a definite pitch, such as a timpani, and those with an indefinite pitch, such as a triangle.

9 Pianos, Pipe Organs, and Harps

Diplomacy without arms is like music without instruments.

FREDERICK THE GREAT,
PRUSSIAN RULER AND FLUTIST (1712–1786)

Pianos

Until the twentieth century, orchestras often did not include a piano. Today the piano is most often used as a solo instrument. There have been many arguments over whether a piano is a stringed instrument or a percussion instrument; it is also considered to be a keyboard instrument. When a piano is included in an orchestral piece, it is technically considered to be a member of the percussion section.

Piano interior

Piano pedals

A piano is essentially a harp laid sideways in a wooden case that has a keyboard made up of eighty-eight black and white keys. Touching the keys causes felt-covered hammers to strike the strings and then spring back. There are also three pedals on a piano: the damper pedal on the right; the soft pedal, called the una corda, on the left; and the sostenuto pedal in the middle.

The damper pedal raises the dampers off the strings and holds them off. (A damper is a small, felt-covered block that drops onto the piano string to stop it from vibrating.) That way, when the fingers are removed from the keys, the sound does not stop. The damper pedal is used for playing legato (a smooth, graceful, connected style) or for allowing two tones to sound at the same time. The una corda pedal allows only one string to be played (this affects only the higher notes, which are double- or triple-strung), therefore reducing the volume of sound. The sostenuto pedal sustains or holds sounds.

Bartolomeo Cristofori, an Italian instrument builder, is credited with inventing the piano in the early 1700s. The piano's ancestors are the harpsichord and the clavichord, but in both of these instruments the strings were plucked instead of being struck by hammers.

A harpsichord in the Flemish style

Today, pianos have become one of the most important instruments; they are employed as solo instruments, as accompaniment (support) to other instruments or voices, and as an aid in composing music, and they are able to perform just about any style of music. Electric pianos and electronic keyboards that reproduce piano sounds are available nowadays.

Pipe Organs

The hydraulis, an ancient Greek instrument, was the ancestor of the pipe organ; it was invented in 246 BCE by Ctesibius of Alexandria. The word "hydraulis" is from the Greek words for water (*hydro*) and pipe (*aulos*). When it was operated, a large water-containing chamber regulated the pressure of the air that was sent through a keyboard to pipes. This instrument was widely used throughout the ancient world.

A pipe organ is both a wind and a keyboard instrument. It is called a pipe organ because it produces sound by causing air to flow through pipes. The air is stored in wind chests, supplied by a bellows or an electric fan, and then made available to specific pipes. Knobs called stops control the pipes to allow certain tones selected by the organist to be heard. The keys are touched to produce the tones. Typically a large instrument, an organ has several keyboards, including a pedal keyboard.

Organ pipes

The console of the pipe organ at the United States Naval Academy Chapel

Pipe organs are designed and built individually to fit the architectural space in which it is to sit and to meet the needs of the organization buying the instrument. Usually these instruments are housed in churches and other places of worship, and sometimes in concert halls. The largest theater-style pipe organ ever built is in Boardwalk Hall in Atlantic City, New Jersey.

Harps

One of the oldest instruments, the harp is found in differing forms throughout the world. The word "harp" developed from Anglo-Saxon and Old Norse words whose root means to pluck. This instrument has strings stretched across an open frame that are plucked or strummed with the fingers. Harps vary in size and structure. The classical harp has seven pedals at its base, while the folk harp or lever harp has no pedals.

Portrayed in ancient sculptures and mentioned in early writings, harps were played in the lands of Babylonia and Mesopotamia; burial chambers in Mesopotamia contained several harplike instruments. A wall painting containing a picture of a harp was found in the tomb of the Egyptian pharaoh Ramses III (1198–1166 BCE). Five thousand years ago, a harp used in Egypt consisted of six strings attached to a curved wooden body with small pins. The harp was the traditional instrument of the bards (poets and musicians) of England and Ireland; it became the national symbol of Ireland.

The harp is not a standard member of the symphony orchestra, and it is played mainly as a solo instrument. When an orchestral work does include the harp, the staff on the score is written under the percussion instruments. Chords are usually performed in broken form on a harp, with the notes being sounded one after the other rather than simultaneously; from this comes the Italian term for a broken chord: arpeggio, meaning in the style of a harp.

Harp

In the seventeenth and eighteenth centuries many different types of harps were constructed. Today a classical harpist (or harper) usually plays the concert or the pedal harp, which was an innovation of Jacob Hochbrucker (1673–1763). Hochbrucker's improvements allowed a harpist to produce two pitches from each string, since the pedals change the pitches of the strings. Further changes were made to the harp in about 1750 in Paris by the harp makers Georges Cousineau (1733–1799) and his son Jacques (1760–1824), who added extra pedals. Sébastien Érard (1752–1831), a French instrument maker, created a mechanism that enabled each string to be shortened by one or two semitones; this improvement allowed a harpist to perform in any key.

The size and shape of the harp is an important factor in the sounds it produces, since the length of each string determines how high or low a sound it can make. A modern concert harp is about seventy inches tall and forty inches wide, and it weighs about eighty pounds. The electric harp is one of the latest steps in the evolution of this instrument.

10 Operas and Oratorios

It is so important for people at a young age to be invited to embrace classical music and opera.

LUCIANO PAVAROTTI, ITALIAN TENOR (1935–2007)

Operas

Ancient Greek dramas inspired another form of music: opera. The first operas were based on Greek mythology. Using music to present a drama has been a custom throughout the ages in all cultures. Dramas set to music have related goals: entertainment and/or education. An opera is a play set to music; it can be serious (called "opera seria" in the eighteenth century) or comic (sometimes called "opera buffa" or "opéra comique"). Operas create a special magic due to the combination of the drama, the special effects, the elaborate scenery, the magnificent voices, and the fantastic music. Attending a live performance of an opera creates an excitement that cannot be easily explained.

With the coming of the Renaissance, interest in non-church music increased. The courts staged entertainment for the nobility that ranged from simple plays to dramatic great spectacles. Opera was created in Italy. The first work now known as an opera was performed in 1597; however, the word "opera" was not used until 1639. It comes from the word *opus*, meaning "work," and is a shortened form of the Italian *opera in musica*, which means "works in music." This musical genre became popular in the 1620s and quickly spread throughout Italy.

Interior of an
opera house

In the late sixteenth century a society of Italian scholars called the Florentine Camerata became interested in ancient Greek tragedies and choruses. The members of the Camerata believed that portions of the Greek dramas had been sung instead of spoken. They wanted to return to this tradition, but they had no idea how the music had actually sounded. The concept of the ancient Greeks presenting their plays set to music was very appealing to the Camerata, so they wrote music to accompany stories.

The score of one of the earliest attempts at writing opera has survived; it is titled *Eurydice* and is based on a play by Ottavio Rinuccini. Jacopo Peri (1561–1633) set this play to music in 1600 for the wedding of King Henry IV of France. A libretto is the text or words of an opera or oratorio. It is derived from the Italian word *libro*, meaning book. Rinuccini was the first librettist.

In 1607 the first work to be considered a true opera, *L'Orfeo, favola in musica* (Orpheus, a Legend in Music), was composed by Claudio Monteverdi (1567–1643), an Italian composer whose style straddled the very end of the Renaissance and the early baroque. The Greek myth of Orpheus and Eurydice has been the subject of more than thirty operas. Monteverdi's *L'Orfeo* is based on the ancient Greek legend of Orpheus, the greatest musician in the world, who seeks to rescue his love, Eurydice, from the underworld. This work contains all of the elements that are required to consider a musical work an opera: a combination of singing, acting, orchestral music, costumes, scenery, and frequently a ballet or some other form of dance. While William Shakespeare (1564–1616) was writing his plays, Monteverdi was composing his music.

Opera began as entertainment for the nobility; however, it rapidly came to be admired by all the people. This new genre of music became very popular throughout Europe. In 1637 the first public opera house opened in Venice, Italy, and by 1700 at least sixteen more theaters had been built in Italy. Between 1637 and the end of the century, 388 operas were produced in Venice. Opera grew quickly in popularity, and by 1700 other European countries, including Austria, France, England, and Germany, had constructed opera houses.

Jean-Baptiste Lully (1632–1687) was a composer who had been born in Italy but lived in France during the baroque era. Working for the court of Louis XIV, Lully composed operas that were more suited to the French language and French tastes. With the librettist Philippe Quinault, he succeeded in establishing a new and essentially French type of opera known as *tragédie lyrique* (lyric tragedy). Lully created sixteen operas, each containing five acts. His French-style works exhibited several differences from the Italian style of opera. His operas contained elaborate ballets and *divertissements* (entertainments that interrupt the plot), which appealed to French audiences. The composer established a form for his overtures that is known as the French overture. It consists of two parts: the first is a slow and majestic section with dotted rhythms. The second part, which may contain a theme taken from the first section, is livelier and contrapuntal. The French overture was one of the most influential musical patterns of the baroque period.

Opera is expensive to stage and perform because it involves elaborate sets, special equipment and technicians to operate this equipment, singers, an orchestra, and a large theater. Many operatic works incorporate lavish scenery, complex staging, and spectacular displays. Opera requires the audience to accept certain operatic conventions; for instance, the people on the stage are always singing the words instead of talking. There are exceptions to these conventions, but for the most part, they have been followed by all operatic composers.

All of the dialogue in an opera is either sung or recited in recitative, which is a style of vocal music that is in between speaking and singing. The recitative sets up the scene for the aria, which is an elaborate melody. The music in opera is continuous, with set pieces such as solos, duets, trios, quartets, quintets, and so on, and choruses. Some operas are called number operas; this is a term for an opera consisting of individual sections, known as numbers, which contain the arias, duets, ensembles, and recitatives that make up the entire opera. A solo is presented by only one performer, duets employ two, trios have three performers, and so on. A chorus is a group of people singing together (at the same time). A group of two or more singers performing together is called an ensemble. In ensemble pieces the singers create an interaction of separate melody lines. The chorus can perform by itself or interact with a soloist. Just as in Greek dramas, the chorus may comment on what is happening in the opera or become part of a scene. The chorus adds to the dramatic effect of the story. Many operas include dancers as well.

Bel canto, which means beautiful singing in Italian, is an elegant Italian vocal style of the eighteenth and early nineteenth centuries. This style emphasized a smooth movement of the voice and an effortless performance of musical embellishments. Many Italian composers of that time wrote their operas keeping the bel canto traditions in mind. Singers who were able to achieve the goals of bel canto drove their audiences wild.

Opera poster

An overture is the introduction to a musical work presented by an orchestra. The overture might contain some of the themes and motifs (melodic subjects) of the music that will be performed, to give the audience a hint of what is coming. Operatic overtures set the stage for the entertainment that lies ahead. The orchestra performs the overture and then provides the accompaniment for the singing that follows. It establishes the mood for the scenes and acts with preludes (introductions), interludes (inserted pieces), and postludes (concluding pieces). Composers of operas include many instruments to accompany the singers; however, the number of instruments used in each opera varies according to what the composer decides to include.

Opera singers are categorized by the types of voices they have. Female voices are classified, from the highest voice to the lowest, as soprano, mezzo-soprano, and alto; a coloratura, which is a type of soprano, is the highest female voice and has the greatest ability to perform trills, which are rapid alterations between two notes. Male voices are classified, from highest to lowest, as tenor, baritone, and bass. Sopranos and tenors usually portray the heroes of the opera, while the other voices are typically the parents, friends, evildoers, and criminals.

Composers often wrote dozens of operas; some remain popular today, while others had only a few performances and then disappeared from the stage. Operas have been written in many different languages. Numerous countries have developed their own operatic traditions.

Opera Houses

The Metropolitan Opera is located at Lincoln Center for the Performing Arts in New York City and is the most famous opera house in the United States. The repertoire (supply of works) of the Metropolitan Opera, sometimes called the Met, includes all of the most important operas. The Met also commissions new operas to be written. In 1995 the Met installed devices on the seats so that the audience could easily follow the libretto in English: the translation appears on individual computerized screens mounted behind each row of seats. This innovation is catching on in many opera houses. Opera houses are found in larger cities throughout the world.

Odessa Opera Theater, Odessa, Ukraine

La Scala, Milan, Italy

Oratorios

A musical genre that is similar to opera is called oratorio. Oratorios were named for the place they were first performed: an oratory (prayer hall). They are large-scale musical compositions performed without the costumes, scenery, and acting that operas have, but oratorios do employ an orchestra, soloists, and a chorus. Usually the chorus has a more prominent role in an oratorio than in an opera. Oratorios are strictly concert pieces and are most often based on biblical or religious subjects. In this respect, they resemble the mystery and miracle plays of the Middle Ages.

Emilio de' Cavalieri, an Italian composer who lived in the sixteenth century, is credited with creating the forerunner of the first oratorio, *La rappresentatione di anima e di corpo* (The Representation of the Soul and the Body). This piece, written in 1600, was a religious work that made use of acting and costumes, so it was not a true oratorio. Cavalieri is also celebrated for his contribution to the development of the new recitative style.

Giacomo Carissimi was a significant composer who lived in the seventeenth century; he is regarded as the originator of the oratorio. His musical compositions were religious, reflecting the fact that he was a priest, and did not employ acting or costumes. *Jephthah*, the most well-known of his oratorios, is based on the story found in the biblical Book of Judges. This work established the oratorio genre.

Oratorio societies exist around the world. Many oratorios were written by operatic composers; for a time oratorio and opera flourished side by side, but gradually they took different paths. The best-known oratorio is George Frideric Handel's *Messiah*, which contains the Hallelujah Chorus. In 1888 a recording was made on a wax cylinder, a technology developed by Thomas Edison, of Handel's oratorio *Israel in Egypt*. It is the first known piece of recorded music.

11 The Renaissance, Baroque, and Classical Eras

Great music is that which penetrates the ear with facility and leaves the memory with difficulty. Magical music never leaves the memory.

SIR THOMAS BEECHAM, CONDUCTOR (1879–1961)

Classical is a term used to cover music that has been composed within an established tradition and intended as a major art form. The word "classical" indicates that a certain level of excellence has been reached. The word further implies a high level of craftsmanship and the universal appeal of this work. Classical-music composers and their works are defined by the musical periods to which they belong. Musical eras reflect the type of musical style that was popular in the culture of that period.

In order to understand the changes in music over time, we must look at and be aware of the important historic events that shaped and produced those changes. As composers explored, enriched, and refined their compositions, many developments and events impacted the culture and customs of the societies in which they lived. These changes influenced the composer's lives, the way they wrote their music, and the way music was presented. Scholars disagree somewhat as to when one musical style period ends and the next begins, and the periods do overlap. Since each period leads into the next, and each period represents an idea of genre, style, and tastes, the dates are simply a guideline to the main periods in the history of Western music.

Major Musical Eras

Renaissance: 1450–1600

Baroque: 1600–1750

Classical: 1750–1825

Romantic: 1800–1900

Modern: 1900–present

The Renaissance: 1450–1600

BACKGROUND

The Renaissance was an era of new beginnings in Europe. The word "Renaissance" is from the Italian word meaning rebirth. What was being reborn was the tradition of intellectual exploration and artistic experimentation that sixteenth-century thinkers and artists believed had been lost during the era called the Middle Ages. The Middle Ages got their name because they came in the "middle" between the time of the ancient civilizations of Greece and Rome and the rebirth they inspired in the Renaissance, when there was a fresh focus on knowledge and the arts. The Renaissance stressed individual achievement and a belief that humans were reasonable beings capable of truth and goodness. During this era the attention and interest of scholars and educated people moved away from the rigid values that had been enforced by the inflexible religious beliefs of the Middle Ages, when free and honest study of science and the arts was not allowed. Renaissance scholars sought to advance the concept of humanism, which demanded a search for truth and factual evidence.

Artists, musicians, poets, and philosophers were financially supported by patrons who were either members of the aristocracy, organized groups such as guilds, wealthy merchants, or the church itself. Until the eighteenth century, musicians were not able to pursue their work outside of the patronage system. The patronage system had permitted the powerful and the wealthy people a say in the art that was produced for them. This often created conflict between the patron and the artist.

The Protestant Reformation began in the sixteenth century as a protest movement to transform the Catholic church. The Reformation led to the final break between the Middle Ages and the rise of modern Europe. The object of the Protestant reformers was to alter some of the practices of the Catholic church and bring it more in line with the new secular thinking, which was closer to the ideals espoused by the Renaissance. When this change did not happen in the Catholic church, new types of Christian churches and doctrines were established that reflected the concepts that led to the Enlightenment. The Reformation shattered centuries of a common faith and religious unity throughout Europe.

The printing press, invented by Johannes Gutenberg (1398–1468), made it possible for information to be communicated and distributed more easily and cheaply. This revolutionary method of printing now made affordable books available to all, and literacy increased throughout Europe. The printing press helped to spread the new belief systems, the scientifically based concepts about the universe, and the intense interest in reason and logical thought produced during the Renaissance. Scientific investigation and discoveries flourished during this period. The compass was developed and made the exploration of distant lands possible. Medical knowledge also was advanced. Artists turned their attention from the religious to the real world and began depicting scenes from daily life. New mathematical concepts were developed. The Renaissance reshaped the cultural climate of the Western world.

Leonardo da Vinci (1452–1519) is considered the perfect model of a man of the Renaissance. He was an artist, an inventor, an engineer, a scientist, and a mathematician. Leonardo's accomplishments represented that which all intellectuals of the Renaissance believed a human being should hope to achieve. Famous for his great intelligence, fabulous art, brilliant inventions, astounding creativity, and vast curiosity, Leonardo still inspires feelings of awe.

Statue of
Leonardo da Vinci

RENAISSANCE INNOVATIONS IN MUSIC

Throughout the Renaissance music underwent dynamic changes. In earlier times the voice was considered the principal means of presenting music, and instruments were employed to accompany the human voice. This era also enjoyed a cappella music, or voices without any instrumental accompaniment. Many a cappella pieces were written in a continuous imitation polyphonic style, where the voices repeatedly imitated one another in an overlapping fashion.

During the Renaissance composers began to write instrumental music. The recorder, the viol, the virginals (an instrument in the harpsichord family), and the lute were popular. In the early years of the Renaissance instruments were grouped together because they were in the same family; later in this era instruments of different types were combined in ensembles.

New musical instruments were invented and developed. Advances in metalwork were incorporated into brass instruments, whose design began to approach that of the instruments that we use today. The trumpet had been used from the earliest times of recorded history for religious and ceremonial occasions. Until the fifteenth century, instrument makers did not bend brass tubes. In the early part of that century, as techniques of metalwork improved, an S-shaped trumpet was fashioned; later it was followed by a folded trumpet, and in time a slide trumpet was created. The trombone (Italian for big trumpet) was developed out of the slide trumpet early in the Renaissance era. The first trombones were tenor instruments, like the modern trombone, and were used in bands and church services.

The viola da gamba (literally, "leg viol"), a bowed stringed instrument held between the knees (much like the cello), was crafted in the late fifteenth century. It had six strings made of gut that were stretched over a bridge, and its back was flat. Viols were constructed in four sizes: treble, tenor, bass, and double bass. They became well-liked ensemble instruments throughout Europe.

A bass woodwind instrument known as a dulcian, also called the curtal, was produced in the sixteenth century. The dulcian was a double-reed instrument that, owing to its more convenient size, probably took the place of the shawm. This instrument was the ancestor of the bassoon.

The use of the printing press with movable type also affected music, since now music did not have to be painstakingly copied by hand. As the prosperity of merchants and tradespeople rose, they began to have money left over, after their basic needs were met, to spend on the arts and education. The middle and upper classes wanted to follow courtly fashions. They wished to become skilled in music because it was one sign of being a well-rounded, well-educated person.

RENAISSANCE MUSICAL GENRES

Although Renaissance musicians continued to write sacred music, many stopped composing only religious music and began writing in secular genres including the madrigal and the chanson (a polyphonic French song usually set to poetry). The madrigal was one of the most popular genres of music during the Renaissance and was an important part of secular (non-religious) music. Madrigals were compositions for several voices; they were usually short (rarely more than twelve lines), lyrical, and rich in harmony. Frequently love was the subject of the text. This genre thrived in the British and Italian courts. Since madrigals often told a story, Renaissance composers sought to make the words of the text more clearly understood. They created music in which the phrasing of words was more speechlike and the accompaniment highlighted the words. Madrigals usually were the songs chosen by the traveling musicians who entertained at the courts, fairs, and other festivities. By playing these love songs and telling stories through music, the traveling musicians brought these new musical genres to the people.

Outstanding composers of this era included Guillaume Dufay, Josquin des Prez, Roland de Lassus, and Giovanni Pierluigi da Palestrina. The Flemish composer Lassus (1532–1594) and the Italian composer Palestrina (1525–1594) were masters of Renaissance polyphony, in which all voice parts are given equal importance. Lassus produced over two thousand pieces of music, and he influenced many later composers. Palestrina was the most famous Italian composer of his time and was celebrated especially for his contrapuntal (two or more voices heard at the same time) composition. Both men were composers of Catholic church music, but in addition to masses (the central service of the Catholic church), motets (pieces with one or more voices), and hymns (songs of praise), they also wrote a number of secular madrigals. Renaissance composers also wrote pieces that accompanied dancing.

Josquin des Prez applied the canon, a technique used by earlier composers, to his works which contain themes using continuous imitation in their structure. The repetition of a melody in different voices was a contrapuntal device that he perfected in his music. This technique was the forerunner of the modern fugue. He is also noted for his motets, which often used this device.

The French chanson was generally written for three or four voices. This was also a very popular kind of secular, polyphonic, lyrical ballad, often accompanied by instruments. A wide variety of themes were explored in chansons, including courtly love and descriptions of heroic figures.

The Baroque Era: 1600–1750

BACKGROUND

The word "baroque" means elaborate. The music of this era was very ornate. It was the era of such composers as Claudio Monteverdi, Johann Sebastian Bach, Antonio Vivaldi, George Frideric Handel, and Domenico Scarlatti. These 150 years saw many great changes and daring adventures. During this period Europe was in turmoil: numerous countries and often various factions within a country clashed. Calls for religious reform created conflict and tension in society. The conquest and settlement of overseas empires caused distrust and competition between the European countries. During this time period the basis of Europe's economy was transforming from agriculture to industry, and the rising middle class was becoming a thriving, free-thinking, and better-informed group. The far-reaching control, power, and authority of traditional monarchies were being questioned by the people.

The baroque era was an age where reason and logical thought were major issues. Nicolas Copernicus (1473–1543), Johannes Kepler (1571–1630), and Galileo Galilei (1564–1642) advanced research regarding the universe. Copernicus is called the founder of modern astronomy. While he lived he was afraid to make his work available to others, since he feared that he would be accused of challenging accepted religious beliefs. He had good reason to be afraid, because the Inquisition, established by the Catholic church, was able to interrogate anyone whose beliefs or practices were different from the opinion of the church, and the punishment for any suspected deviation from such beliefs, called heresy, was extremely severe. In 1530 Copernicus published his work *De Revolutionibus*, which asserted that the earth rotated on its axis once daily and traveled around the sun once yearly. This remarkable concept was in total opposition to the philosophy supported by the church. The most important result of Copernicus's work is that it forever changed human beings' view of themselves within the universe.

Johannes Kepler, building on the discoveries of Copernicus, theorized that the Earth and other planets travel about the sun. This German mathematician and astronomer was the first to accurately describe the movements of the planets about the sun in elliptical orbits. In 1609 he published *Astronomia Nova*, explaining his discoveries. He also did valuable work in optics and geometry, and his book *Stereometrica Doliorum* formed the basis of integral calculus.

The telescope was invented by the Dutch and improved by the Italian astronomer Galileo Galilei. He was the first to employ it to systematically examine the heavens. Galileo made a chain of important discoveries using his telescope, including the moons of the planet Jupiter and the phases of the planet Venus.

Also a believer in Copernican theories, Galileo was brought before the Inquisitors of the church and forced to renounce those views. He was sentenced to house arrest for the remainder of his life. Galileo died in 1642, the year Isaac Newton was born.

Sir Isaac Newton (1642–1727), an English mathematician and physicist, formulated fundamental laws regarding gravity and motion. Newton was the greatest English mathematician of his generation. He described planetary motion and also developed a new theory regarding light and color. Newton studied the mathematics and the physics of the French philosopher and scientist René Descartes (1596–1650), another brilliant mind of the baroque era. Descartes's work influenced many of his contemporaries; his fame as a philosopher, a mathematician, and a physicist has survived the centuries. He was a highly original thinker whose philosophy led to a more rational and scientific method for conducting research.

BAROQUE INNOVATIONS IN MUSIC

Baroque music reflects all of the revolutionary philosophy of the era. The work of these great minds (and many more) influenced the composers of the baroque era. A major transition from the Renaissance period to the baroque was the shift of attention from independent parts of equal importance to a single melody with chords that accompanied it. This movement from polyphony (one-line voices that were interwoven) to homophony (having a single melodic line with accompaniment), also called monody (meaning one song), was a major change in musical structure. The members of the Italian scholarly group known as the Florentine Camerata were the major promoters of this change; they wished to boost the emotional power of the words in the dramas that became the basis of opera. Now the emphasis was on the melody, the text, and an underlying chordal harmony.

Basso continuo, meaning continuous bass, was played throughout a musical work. At least two players were necessary, and one had to play an instrument that could produce chords, such as an organ or a harpsichord. Often, instead of writing out the specific notes of the chord, composers wrote a number below the bass note to indicate the chord to be played. This musical shorthand, called figured bass, allowed the performer to fill in the harmony. Continuous bass is a principal feature of baroque music.

During the baroque era the members of the middle class created their own forms of entertainment, since they were normally excluded from the festive activities of the nobility. Baroque musicians still served under their noble patrons, the state, or the church. Because all artists were dependent on the sponsorship of the church or the wealthy aristocracy, most performances were held in the churches, palaces, and grand halls of their patrons. Eventually, during this era, public concerts or opera performances became more common, and the middle class could attend.

Many instruments were further developed during this era. The baroque harpsichord was a stringed keyboard instrument; unlike the piano, however, its strings were plucked by a quill. It often had two keyboards and three sets of strings. The harpsichord was the main instrument used in the basso continuo. It is one of the most distinctive sounds of the baroque era and was a favorite instrument of baroque composers when they created solo music.

During the baroque period the violin became the leader of the stringed instruments, and its sound became the major timbre in ensemble music. Antonio Stradivari (1644–1737) of Italy constructed violins that are still in great demand among professional violinists today; in 2006 a Stradivarius violin was sold at auction for a price of over $3.5 million. The Stradivarius studio in Italy became famous for the quality of the instruments produced there. Stradivarius violins were constructed to produce a richness of sound that cannot be duplicated even today. Stradivari's craftsmanship and originality were evident: he improved the arch (the curving of the top), the bridge, the position of the sound holes, and even the varnish. Stradivari sought to make perfect instruments; his finest instruments were made after 1700. He produced over one thousand instruments, including violas, mandolins, and cellos.

One of the most significant transformations in music came about during the baroque era: the idea of the orchestra. The modern concept of an orchestra began in the late sixteenth century, when composers began writing music for instrumental groups. Baroque orchestras consisted mainly of strings, with some woodwind instruments. They did not include a brass section: valves were not added to brass instruments until the nineteenth century, so baroque brass instruments were limited in their usefulness. However, brass instruments were at times included in an orchestral piece for a specific purpose.

Baroque woodwinds were all made of wood and had few or no keys. Flutes now replaced recorders; oboes and bassoons became the principal woodwind instruments of the orchestra. Throughout medieval times an instrument called the shawm, a double-reed instrument with seven finger holes and a range of about two octaves, was popular. Shawms were used during the Middle Ages and the Renaissance, but they were gradually replaced in the baroque period by the oboe. In this period the woodwind instruments were made in three or four sections instead of a single piece of wood, reeds were improved, and keys were added.

The Stradivarius
Spanish II, 1687–89

The makeup of a baroque orchestra often depended upon which instruments and players were available. Baroque composers did not always propose which instrument should play a specific part, so any available instrument that had the proper range was employed. During this era the orchestra was much smaller than the orchestras to which we are accustomed today. The small size of the orchestra compelled the composers to pay close attention to the balance of the sounds and the blending of the timbres. It was in the opera houses that the role of orchestra became important, because composers had to consider the dramatic effects of the accompanying music and the way it worked with the voices.

Another important feature of the baroque era was improvisation, which is the art of creating or making up the music as one plays. Composers of both vocal and instrumental music often merely outlined the melodic line, with the intention of having the performer invent his or her own ornamentation. This practice allowed the performers a great deal of freedom and an opportunity to add to the composition. Eventually composers felt it was necessary to assert their authority over the music they had written and to reclaim their right to choose how all of their music was to be performed. Improvisation is still customary today in jazz.

With the increased interest in developing and improving instruments there was also a strong desire to become masters of these instruments. During the baroque era the rise of virtuosity increased the importance of instrumental music. The word "virtuoso" (plural: virtuosi) is Italian, and it means a person who is an expert and outstanding performer. Most baroque composers were also brilliant virtuosi on their chosen instruments.

BAROQUE MUSICAL GENRES

Vocal musical genres of the baroque era included opera, oratorios, the chorale, and the cantata. The chorale originated as a hymn (a song of praise associated with worship) with very melodic tunes used by German Protestants. Martin Luther (1483–1564) was a leader of the Protestant Reformation in Germany. Sometime after he became a priest in the Catholic church, he realized that he was opposed to some of the church's views and teachings. At first Luther and other reformers attempted to make changes from within the church, but the debates became bitter conflicts and soon caused a complete break from Catholicism.

Lutheran Protestants conducted services in German rather than Latin. Luther and his assistants wrote the first chorales used by his church. The chorales were intended to be sung in unison (as one voice) by the congregation; therefore, the music is simple, and the same melody is repeated for each verse. Many of the tunes they originally employed were taken from Catholic church chants. Eventually the chorales were performed in four-part harmony, with each chord containing four notes; this created four melodic lines. This type of harmony echoed the trend in this era to present one melodic line accompanied by harmony.

A cantata is a work for singers, chorus, and instruments. It can be either religious or secular and usually contains several movements. These large-scale vocal works contain solos, duets, and choruses and include orchestral or keyboard accompaniment. Cantatas began in Italy but became very popular in Germany, where they grew into the most important type of Lutheran sacred music and were made a central part of the religious service.

Instrumental musical genres of the baroque era included the suite, the concerto grosso, the toccata, and the prelude. A suite is based on dance music; it contains several movements that are all written in the same or closely related keys. A baroque suite might include five to twenty-five different dances, for which the suite's various movements were named. The standard suite contained at least the allemande, an elegant German dance; the gigue, a lively and spirited Irish or Scottish jig; the courante, an energetic French dance; and the sarabande, a slower dance in triple time. Suites often mixed together both lively and elegant dance types to give variety to the music. Rhythm is an essential factor in a suite, just as it is in any type of dance.

In the concerto grosso the idea of contrast in music reached a peak. This musical genre is antiphonal (from the Greek meaning opposing): a group of instruments performs in contrast with another group that plays a response to the first group. Usually the groups were divided between a small group of soloists, such as a string trio (two violins and a cello), and the full orchestra (called tutti, meaning all), which generally was the strings and, perhaps, some woodwinds.

The toccata is commonly written for a keyboard instrument; the word derives from the Italian *toccare*, meaning to touch. Baroque toccatas were composed for the organ or the harpsichord with complicated passages and elaborate runs that emphasized the virtuosity of the performer. Toccatas originated in Italy, but it was in Germany that this genre was fully explored and developed.

The prelude is a relatively free-form type of music and was not as restricted by the rules that governed other musical genres. It is a short piece that might serve as an introduction to several movements that are usually longer and more complicated. A prelude is similar to an overture, which introduces an opera or an oratorio. Preludes are expressive pieces that display variety and often include some improvisation. Other musical genres cultivated during the baroque era include the fugue and the sonata. Because these compositions underwent many changes from the baroque to the classical period and continued to evolve, they will be discussed later.

The Classical Era: 1750–1825

BACKGROUND

The early part of the classical era in music is called the rococo (from the French word *rocaille*, meaning a type of shell), suggesting the decorativeness and gracefulness of this era. This musical period originated in France, where it was also called *style galant*, or courtly style, in reaction to the ornate and technically complicated music of the baroque. The object was to present music in a lighter style with an emphasis on simplicity, order, and a more natural feel. In the eighteenth century this French reaction to baroque music reached Germany and Italy. As the baroque era entered its final phase, the classical era was becoming well established in Western Europe.

From the eighteenth to the early nineteenth century the countries of Europe were at the height of their global power and influence. But during the classical era the old social order started to break down. The development of steam power allowed goods to be produced by a new manufacturing industry, and the shift, already in progress, from a farming-based economy to a modern industrial system moved ahead quickly. The beginnings of the Industrial Revolution had a dramatic impact on the expansion of technology, the rapid growth of cities, and the cultural climate.

The classical era in music encompassed the same time period as the American and French Revolutions. European society was changing, partly because of the prosperity created by the new lands in the Americas that the European countries had discovered, conquered, and settled. Improved economic conditions overall allowed more people to acquire wealth. A successful and growing middle class required reasonable control over its expanding economic opportunities and was seeking greater individual freedom. As the era advanced, more people became involved in banking, investing and finance, and professional and business projects. The middle class was now able to become more engaged with the arts. One of the key developments of the classical period was an increase in the number of public concerts. Concert societies flourished in London, and similar groups were founded in France and Germany. Composers attracted large audiences for these concerts; now composers could organize concerts that would display their work.

In the eighteenth century the objective of the French writers of the *Great Encyclopedia* was to organize all knowledge and to examine information in a rational and useful way. The goal of these intellectuals was to use methods that made the investigation and exploration of any subject a systematic and orderly process. This philosophy was central to the thinking of the scientists and scholars of this time and is why the era is called the Age of Enlightenment. The aim of these great thinkers was to use human reason to combat ignorance, superstition, and tyranny in all aspects of life in order to establish a better world.

Until the eighteenth century the behavior and beliefs of the common people were regulated by the doctrines of the church and by the aristocracy, both of which claimed to have inherited the right to control the lives of the lower classes. During the Renaissance, in fifteenth- and sixteenth-century Europe, a group of thinkers known as humanists arose and celebrated the ability of human beings to explore the world without being required to accept as true an approved way of thinking determined by the religious and governmental establishment. Humanitarian ideals expanded during the Enlightenment. Humanism seized upon the methods, based on observation and facts, that were being employed in science and applied them to politics, religion, and art.

During the Enlightenment, the contributions of the scholars, scientists, philosophers, musicians, architects, and artists during past eras, including the Renaissance and baroque periods, were studied and expanded to create fresh ideas and images. The thinkers of this era sought freedom, in all of its expressions, and tolerance for new or unique inspirations. These social and intellectual reformers questioned the authority of the people and policies that controlled the destiny and thoughts of their cultures. Viewing the world in a truthful and natural way became an important factor in art.

John Locke (1632–1704) was an Oxford scholar, a physician, an economist, and one of the greatest philosophers of the late seventeenth and early eighteenth centuries. He was among those who chose to employ reason in a search for truth. Locke believed that all people should be independent and treated equally; he also held the opinion that a government must have the consent of those it governs. He influenced the direction of political thought that led to the American Revolution that began in 1775, and to the crafting of the American Constitution.

The French philosopher and author François-Marie Arouet—known by his pen name, Voltaire (1694–1778)—was a towering figure of the Enlightenment. He represents the goals of the era. His enormous output of writings include fifty-six plays, dialogues, historical writings, novels, poetry, essays, scientific papers, philosophical works, and many pamphlets. Voltaire promoted liberation from the existing traditions of European society, which restricted people, and sought reform of the social, cultural, political, and legal institutions that were in place. He criticized a society in which all power lay in the hands of the king, the nobility, and the church. Voltaire rejected the idea of organized religion; he believed in religious freedom and in the separation of church and state. Because his writing criticized both the monarch and the Catholic church, he suffered constantly from the fear of being arrested and imprisoned. Voltaire spent time in England, where he was impressed by the greater freedoms enjoyed by the British people and the writings of William Shakespeare and Isaac Newton.

Benjamin Franklin (1706–1790) was one of the founding fathers of American independence. Franklin was born in Boston but made his home in Philadelphia. He was a scientist, a printer, a humorist, a businessman, an inventor, a statesman, and a remarkable man of the Enlightenment. Talented and brilliant, with countless interests, Franklin made important discoveries and advancements. Among his many inventions were bifocal eyeglasses, the lightning rod, a wood-burning stove, and an odometer (to measure the length of postal routes). He was also a musician and played several instruments, including the violin, the harp, and the guitar.

Ben Franklin had a great effect on the future of the United States of America; he was the only person to have signed all four of the documents that helped to create the United States. Franklin became an international celebrity; he crossed the Atlantic to Europe eight times and negotiated treaties for the new United States with England, France, Germany, Spain, and Sweden. Franklin was America's first ambassador to France and convinced the French to support the American Revolution against England.

The yearning to systematize all knowledge also affected the attitudes of classical composers. The ornate baroque style was transformed into a new approach reflecting organization, clarity, naturalness, purity, and balance. The superstars of music in this era were Joseph Haydn, Wolfgang Amadeus Mozart, Ludwig van Beethoven, and Franz Schubert. They pioneered new pathways for music, using the past as stepping-stones.

CLASSICAL INNOVATIONS IN MUSIC

A fresh way of thinking began in music. The elaborate counterpoint that dominated the baroque era gave way to themes and motifs. The basso continuo that had been an important component of baroque music was replaced by a flexible bass line. Polyphonic writing was abandoned in favor of a homophonic texture, a single melody with chords.

Many more elements of a piece were written out by the composer; improvisations and embellishments by performers became less and less lengthy, and less and less elaborate. Composers established contrasts between sections within movements to create clearer divisions between parts. They intensified the use of rhythm and silence. During the classical era, large instrumental music genres were produced, and composers added titles that identified their works clearly.

Alterations and modifications were made to instruments during the classical era thanks to new demands being made on the expressive capabilities of the various instruments. The orchestra was also enhanced. Johann Joachim Quantz (1697–1773) and Johann George Tromlitz (1725–1805), German flutists (also called flautists), are credited with many improvements to this instrument. Flutes were originally made of wood; in the nineteenth century they began to be manufactured in silver. Flute makers improved flute design and added keys to make it easier to play. Their innovations allowed the flute to rise to a position as the most popular of wind instruments.

During the baroque era the innovations of the German Johann Christoph Denner (1655–1707), who was working to improve the single-reed instrument called the chalumeau, led to his invention of a new instrument: the clarinet. His innovation of the speaker key gave the clarinet a larger register. Adding the clarinet to the orchestra became common practice around 1780 as improvements were made to the instrument, including the addition of more keys, smaller finger holes, a narrower mouthpiece, and experiments with tone holes. This allowed the wide range and unique sound of the clarinet to develop.

A more extensive use of brass began in the classical era. Toward the end of the seventeenth century, inventive adaptations to the sixteenth- and seventeenth-century hunting horns permitted them to enter the orchestra. Horns and trumpets became partners. The trumpet, as the soprano of the brass family, is its highest-pitched member. Early versions of this instrument had straight, narrow tubes and lacked finger holes. Once mechanical improvements were made to the trumpet, it was in demand as an orchestral instrument. Valves were not added until later.

Beethoven made the trombone a standard member of the orchestra. The trombone has a movable slide that takes the place of valves, since the movement of the slide alters the length of the vibrating air in the tube. This instrument first appeared in the fifteenth century, and the construction of the instrument has remained the same. (The brass section of the orchestra as we recognize it today was not complete during this era, for the tuba had yet to make an appearance.)

The percussion section of the classical orchestra reflected the tastes and trends of the era. The timpani is also known as the kettledrum; this was the first percussion instrument of the orchestra, starting in about 1600. Timpani were made of calfskins stretched over large copper bowls and held in place by a metal ring. Adjustable screws enabled them to be tuned to specific pitches. These drums were often teamed with trumpets to provide military effects to a work. Beethoven was the first composer to use the timpani as a solo instrument.

The piano replaced the harpsichord as the most popular keyboard instrument. The piano was developed by an Italian instrument maker, Bartolomeo Cristofori (1655–1731), who changed the plucking mechanism of the harpsichord to the hammer action that strikes the stings of a piano. The instrument was not immediately accepted by the composers of the classical era, because they still felt that the harpsichord was a superior instrument. As the design and capabilities of the piano improved, it became widely accepted as the instrument of choice for musicians and composers.

The classical orchestra contained about thirty-five instrumentalists. The heart of the classical orchestra was the string section; it was backed up by the woodwinds. The brass section helped to maintain the harmonies, and the timpani added rhythmic life. The object of composers was to blend all of the instrumental groups but still present a variety of musical texture and color.

From 1743 to 1778 the famed orchestra of the court at Mannheim introduced extraordinary changes in orchestral technique and compositional styles. This German orchestra had fewer than fifty musicians, but it became the model for later orchestras. It was famous throughout Europe for its large size, its thorough preparation, and its excellent musicians. The Mannheim orchestra usually contained twenty violins, four violas, four cellos, and four basses. The strings were joined by two flutes, two oboes, and two bassoons. One trumpet and four horns rounded out the orchestra. Occasionally a harpsichord or timpani would be included. New musical techniques introduced by the orchestra included an innovative treatment of dynamics that was soon reproduced by orchestras all over the continent. Instead of baroque-style dynamics, which were either loud or soft, the Mannheim orchestra introduced the use of a growing crescendo created by the whole orchestra that slowly propelled the music toward a climax.

CLASSICAL MUSICAL GENRES

Classical composers sought balance and proportion in their works. Their compositions were carefully planned to reflect the structural logic of the music. The elaborateness and ornamentation that had been preferred by the baroque composers were discarded in favor of simplicity and elegance. In the classical era, instrumental genres were favored over vocal genres. The sonata, the symphony, and the concerto were the standard genres used during this era.

The sonata is credited with having the most influence over the development of orchestra music. This genre is a series of several movements and was employed by baroque composers, but it reached new heights in the classical era. Early in the baroque era, the sonata used a single theme that was expanded through the use of contrapuntal techniques throughout the work. By the classical era, it had come to be firmly based on the development and expansion of two themes or theme groups that were set in contrasting sections of the movement. The contrast causes a conflict between the themes until this contrast is resolved in the final section of the work.

The classical symphony developed out of operatic overtures. It became a large-scale orchestral work and one of the most important musical genres. Symphonies in the early classical period followed strict rules; there were three movements: a faster opening movement, a slower middle movement, and a fast final movement. Therefore, the moods in the three movements of a symphony contrast as the themes unfold, expand, and develop.

The concerto genre was used when a soloist performed with an orchestra; the work focused on the featured solo performer. The cadenza is an elaborate, usually improvised passage in the concerto that provides the virtuoso with an opportunity to shine. Prior to the nineteenth century, the featured soloist was most likely to be the composer.

CLASSICAL DEVELOPMENTS IN OPERA

Christoph Willibald von Gluck (1714–1787) was a German-born musical theorist as well as a composer. In 1761, after traveling all over Europe, he came to believe that the kind of opera that had become fashionable during the baroque era contained too many unnatural, exaggerated and unbelievable elements, and that the performers had become more important than the actual work. He concluded that the function of the music was to serve the needs of the story. This was the type of thinking that the realists of the Enlightenment expected and encouraged.

Gluck's new style of opera integrated his ideas for a union of the music and the drama. He made the division between aria and recitative less severe by having the orchestra accompany the words that were recited. Gluck transformed the overture to make it more connected to the drama; he simplified the plot and incorporated the dancing to the purpose of the opera. He also increased the role of the chorus. On October 5, 1762, his first "reform opera," *Orfeo ed Euridice* (Orpheus and Euridice), premiered. Gluck and other operatic composers set a new direction for this art form. They provided it with a purity, unity, and elegance that was groundbreaking for serious opera.

12 The Romantic and Modern Eras

*A composer's horizon cannot
be far-reaching enough.*

PAUL HINDEMITH, COMPOSER (1895–1963)

The orderliness and discipline that characterize the arts of the classical era are in contrast with the disturbances and disorder of the revolutions that were occurring in Europe and the New World. Much of the work did not relate to the unrest and instability of the epoch. Beneath the surface of elegant courtly manners and highly polished style rumbled tremors of conflict. The vibrations caused by this earthquake began shaking the world. A great challenge arose to confront the ancient institutions and their traditional way of conducting politics and commerce. Revolutionary ideas had surfaced, struggled, and succeeded; a path of change broke out that led to the modern world.

The Romantic Era: 1800–1900

BACKGROUND

The romantic era spanned a century that declared the superiority of passion and emotion over reason and logic. The liberty to express feelings in place of the classical emphasis on restraint and control was the romantic model for the arts.

The eighteenth-century transfer of power from the aristocracy to the people and the change from an agricultural to an industrial society highlighted the importance of the individual. Now standards of behavior were no longer based on a formal courtly style, but were dictated by the rules of free enterprise and the rights of the common man. The slogan of the French Revolution, "Liberté, égalité, fraternité, ou la mort" (liberty, equality, brotherhood, or death), inspired this new direction. The fundamental ideals of this era were faith in human beings and their destiny, awareness and sensitivity to the beauty of nature, and concern and compassion for human suffering.

In contrast with the classical scholars' looking to ancient Greece for inspiration, the romantics sought to reexamine the thinking of the Middle Ages. That lengthy period of European history, which lasted from the breakup of the Roman Empire in the fifth century BCE until about the middle of the fifteenth century, takes its name from the romances—heroic narratives that originated in medieval literature. The world of nature was viewed as a source of mysterious powers. Fantastic creatures and folk tales replaced the gods and myths of the ancient Greeks. The legends recalling Robin Hood and his "band of merry men" and King Arthur amid his "Knights of the Round Table" replaced the heroes of the classical era. Glamorizing the past allowed the romantics to conceal their feelings of frustration and disappointment with the present.

The revolutions did not bring about the splendid society that had been expected; the new freedoms, in reality, brought mixed blessings. The Industrial Revolution took people off the land and placed them in airless factories where they performed mindless work. The French and American Revolutions did not make all men equal or even free. The optimistic future forecast by the thinkers of the Enlightenment gave way to doubt and disappointment.

The arts were still largely supported by wealthy aristocrats or by the church; this patronage system required the artist to produce work that would please his patrons. As this system changed, the artist began to labor for a broad audience consisting of his equals; in other words, the artist needed the support of the public. In this setting, each artist emerged as a distinct personality with an enthusiasm for creating what he or she deemed significant. Bolstered by this creative freedom, inventive romantic genres expressed the spontaneity, individuality, and temperament of the artist.

European history between 1800 and 1815 is labeled the Napoleonic Era because the early years of the nineteenth century in Europe were defined by the ambitions of Napoleon Bonaparte (1769–1821), the French emperor who wished to liberate all of Europe. His dream was to create a federation of free peoples in a Europe that would be united under a liberal government. The object of his Napoleonic Code was to replace existing laws with regulations that applied to all people. The most important principle of this civil code was that every person would be equal before the law. Napoleon's goals of equality and liberty inspired the artistic community. After he was captured and sent into exile, where he eventually died, his contribution to European civilization actually increased, because the principles Napoleon had championed were the triumph of ambition, talent, and determination over birth status.

The romantic scholars emphasized imagination; this can be easily recognized in the works of William Blake (1757–1827), an English painter and poet. Blake saw the world through the extremes of good versus evil; he was sensitive to the difficult problems that people faced. He was a Libertarian, a political doctrine declaring that every individual should be free to do as he wishes as long as what he or she does will not affect the rights of others. In the nineteenth century women had no individual rights, and slavery was an institution. Blake, through his writing and artwork, sought universal equality for women and for people of all races.

Sir Walter Scott (1771–1832) was a Scottish novelist and poet who based his themes on historical events and glamorized the past. Published in 1810, Scott's poem *The Lady of the Lake* refers to legends about King Arthur and established the author's popularity throughout Europe. He wrote twenty-seven books, including *Ivanhoe*, a tale of chivalry depicting the manners and gallantry that Scott believed existed in twelfth-century England. The story portrays the qualities of bravery and courage that Scott attributed to that earlier era. A yearning for a heroic past that contrasted utterly with the realities of the present was a recurring theme among many writers of this period.

There were, however, other writers who examined the dreadful circumstances of many people's lives. The poor and the lower levels of society experienced terrible problems with housing, sanitation, clean water, and hunger. Charles Dickens (1812–1870), the foremost novelist and social commentator of the Victorian era (the period of the English Queen Victoria's rule, 1837–1901), wrote novels that criticized those alarming living conditions. *Oliver Twist*, his 1838 novel about the use of child labor and children trained by criminals to work as thieves, illustrated the need for Victorian society to examine and deal with the sharp differences that existed between the more privileged classes and the people who lived in poverty.

The taste for medievalism was felt throughout all aspects of nineteenth-century life. A renewed interest in the Middle Ages was seen in the Gothic Revival style of architecture and in the focus on dark subject matter with mystical and dramatic themes in the works of art. Johann Heinrich Füssli (1741–1825), known as Henry Fuseli in England, was a Swiss-born painter and an art critic. His work exhibited the great interest of the era in the supernatural, the weird, and the fantastic. The tales of Edgar Allan Poe (1809–1849), an American author, reflect the same appeal of gloomy, gothic tales of mystery and horror. Poe popularized the short story. He was also one of the earliest mystery writers, and his book *The Murders in the Rue Morgue* (1841) is one of the first detective stories.

The increasing importance of science had a significant impact worldwide. Charles Darwin's (1809–1882) *The Origin of Species* led to changes in the beliefs of the time and afterward. Darwin was a British naturalist who spent the years 1831–36 on a scientific expedition that took him around the world. His findings during this journey led to his theories of evolution, which were extremely controversial and dealt a tremendous blow to the prevailing ideas of creation in the nineteenth century. Darwin's work had a huge impact on religious thought and scientific research.

The year 1848 was the beginning of a series of uprisings that led to another major movement sweeping through Europe at this time: the rise of nationalism. This movement is defined as pride in the interests or culture of one's nation and a desire to realize the goals of that nation. Until this period, many people felt loyalty to their local traditions, their religious groups, and regional authorities. Often there was no state that contained and included all the people of a specific nationality, so there was no political allegiance to a particular country. The French and American Revolutions, the growth of commerce, and the new theories about the rights of people caused nationalism to take hold and spread, and many Europeans struggled to liberate their country or to create a national identity. Encompassing the American Civil War (1861–65), the romantic era also dealt with the issue of slavery. Abraham Lincoln, the sixteenth president of the United States, guided the country through this devastating experience.

ROMANTIC INNOVATIONS IN MUSIC

The poetry, prose, paintings, and politics of the romantic era satisfied the needs of the society. It was the music of the period that fulfilled the demands of the emotions. The nineteenth century saw a departure from the musical genres that the classical composers had treasured; a new vision arose that music should be lyrical (melodious) and should therefore "sing." Melodies became longer, far more emotional, and more dramatic. In this era, composers strove to make their instruments duplicate the human voice. This model for melody is still admired today, and a number of themes from the work of romantic composers have found their way into popular music.

Many composers looked to their own backgrounds and locales for inspiration. The colorful ethnic music of folk songs and dances were often incorporated into compositions influenced by the rise of nationalism. Instrumental music was the central focal point of the nineteenth century, and within this focus was the intent to expand music's expressive potential.

New vocabulary terms were employed to express the feelings and atmosphere that the composer intended to set in the music he composed. Words were added to the musical dictionary that suggested the moods that the composer wished to transmit. The employment of sentimental words such as con amore (with love), lamentoso (mournful), mesto (sad), and gioioso (joyful) communicated these suggestions from the creator of the piece to the musicians.

Composers of this period also sought a greater range of sound. They widened the dynamic range to create dramatic contrasts between musical ideas, opposing loud against soft or creating swift or gradual changes in the dynamics. The composers of the nineteenth century indicated dynamic notations far more often, and more specifically, than composers had in the previous century. At this time, too, more complex rhythms were introduced. Tempos became more extreme and were often varied within a composition. Romantic composers abandoned the classical view of strict tempo; they called for accelerando (getting faster), ritardando (gradually slowing the tempo), and rubato (slowing down or hurrying up the tempo).

Musicians also were able to receive better training as more musical academies were established. There were now virtuoso performers who were not also composers. Women were reluctantly given some opportunities in music, chiefly as performers but some composed as well. Fanny Hensel (born Fanny Mendelssohn, 1805–1847) and Clara Schumann (born Clara Wieck, 1819–1896) were two accomplished musicians who encountered the widespread attitude against allowing women to have a professional role in music. Hensel, the sister of the great musician Felix Mendelssohn, was a German pianist and a composer of lieder and chamber music, yet most of her work was never published. Schumann, also German born and the wife of the composer Robert Schumann, was a virtuoso pianist who began her public career at the age of nine and continued to perform for the next sixty years. She was also a skilled composer whose compositions include a piano concerto, choral pieces, and solo piano works.

New harmonies were tested; some of these harmonies were dissonant (a disharmonious combination of sounds) and harsh, creating a build-up of tension and color. Chromatic harmonies and more accidentals were employed in this era. These innovative harmonies added to the romantic emphasis on mood, tone, and atmosphere.

ROMANTIC MUSICAL GENRES

In the romantic period formal musical structures were expanded. Free forms were created including the fantasia (a large piece that has no particular form), the rhapsody (a free-flowing piece inspired by romantic ideas), the impromptu (a short, freestyle piece) and the nocturne (a piece that has a dreamy quality). New types of symphonic works were created such as the tone poem (a descriptive piece), which is also known as a symphonic poem. These structures were visualized as a way to tell a story through music. The symphonic poem was a large work for orchestra that evoked images; therefore, this genre was identified as program music, meaning music that describes something or tells a story.

There were other types of program music as well. Incidental music was not well named because the music was not truly incidental. Its function was to operate as an overture or as a diversion between acts or scenes in a play. It evolved into a genre that enhanced the drama and improved the total production. Concert overtures were also a product of the theater. Some overtures to operas or theatrical plays became so well liked that they were performed independently in the concert hall as program music. The fondness for this genre caused composers to create pieces that had the same sensation as an overture but were actually one-movement pieces that did not really introduce anything. These works were generally based on a literary theme, and they became identified as concert overtures. Just as the concert overture fulfilled a need, the program symphony also satisfied the romantic idea of what a symphony should be. In the early development of this genre the music was associated with a literary theme; however, as the century advanced, this requirement was discarded.

Short and lyrical genres entered the repertoire (compositions that are prepared for performance). The romantic stress on lyricism created a new genre: the art song. Differing from an aria or a ballad, the art song combined romantic poetry with accompanying music. This genre became known throughout the world by the German word for song: lied (pronounced "leed").

In this era the piano enjoyed great popularity, and romantic composers wrote many lyrical pieces for the instrument. The piano was improved by the addition of metal frames and thicker strings. Piano recitals (concerts) were well attended. Dances such as the waltz and the polonaise evolved into independent compositions expressly created for the piano. The etude (a French word meaning study) was written and designed for training, practice, or displaying technique, since many amateur musicians could now afford to own a piano. These are technically challenging pieces that require a great deal of skill but also have artistic worth as entertainment. Etudes have also been written for other instruments; however, the majority were composed for the piano.

ROMANTIC DEVELOPMENTS IN OPERA

A blending of the arts was eagerly sought by the romantics. Literature and painting were incorporated into the musical experience in order to suggest a total picture. Composers wrote works that described unusual and faraway lands and people. Opera underwent considerable changes in this era as romantic composers brought their innovative thoughts and experiments to this setting. This is where the blending of the arts could be realized, and all of the elements that make up the romantic style were brought to the operatic stage.

A focus on nationalism, nature, folklore, medieval tales, and the supernatural, along with a concentration on intense color and emotion, is found in romantic operas. Many operas focused on tales of national heroes or on a particular national event; the public often saw great political meaning in a work, and some piece it would become a symbol of patriotism. Giuseppe Verdi (1813–1901) was the most influential Italian opera composer in the nineteenth century. The chorus "Va, pensiero" (Fly, Thoughts; also called Chorus of the Hebrew Slaves) from his opera *Nabucco* (Nebuchadnezzar), which premiered in 1842, became a song of freedom for the Italian people. The Italians identified with the Hebrew slaves and their situation as it was depicted in this work. The Italians associated the circumstances of slavery with the fact that they were unable to reunite with Lombardy, a section of Italy that was then under Austrian rule.

Toward the end of the century, a less exalted style of opera called verismo (meaning realism) became popular in both Italy and France. This style attempted to portray real life and may be illustrated by the work of the Frenchman Georges Bizet (1838–1875), whose *Carmen* premiered in 1875. The characters in *Carmen* are very real, the action is swift, and the music reflected the Spanish setting and fit the interactions of the characters in the opera.

Richard Wagner (1813–1883) incorporated all of the features of the other romantic opera composers, but he also introduced innovations that led opera out of the nineteenth century and into the next. Although he wrote a few symphonies, Wagner is mainly known for his operatic works. A German composer and conductor, Wagner wished to bring to opera a total unity of the drama and the music. In his works he achieved this goal more fully than in any operatic work created before his time. Wagner often wrote his own libretti and filled them with German heroic characters and idealized Norse legends. Mystical symbolism glorifies the German land and people in Wagner's operas.

In Wagner's operas there is a continuous flow of music, without any distinction between aria, recitative, ensemble, dance, and chorus. The orchestra is not just an accompanist, but a definite participant in his operas: Wagner employed the orchestra to introduce themes called leitmotifs, or leading motives, that run throughout the work. Each leitmotif has a specific meaning that suggests a character, an object, or an idea. For example, a river may have its own leitmotif, and so may the idea of fate. These motives are developed and vary throughout the piece, transforming themselves as the drama evolves to trace the course of the story. These musical themes take on a symbolic life of their own. Although Wagner was a very controversial figure—even after his death—he brought opera to great new heights and had an overwhelming impact on the music of the twentieth century.

Distinguished romantic composers included Gioachino Rossini, Giacomo Meyerbeer, Hector Berlioz, Felix Mendelssohn, Frédéric Chopin, and Franz Liszt. Because the late romantic era also encompassed the nationalist movement, many composers reflected the background, history, and struggles of a country in their music. This nationalism was a strong source of inspiration for many great composers including Pyotr Ilyich Tchaikovsky, Mikhail Glinka, Bedřich Smetana, Antonín Dvořák, Edvard Grieg, and Jacques Offenbach. Romantic music produced a grand style that contained the seeds that sprouted in the modern era.

The Modern Era: 1900–Present

BACKGROUND

In the early twentieth century the world encountered a period of rapid change. An intense mix of competition and conflict between the different countries of Europe led to additional disorder. Industries and commercial activities began to grow rapidly, taking huge leaps ahead and upsetting the social order of the past. Insightful investigations in science brought about new discoveries, often leading to inventions that were then put to use in everyday life. The post-romantic period was a bridge to the works of the twentieth century. In this century newcomers entered the world of the arts that for centuries had been dominated by Italy, France, and Germany. These modern artists emerged from many places, including Scandinavia, Russia, Spain, and the United States.

World War I (1914–18) changed the face of Europe and transformed Western civilization. This war was also the first major conflict to be fought in the technological age. The rapid progress of technical knowledge produced some unexpected and far-reaching consequences. Many of the advancements made by scientists, engineers, and the military were in time applied to civilian uses. Advances were made in all aspects of life.

The technological revolution altered the way people lived. This era saw countless scientific developments that, by the early years of the twentieth century, had reached even the most remote corners of the globe. Guglielmo Marconi (1874–1937), an Italian, experimented with a method of employing radio waves to transmit signals, which led to the invention of the radio. Thomas Alva Edison (1847–1931) was an American inventor whose improvements and inventions modernized the world. Among his designs were the electric light bulb and the phonograph. Alexander Graham Bell (1847–1922) was another great thinker who paved the trail to the modern world. Born in Scotland, Bell settled in Boston, Massachusetts, where he invented the telephone.

Albert Einstein (1879–1955) published his book *Relativity: The Special and General Theory* in 1905. This scientist, who fled the Nazi regime in 1933 and came to the United States, made a gigantic contribution to the current understanding of physical reality. Sigmund Freud (1856–1939), the founder of psychoanalysis, had a clear impact on our comprehension of how the human mind functions. His conclusions changed the treatment of mental disorders.

The United States emerged from World War I as both a financial and a military force. After this war, the entire international structure of power was altered. European countries and the United States raced to expand their economic and political influence, either through conquest or by applying measures that took advantage of the resources of other countries. European nations sought to expand their influence in Asia. The French worked to extend their control over Indochina. European and American manufacturers pushed their governments to expand their global influence, since they needed larger markets for the sale of their products and cheap labor to produce their goods.

While the peoples of most European countries were enjoying new freedoms and benefiting from the economic and scientific advances of the twentieth century, trouble was brewing in Russia. World War I found the Russian people dealing with even more tyranny, hunger, and unrest. A backward monarchy was still in control, and the Russian people were severely oppressed. Fighting in World War I added to the misery of the starving Russian people, leading them to stage riots and strikes. As their hunger and anxiety intensified, the Russian people began demanding an end to the war and the overthrow of the dictatorial czar. Large numbers of demonstrating Russians were killed or arrested in the streets by the czarist police force. In the face of these massive protests, Russia withdrew from World War I. The Russian Revolution began in 1917; in March of that year, Czar Nicholas II abdicated his throne, and a new government was in place.

All of the great changes in communication that were now in place allowed the swift delivery of these concepts and inventions throughout the modern world. New trends in art and music blossomed throughout Europe. The seeds that produced these blossoms had been sown in the decades that led up to the new century. Artists looked for novel ways to create and produce their work. Many artists gathered in Paris, for it was the center of innovative ideas. A new style called impressionism discarded the formulas that had been valued during the romantic period and came up with a fresh approach to art. These painters deposited on canvas their impressions of what they saw; they were interested in how things constantly changed in appearance. This approach placed a great emphasis on the use of unmixed colors and the effects of light on a scene. Impressionists painted hazy pictures that allowed the viewer to sense a setting even though all the details were not portrayed. The Impressionist painters were not interested in the mythological heroes of the romantics; they preferred to illustrate real life in their work. The compositions of these artists depicted everyday scenes such as people sitting at a table. Claude Monet (1840–1926) was a Frenchman and a leader of this movement. His paintings portrayed his observations of ordinary, middle-class people or the splendor of a landscape.

The French composer Claude Debussy (1862–1918) was labeled an "impressionist" (a term he disliked) on account of his ability to portray a specific atmosphere in his music. Debussy was influenced by Asian music and by the work of Richard Wagner. His work includes sequences of unresolved dissonant chords and unusual chord progressions. Debussy employed a whole-tone scale, in which each note was separated from the next by a whole step. Music that uses this scale is neither major nor minor, but moves between both. One of Debussy's finest pieces was a groundbreaking orchestral composition that he titled *La mer* (The Sea). In this symphonic portrait Debussy captured the character and temperament of the sea. Debussy wrote mood pieces, short and flexible works that suggested powerful images.

Impressionist music was well received in the first quarter of the twentieth century. It was treasured by audiences and inspired many musicians but eventually lost its novelty and was replaced by a complete change that pulled away from all the musical traditions of the past. The new music of the mid-twentieth century launched a drastic and rapid change from all that had come before. It began as a reaction against romanticism and developed into a rebellious, individualistic style.

Radical harmonic systems were introduced by Arnold Schoenberg (1874–1951), an Austrian composer who moved first to France and then to the United States after the Nazis came to power in 1933. Schoenberg developed a system that was atonal (without a key center); it offered freedom and allowed any combination of chords. This development was a turning point in Western music. In Schoenberg's system the twelve pitches of the octave are seen as equal, and no tonality is given the importance that it occupied in classical harmony. With this twelve-tone technique a composer could create a composition based on a series using all twelve notes of the chromatic scale in an order decided upon by the composer. Many people felt that this atonal quality made the music seem confused and disorganized, since there was no definite key.

A similar movement arose in art. Works of art no longer depicted nature as it is witnessed by the eye or a camera, but in an abstract way. Cubism was another novel artistic style that developed in the early part of the twentieth century. The Spaniard Pablo Picasso (1881–1973) and the Frenchman Georges Braque (1882–

1963) were the originators of this style, which portrayed objects and people in a flat, two-dimensional manner. On Cubist canvases you can view several sides of an item simultaneously.

Georges Braque,
Violin and Candlestick,
1910

As the century progressed, the aftereffects of World War I became evident. A worldwide economic depression overwhelmed the Western countries; in 1929 the New York stock market crashed, banks closed, and many businesses failed. Millions of people were unemployed, and governments eagerly sought solutions to the extreme economic problems during this period, which is known as the Great Depression.

In Germany the situation was worsened by the trauma of having lost World War I and by having signed a treaty that restricted its economy. The German people experienced severe shortages, massive unemployment, and huge inflation. The National Socialist Party (the full name of the Nazi Party) under Adolf Hitler promised the German people that he could solve all of their economic and social problems. In 1933 Hitler became the leader of Germany; the Nazi Party, an intolerant and racist political group, abolished basic freedoms, including freedom of the press, and fashioned a police state. Germans flocked to join the Nazi Party in the belief that Hitler had the answers to all their troubles.

In 1939 Germany invaded Poland, and after that Great Britain, France, Australia, and New Zealand declared war on Germany. In 1940 the Nazis signed a pact with Japan and Italy agreeing that their governments would "establish and maintain a new order of things calculated to promote the mutual prosperity and welfare of the peoples concerned." Germany then formed a union with Austria; soon the German army conquered Poland, Denmark, Norway, Belgium,

Holland, France, Yugoslavia, and Greece. In 1941 the German army attacked the Soviet Union. The United States entered the war later in that same year, after the Japanese attacked Pearl Harbor on December 7. World War II was the largest war in history and spanned much of the globe. The vast resources of the United States, plus its military strength, helped to defeat the armies of Japan, Italy, and Germany. Nazi Germany surrendered on May 8, 1945. The Japanese admitted defeat shortly after the United States dropped atomic bombs on two Japanese cities, Hiroshima and Nagasaki, in the summer of 1945. Peace was finally realized, but after all of the turmoil caused by this massive war, no one felt confident about the future.

At the conclusion of World War II other conflicts arose. The "cold war" was a clash of ideological principles between the United States and the Soviet Union that began in 1945. The Russian Revolution of 1917 had placed a Communist system in control that was hostile to the economic policies and political ideals of the Western countries. The Communist system was a single-party dictatorship that was seen as a serious threat to democracy and liberty. Throughout the years of the cold war the United States and the Soviet Union competed with each other in an attempt to gain influence over people in other countries and to surpass each other in the exploration of outer space and the development of nuclear weapons. Suddenly, in late 1991, after years of bloodless battles and psychological conflicts with the West, the Soviet Union collapsed. The breakdown of the Soviet empire transformed the map of Eastern Europe and ended this global contest.

In the mid-twentieth century, technological, medical, and scientific advances continued at a frantic pace. The *Nautilus*, a nuclear submarine, was launched in 1955. The space race was heated: in 1958, three months after the Soviet Union launched their first satellite, Sputnik, the United States sent a satellite of its own into orbit. The Apollo astronauts landed on the moon in 1969. Optical fiber was created in 1970 and revolutionized the communications industry. In 1951 the first commercial computer was sold; the development of the computer transformed everything in our lives. Bill Gates and Paul Allen began writing computer software; their company, Microsoft, was founded in 1975. That year the personal computer industry started and quickly prospered. In 1967 Christiaan Barnard performed the first heart transplant, and in 1982 Robert Jarvik implanted the first artificial heart in a patient. The Hubble telescope was positioned in space in 1990, allowing observation of the universe, and one year later the World Wide Web was developed, allowing observation of the universe of the Internet.

The countries of the Western world face new challenges in the beginning of the twenty-first century. Political, social, and economic problems plague the world. Key events in the new millennium include the rise of terrorism and the violent attacks of terrorists throughout the world, as well as the response of the major powers to these assaults. Another immense concern is the worldwide dispute over the positive and negative effects of economic globalization and international trade, which creates tensions between countries. The atomic age has opened new doors but has also presented severe problems. The possession of nuclear arms and the attempts of some countries to acquire them have caused tremendous fear. The issue of global warming occupies center stage.

Technological advances occur rapidly in the modern era. The effects of technological change transform the way people and countries interact; a greater interdependence and interconnection of all peoples has been made possible by these developments. Progress in science and engineering makes an impact on everyone. In 1982 the first digital audio disc was made available to the public. In 2001 Apple Computer introduced the iPod, a portable music player; a few years later, you could download music and listen to it on your iPhone. With each passing year these technical advances increase; today our world relies greatly on technology.

MODERN INNOVATIONS IN MUSIC

Even more innovative styles of classical music emerged after World War II. Melodies and rhythms appeared that did not have a symmetrical structure. Modern composers were not concerned about a balance of repetitions and contrast. They did not automatically believe that harmony had to be harmonious. Music became much more personal, and all avenues of experimental music began to be tested.

Modern composers range from the avant-garde to people still writing in more traditional styles. Today there is an extensive field of old and new musical concepts and experiments upon which to draw for inspiration. Many contemporary composers have harnessed the latest amazing technologies to create their masterpieces.

Arnold Schoenberg ignored the rules of traditional harmony, while Samuel Barber remained a romantic lyricist and wrote his music in traditional genres. The music of by Charles Ives predicted many twentieth-century musical techniques. Igor Stravinsky's daring harmonies, dynamic rhythms, and creative use of tonality altered modern music. Edgard Varèse, considered the father of electronic music, was intrigued by the development of the tape recorder. The minimalists Philip Glass and Steve Reich compose rhythmic, repetitive works that change very slightly and very slowly. The unusual works of John Cage presented a very different view of music: he sometimes used common household objects in his experimental pieces. Each modern composer has contributed his or her own ways of thinking "outside the box" and innovative methods of performing and presenting music.

MODERN MUSICAL GENRES AND STYLES

Musique concrète (a French phrase meaning, literally, "real music") was composed by recording real-world recorded sounds and editing them together to form a work. This was the ancestor of electronic music. Machine music (also known as industrial music) developed out of the sounds of the machinery that characterized our industrial society. In art, many sculptors and painters looked toward the works of less industrialized societies for inspiration. Musicians sought out folk melodies and the rhythms of other cultures. Another trend in modern music that was popular during the twentieth century was primitivism. The idea behind this movement was to portray the imagery of an earlier time in history. Sergei Prokofiev's *Scythian Suite* is an example of an imaginative musical portrayal of prehistoric man in Russia.

Minimalism (also called process music) was another ultramodern classical music trend that began in the later years of the twentieth century. This development was connected to other movements that emphasized simplicity. Minimalism stressed the repetition of motifs, simple rhythmic and harmonic structures, long tones, and a limited use of materials.

Music in the technological age is far more readily available than ever before. Our cars are equipped with CD players; our homes are built around entertainment centers featuring the latest high-tech equipment; images and music can be downloaded to a tiny portable media player or to a cellular phone and enjoyed at any time. Software is on hand to help compose music, and a computer can be used to generate digital music. New inventions and technology appear at a dizzying pace.

13 The Great Composers of the Renaissance

*I am not pleased with the courtier
if he is not also a musician.*

THE BOOK OF THE COURTIER (1528),
BY BALDASSARE CASTIGLIONE,
ITALIAN DIPLOMAT AND AUTHOR (1478–1529)

Knowing about the man or woman behind the music provides a framework for further insight into what the composer intended to accomplish; this makes his or her work more understandable for the listener or performer. The great composers were very human and experienced moments of both despair and joy. Their personalities and individual histories are also reflected in their music. Biographical details give us a glimpse of their struggles and triumphs. Often a quotation sums up some special aspect of a composer's life or personal viewpoint. Selecting composers who are representative of their eras is difficult, since there are so many who deserve mention; therefore, this is not an exhaustive list but one based on the composers whose works are most frequently presented in concert.

Masters of the Fifteenth and Sixteenth Centuries

During the fifteenth and sixteenth centuries, musicians of the Burgundian and Flemish schools were considered the finest European composers. From about 1450 until the end of the sixteenth century, these Renaissance men influenced the direction of Western music. They came from countries that are now known as Belgium and parts of France. Moving to other European countries, these men held important positions in the church and in the palaces of the nobility.

GUILLAUME DUFAY

Guillaume Dufay (1397–1474) was a music theorist and composer of the early Renaissance. Born in Cambrai, in northern France, Dufay was a young choirboy at Cambrai Cathedral. There he learned to compose by copying music for the church and by observing other musicians creating music. Dufay became one of leading composers of the Burgundian School, which encompassed parts of eastern France, Belgium, and Holland during the fifteenth century. He had a wonderful understanding of all of the elements that go into writing music. Burgundy was a major site of musical creativity. Dufay wrote seven complete masses, twenty-seven hymns, twenty-two motets, a variety of other liturgical pieces, and eighty-seven chansons (French for song). Dufay was a master of the lyrical genres, and his songs were extremely popular.

In his work, the instruments support the voices and also perform interludes that are independent of the vocal parts. He composed using a more simple style of counterpoint, in which his voices interwove in pleasant harmonies. Dufay was the first to use fauxbourdon (French for "false bass"; pronounced "fo-boor-DOHN") in plainsong; it moved the music away from the chant and into harmony. Fauxbourdon is a straightforward three-part harmony in which the plainsong is in the top voice, with the two other voices providing harmony, one at a sixth and the other at a fourth below the top voice. This technique allowed the melody to stand out from the underlying harmony and was the beginning of modern harmony. Drawing upon of the melodies of folk songs as the basis for religious music was a radical idea in this time period.

Fauxbourdon in *Ave maris stella* by Guillaume Dufay

Dufay was ordained as a Catholic priest, and in 1428 he joined the papal singers in Rome. He was one of the first composers to manage four-voice textures with great skill. Dufay's music bridged the Middle Ages and the Renaissance. He worked while one era was ending and the next was beginning. Almost every composer after Dufay learned from his approach to music, which helped to inspire the style of the Renaissance.

ORLANDE DE LASSUS

Another composer of this period was Orlande de Lassus (1532–1594), who penned over two thousand compositions ranging from masses to love songs. (There are many variations of his name, including Orlando di Lasso, Orlandus Lassus, and Rolande de Lassus.) His works include every major musical genre of the era. Lassus's polyphonic style and flowing counterpoint are the best representation of the music of the later Flemish school.

Orlande de Lassus

Lassus was born in an area that is in Belgium today. At the age of eight he was singing in the church choir. It is said that Lassus had such a magnificent singing voice that he was kidnapped three times so that he could perform in other church choirs, though this is probably a myth. At the age of twelve he left his home to serve the ruler of Sicily. By the age of twenty-one Lassus was appointed to be in charge of the music in a church in Rome, Italy. After a short time Lassus returned to Belgium, where he became part of the court of the duke of Bavaria. He started working there as a singer, but in 1562 Lassus was made director of the court chapel and placed in charge of developing the music of this court in competition with the other musical projects that were taking place throughout the courts of the European aristocracy.

In 1558 Lassus married Regina Wäckinger, the daughter of a maid of honor to the duchess. They had two sons who both became composers. A few years after his marriage, his fame as a composer spread, and other musicians came to Munich, the capital of Bavaria, to study with Lassus. In 1570 the Emperor Maximilian II made Lassus a nobleman, and Pope Gregory XIII knighted him. Many members of the aristocracy offered him excellent appointments, but he decided to remain in Munich. He worked there for thirty-four years as a composer and director of the court chapel, though he frequently traveled outside of Bavaria in search of new ideas and genres. As Lassus aged he began suffering from a deep depression and a breakdown so dreadful that at times his music suffered.

Lassus is recognized for using flexible rhythms that followed the natural intonation of speech, which eased the performances of the singers of his vocal music and his dramatic compositional style. In his five-voice motet *Tristis est anima mea* (Sorrowful is my soul), the counterpoint and elastic rhythms allow the words to flow. Lassus wrote in every genre available to him. Due to his writing in a wide-ranging variety of styles, and because he incorporated the best elements found in European music of the Renaissance, Lassus's works greatly influenced composers of later eras.

CLAUDIO MONTEVERDI

*The end of all good music
is to affect the soul.*

CLAUDIO MONTEVERDI, COMPOSER (1567–1643)

Claudio Monteverdi

An Italian composer whose style bridged the late Renaissance and early baroque periods, Claudio Monteverdi (1567–1643) was born in Cremona, in northern Italy. The music director of the local church taught the youngster about music. When he was fifteen, a leading Venetian publishing house printed Monteverdi's first collection of three-voice motets. They established his reputation, and in 1591 he moved to Mantua, a city in Lombardy, to work as a musician for the court.

As a youth Monteverdi had already published a number of madrigals (secular vocal music), and some even more lighthearted madrigal-like works called canzonettas. In 1599 Monteverdi married a court singer; they had two sons, and also a daughter who died in infancy. In Mantua, Monteverdi continued to compose madrigals.

In 1600 a respected composer, writer, and music theorist wrote a critical article about the "crudities" and "contrapuntal license" that were to be found in the secular works of a composer that he refused at first to name. The critic declared that this particular composer's contrapuntal unorthodoxy was objectionable and provided examples from Monteverdi's books of madrigals to prove his point. Monteverdi responded to this attack in the introduction to his fifth book of madrigals, published in 1605. It is in this book that we see the change from the Renaissance to the baroque style in music. Monteverdi's reply stated that music consisted of two styles: the *prima prattica* (first practice), which was the

Renaissance style of seamless counterpoint between voices that were equal in importance; and the *seconda prattica* (second practice), which was the new style of a melody accompanied by a harmonized bass line. The traditional rules of counterpoint had changed, and the new way of thinking sought to allow the words of the text to be understood and emotions to be displayed.

A few years before 1600, groups of Italian scholars, writers, and musicians began to meet to talk about the nature and direction of the arts. One group of Florentine intellectuals, known as the Florentine Camerata, discussed their concept for a revival of ancient Greek drama; their idea was to set the ancient Greek dramas to music. This led to the development of opera.

In 1607 Monteverdi composed *L'Orfeo, favola in musica* (Orpheus, Legend in Music) as part of the celebrations of a religious carnival. The work's premiere challenged all of the existing musical conventions of the time; the composer had crafted *L'Orfeo* as a sound and logical musical genre. Monteverdi used dynamics and dissonance to communicate human emotion. He also created recitative as an expressive device; as he stated, "The text should be the master of the music, not the servant." *L'Orfeo* is regarded as the first great opera.

One year later Monteverdi completed his second opera, *L'Arianna*, for a ducal wedding celebration in Mantua; unfortunately, most of this work has been lost, and only the famous "Lamento d'Arianna" (Arianna's Lament) survives. "Lamento d'Arianna" is a prime example of monodic (a single line of melody) composition of the early seventeenth century. Monteverdi later arranged it as a five-part madrigal. The composer was reluctant to return to Mantua after his wife's death, but he came back to supervise the production of *L'Arianna*, which was performed in 1608.

In 1613 Monteverdi was appointed music director at Saint Mark's Cathedral in Venice. There he composed a splendid collection of sacred works that helped to spread his fame throughout Europe. In 1632 he took orders as a Catholic priest. Monteverdi spent the rest of his life in Venice, where he composed three more books of madrigals. In 1637 public opera houses were established in Venice; *L'Arianna* was performed in that city in 1640.

Monteverdi died in Venice in 1643 at the age of seventy-six. He is considered to be a composer of the late Renaissance and early baroque. His work demonstrates the changes in music that occurred in the final years of the sixteenth century and the first years of the seventeenth. Monteverdi employed dissonance, texture, and instrumental color to construct drama and expressiveness. He used abrupt key changes to create contrast between the characters in his operas. His works represent a move toward the new style of monody. Monteverdi composed nine books of secular madrigals, in many of which he also introduced a continuo part. His greatest legacy, however, is his contribution to opera, which influenced Italian composers for over two hundred years.

14 The Great Composers of the Baroque Era

Music is the universal language of mankind.

HENRY WADSWORTH LONGFELLOW,
AMERICAN POET (1807–1882)

Masters of the Baroque Era

The transition from the music of the Renaissance to the baroque included a transfer of interest from a texture of independent parts that were equally important (polyphonic) to the concept of a single melodic line with chords accompanying that line which move together (homophonic). In 1600 a group of Italian musicians known as the Camerata wanted to free themselves from the complex contrapuntal style and compose music that was written for only one voice. They believed that this style, known as monophony, imitated the Greek art of music and drama. Their aim was to increase the power of the words by having the music allow the text and its meaning to be clearly understood. This thinking led to the invention of opera.

Baroque mask

JEAN-BAPTISTE LULLY

Jean-Baptiste Lully (1632–1687) was born in Florence, Italy, but he became known as the father of French opera. In 1646 Lully, an accomplished violinist, guitarist and dancer, was brought to France by a nobleman who noticed his talent. There he began studying composition and was able to learn from several important musicians in Paris. Lully became the favorite musician of King Louis XIV, and in 1662 he was appointed to the post of Master of Music of the Royal Family. He was now the most important composer in France.

Jean-Baptiste Lully

Lully created magnificent entertainments, crafted on a grand scale, for Louis XIV and his courtiers. Lully's operas and ballets were performed at the spectacular court of Versailles in an outdoor marble courtyard lined with orange trees. His innovations included a style of recitative that was accompanied by the active participation of the orchestra, as opposed to the Italian recitativo secco, which has only a very plain chordal accompaniment. To please the French taste in music, Lully also increased the participation of the ballet and the chorus in his operas.

The style of his overtures, called French overtures, emphasized the use of wind instruments instead of the strings. They were written in four sections: slow, lively, slow, lively. Lully employed straightforward harmonies, melodies, and rhythms and used the orchestral instruments to communicate moods. Although he functioned as a court musician, his pieces were well-known by the ordinary people of France. He created a style that was uniquely French. While conducting one day, Lully accidentally hit himself in the foot with a long stick that he used to beat time; this injury led to his death a couple of months later from gangrene.

HENRY PURCELL

Sing, sing, ye Druids!
All your voices raise.

HENRY PURCELL, COMPOSER (1659–1695)

Born in London, Henry Purcell (1659–1695) is considered one of the great figures of English music. He was the second son of a court musician, and his talent was evident from a very young age. It is claimed that he began composing when he was nine years old.

Henry Purcell

When his father died in 1664, Purcell went to live with his uncle, Thomas Purcell, who made arrangements for his nephew to enter a chapel choir. There he was able to learn from experienced musicians; he became a composer, singer, and organist.

It was at the court of Charles II that Purcell's career began. In 1677 he was appointed composer for the king's violins, and by 1679 he had become the organist at Westminster Abbey. Purcell's works cover a broad range. He composed a large body of choral music for ceremonial occasions. He also wrote many instrumental pieces and was aware of the trends in baroque music in Italy and France. Purcell took the musical developments unfolding throughout Europe and gave them a clearly English flavor.

Known for his lyrical odes and patriotic anthems, Purcell also wrote one opera, *Dido and Aeneas*. First performed at a school for girls in 1689, *Dido and Aeneas* is still considered one of the greatest English operas. The work is a tragedy that has an unusual ending for opera written before the nineteenth century: the heroine dies. In other operas composed during this era, a divine or miraculous occurrence always saves the hero or heroine. Purcell employed dissonance to portray suffering, this is clearly noticeable in the first part of the overture and in the aria "When I am laid in earth," which is known as "Dido's Lament."

Purcell's melodies follow the pattern of English speech; perhaps this was an outgrowth of his extensive experience with compositions that were written for the theater. The composer had worked for many playwrights, supplying the music for more than forty plays. Purcell composed instrumental fantasies and sonatas as well as sacred music. His *Te Deum and Jubilate* was the first hymn ever composed with orchestral accompaniment. He died at the age of thirty-six, leaving behind a wife and three children. Purcell was buried in Westminster Abbey.

ANTONIO VIVALDI

I could write the concerto in all its parts
faster than a copyist could copy it.

ANTONIO VIVALDI, COMPOSER (1676–1741)

Born in Venice, Italy, the oldest of nine children, Antonio Vivaldi (1676–1741) was taught to play the violin by his father, Giovanni, who was also a violinist. Vivaldi was ordained a Catholic priest in 1703 and nicknamed "the Red Priest" because of his hair color. Right after his ordination, he took a position as the

Antonio Vivaldi

violin teacher at one of the famous institutions in Venice that provided shelter for orphaned girls. In 1706 he withdrew from his role as a priest. Eventually he became the music director at this orphanage, and people from all over Europe came to hear the talented young women of the orchestra that he had trained. Vivaldi composed concertos, cantatas, and other pieces of sacred music for this orchestra.

Vivaldi's admirers included Johann Sebastian Bach, who was his contemporary. However, Vivaldi had gained a reputation as a proud man with a bad temper who was overly concerned with money. The composer also had a medical problem, which may have been asthma.

In 1709 Vivaldi's contract was not renewed, so he attempted to spend more time on getting his compositions noticed by the musical establishment. Vivaldi was a leading figure in the development of the baroque concerto grosso; he was a master at the contrast between large and small groups of performers. Vivaldi's concertos provided a model for this genre throughout Europe; he composed more than five hundred concertos. It was the eleventh concerto in this collection of twelve, the Concerto Grosso in D Minor, which most excited the music world. Written for two violins and cello with string orchestra, this concerto grosso begins with dramatic flair, followed by a fugue that displays the composer's magnificent contrapuntal skills. Since the concerto is scored for only stringed instruments, Vivaldi uses rhythm, dynamics, and register (higher versus lower) to produce the required contrasts. This composer was one of those who set the standards for baroque music. Vivaldi died on July 28, 1741, and was buried in a pauper's grave.

DOMENICO SCARLATTI

Reader, Whether you be dilettante or professor, in these compositions do not expect any profound learning, but rather an ingenious jesting with art, to accommodate you to the mastery of the harpsichord.

DOMENICO SCARLATTI, COMPOSER AND HARPSICHORDIST (1685–1757)

Domenico Scarlatti (1685–1757) was a remarkable Italian composer of the rococo era. Born in Naples in the same year as Bach and Handel, he was the sixth son in a family of ten children. Scarlatti lived in Spain and Portugal for much of his life. He was the son of the composer Alessandro Scarlatti, who is considered the founder of the Neapolitan school of opera. Alessandro probably supplied his son's musical training; Domenico was celebrated as one of the finest harpsichordists in the world.

During his early years Scarlatti traveled widely. In 1702 father and son journeyed to Florence, seeking employment for the son in the court of Prince Ferdinando de

Medici. In Florence Scarlatti met the instrument craftsman Bartolomeo Cristofori, who was working on his transformation of the plucked strings of the harpsichord to the hammer action of a piano. It was also in Florence that Scarlatti composed his first three cantatas. Since an appointment was not offered, the young man returned to Naples, where he took his father's position for the following year while his father went on to Rome.

In Venice Scarlatti befriended George Frideric Handel. This friendship has led to a story that is told of the two musicians dueling in a "contest of virtuosity." Handel was reputed to have outperformed Scarlatti at the organ, while Scarlatti outshone Handel on the harpsichord. Scarlatti died on July 23, 1757, at the age of seventy-two, and was buried in Madrid, Spain. The genius of this composer is evident in his 555 short sonatas for harpsichord; he had labeled these pieces "Essercizi" (Exercises). Only thirty of these sonatas were published in his lifetime, the rest were held in the possession of the Portuguese royal family, for whom they had been composed. His works, in their original manuscripts, now are preserved in the National Library in Venice.

Most of the sonatas, which are typically single-movement works in binary form, were paired, with one sonata in a minor key and the other in the parallel (that is, with the same tonic) major key—for example, D minor and D major. The pairs either contrast with or complement each other; for example, a sonata in a slower tempo might be paired with a faster one. Scarlatti's sonatas bond his Italian dramatic temperament with the dance rhythms of Spain. The composer also included features that were unconventional in this era, employing devices such as the crossing of the hands, swift arpeggios, and rapidly repeated notes. His sharp harmonies, irregular phrases, contrasts of texture, and daring modulations reflect the style that has caused him to be known as one of the greatest keyboard composers of the baroque era.

JOHANN SEBASTIAN BACH

I was obliged to be industrious. Whoever is equally industrious will succeed equally well.

JOHANN SEBASTIAN BACH,
COMPOSER AND ORGANIST (1685–1750)

Johann Sebastian Bach (1685–1750) had a tremendous impact on baroque music and on the musicians who came after him. He was our ideal baroque composer, and his music is even more appreciated today than it

Johann Sebastian Bach

was in his life time. Bach was born in Eisenach, Germany, into a professional musical family that had produced organists and members of the town band for over 150 years. He was the eighth and youngest child in the family. Both of his parents died when Bach was still a youngster, so he went to live in the town of Ohrdruf with an adult brother, Johann Christoph, who was an organist. His brother instructed him on a clavichord. Johann Christoph also taught his brother the techniques used in music copying and the repair of pipe organs. The young boy was very inquisitive and learned very quickly.

Bach was able to combine all of the traditions from the Italian, French, and German baroque masters in his music. He produced both sacred and secular works: chamber music, suites, sonatas, and concerti, including the six concerti grossi that he had dedicated to the Margrave of Brandenburg (the Brandenburg Concertos) in 1721. These six concerti are superb models of baroque music and were written during a very pleasant and productive time in Bach's life. Four of Bach's sons became important composers in the following generation: Wilhelm Friedemann and Carl Philipp Emanuel (sons of his first wife, Maria Barbara), and Johann Christoph and Johann Christian (sons of his second wife, Anna Magdalena).

Bach's sacred works reflect his Lutheran faith. This is evident in something the composer himself said: "The aim and final end of all music should be none other than the glory of God and the refreshment of the soul." Some of his chorales are still used in the Lutheran church today. Bach wrote hundreds of pieces of music; his own virtuosity is mirrored in his organ compositions, and his technical ability as a composer is evident in each of his many works. Bach transformed the fugue and he brought the concerto grosso to its highest peak. He created vocal and instrumental pieces that expanded the boundaries of what had been done before. During his final years his health and eyesight declined. Even though he was blind at the end of his life, he continued to work by dictating to one of his students. On July 28, 1750, Bach suffered a stroke and died; he was buried in an unmarked grave.

GEORGE FRIDERIC HANDEL

I should be sorry if I only entertained them;
I wished to make them better.

GEORGE FRIDERIC HANDEL,
COMPOSER (1685–1759)

Born in the same year as Bach and Scarlatti, George Frideric Handel (1685–1759) was another master composer of the baroque era. Although he spent most of his life in England, he was born in Germany, fifty

George Frideric Handel

miles away from Eisenach, the birthplace of Bach. However, the two men never met. Handel's mother supported his wish to study music, but his father wanted him to study law. When, at a very early age, Handel displayed amazing musical talent, his father did not allow him to take music lessons. Thanks to his mother's intervention, though, Handel started his musical studies at the age of seven. He became an accomplished organist and harpsichordist and also studied the violin and oboe.

Handel had begun composing at the age of nine. Still, his father did not feel that music was a good choice of profession and in 1702 sent the young man to the University of Halle to pursue a law degree. After he completed one year at the university, Handel's father died, and this allowed the young man to follow his own wishes. A strong-willed person, he left school and became the organist at the Protestant cathedral for a year. Handel then went to the city of Hamburg, where he joined the orchestra as a second violinist.

Handel did not have a lot of financial success with his operas. He was almost bankrupt when he decided to concentrate on composing oratorios. The music for *Messiah* was written in twenty-four days. It is a masterpiece that still enthralls audiences. This work, with its massive choruses and elegant arias, is the emblem of Handel's oratorios. The composer wrote non-stop until the piece was complete. When *Messiah* was performed in London, the king was so impressed that he stood up during the Hallelujah Chorus—a practice that still is followed to this day.

Like Bach, Handel faced blindness when he entered his sixties. Interestingly, John Taylor, the same oculist who operated on Bach's eyes, undertook the surgery to remove the cataracts that were causing problems for Handel. Also like Bach, after the operation Handel had to dictate his music while others wrote it down. He continued to conduct his oratorios and to give organ concerts. As the performance season ended during Handel's seventy-fourth year, he collapsed in the theater after a presentation of *Messiah* and died a few days later. Handel was buried in London's Westminster Abbey.

Handel lived through the era when the rising middle class was gaining power. England was at the forefront of this social transformation. His move to present oratorios to the public and leave the operas of the court was a sign of that change. His works include about fifty operas, twenty-three oratorios, and a sizable amount of church music, plus his outstanding instrumental pieces. Handel's music bursts with the forceful baroque rhythm; his melodies explode in powerful surges of sound as the voices interweave. While employing only diatonic (firmly rooted in the key) harmony, this master of expressiveness wrote music of exceptional vitality and tone color.

Handel greatly influenced the transition from the baroque to the classical era in music. Beethoven, Mozart, and Haydn learned much from the drama and melodic beauty of his work. It is said that when Beethoven was asked about Handel, he responded, "He is the greatest composer that ever lived. I would uncover my head and kneel before his tomb." Bach and Handel are considered the giants of early eighteenth-century composers. Bach composed intensely religious pieces, while Handel created more worldly music for celebration and festivity. Their paths were very different, but their achievements were equally significant.

15 The Great Composers of the Classical Era

*Music is a higher revelation than
all wisdom and philosophy.*

LUDWIG VAN BEETHOVEN, COMPOSER (1770–1827)

The classical era of music created a culture that was shared by musicians and audiences throughout the Western world. The influence of all that had been achieved before this period began was evident in the music that now was produced. Composers gained insight and inspiration from the work of the previous masters, who had come from many countries, including Italy, England, France, and Germany. These resourceful composers combined all of the knowledge and experience that they had inherited into one musical language that we describe as the classical era of music.

Masters of the Classical Era

FRANÇOIS COUPERIN

We write differently from the way we play, there is an infinite distance between scores and good playing.

FRANÇOIS COUPERIN, COMPOSER AND KEYBOARDIST (1668–1733)

The rococo was the earliest phase of the classical era. The work of François Couperin (1668–1733) illustrates this point in time. He was a French harpsichordist, organist, and composer. Born in Paris into a respected musical family, Couperin was called "Couperin le Grand" (Couperin the Great) to distinguish him from the other family members, who were also well-known. His first teacher was his father, Charles, who was the organist at a church in Paris. Charles died in 1779, and his young son inherited his father's position.

In 1689 Couperin married Marie-Anne Ansault, a young woman from a merchant family. A year later, his *Pièces d'orgue* (organ masses) and a few other works were published. In 1693 Couperin was appointed by King Louis XIV as one of the organists at his Royal Chapel. Since he shared this position with other organists, he also instructed members of the nobility on the harpsichord (called the clavecin in French). King Louis XIV yearned to establish France as the leader of Europe; he also desired to have a deep impact on the arts. He engaged French artists and musicians to accomplish this goal.

During the mid-seventeenth century, a group of keyboard composers called the clavecinists was created in France. Their style reached a peak in the work of François Couperin. In 1716 he wrote a manual that was enormously important for clavecin students. This manual, which the composer dedicated to King Louis XIV, taught the pupil how to finger and phrase the music. It is believed that this booklet influenced Bach's keyboard technique. Couperin was certain that women possessed more of a natural ability to play this instrument. He wrote, "[They] are generally better … at tender, sentimental" passages. Couperin began composing a large number of works, including four books containing over two hundred clavecin pieces. These pieces were very ornamental and relatively short. Couperin gave them descriptive titles such as *Les papillons* (The Butterflies), *Les vieux seigneurs* (The Old Lords), and *Le visionnaire* (The Fortune-Teller). He also composed many religious pieces, much chamber music, and several works for the organ.

Couperin became the central figure of the French clavecin school. He effectively incorporated the French and Italian styles. His clavecin music, brimming with charm and gracefulness, represents the climax of French rococo. Most of his compositions are in binary form; the first section modulating to a contrasting key and then returning to the original key in the second section. His music is regarded as the summit of French court music and displays great refinement. Couperin's music was rooted in the past; it was designed to entertain and delight. Unfortunately, none of his original manuscripts have survived.

JOSEPH HAYDN

I listened more than I studied…
therefore little by little my knowledge
and ability were developed.

JOSEPH HAYDN, COMPOSER (1732–1809)

Joseph Haydn (1732–1809) is called the "Father of the
Symphony" and the "Father of the String Quartet."
He was the second of twelve children in his family,
who lived in the tiny village of Rohrau, Austria, near
the border with Hungary. His father, Matthias, was a

Joseph Haydn

wagon-wheel maker, and his mother, Maria, had been employed as a court cook.
His parents noticed that their son had remarkable musical talent and contacted a
family member who was a schoolmaster and choirmaster in the town of Hainburg.
This relative brought the six-year-old into his school, where he was able to study
the violin and the harpsichord. Looking back on his childhood, Haydn wrote,
"Almighty God, to whom I give thanks for His many mercies, gave me such
facility in music that by the time I was six I stood up like a man and sang masses
in the church choir and could play a little on the keyboard and violin."

At the age of eight Haydn began to sing in the choir of St. Stephen's Cathedral
in Vienna. When his voice changed, he left the choir and moved into an attic in
Vienna. Haydn worked many different jobs to earn a living; he gave music lessons
and was employed as an accompanist for singing lessons. Sometimes Haydn
joined other street musicians, entertaining people with his violin as they walked
by. He also began composing at this time.

In 1761, at the age of twenty-nine, Haydn was appointed Vice Kapellmeister
(assistant director) for the Hungarian Prince Paul Anton Eszterházy, the head of
an extremely powerful and wealthy family known for their patronage of the arts.
Haydn continued in this position for almost thirty years. Prince Nicholas, the
Magnificent, who became the new prince after his brother died, had a new palace
built called Esterháza that matched the splendor of the French palace of Versailles.
In this fabulous four-hundred-seat theater Haydn was in charge of a twenty-piece
orchestra and an opera troupe. Many festivities were held on this estate, so Haydn
was constantly asked for new material. The majority of his symphonies were
written for this purpose.

During his service to the prince, Haydn composed sixty symphonies, five masses, thirty sonatas, eleven operas, one concerto, and many shorter pieces. By the 1780s, even though he was hidden away on the isolated Eszterháza estate, his music had been published all over Europe, and he was a valued composer. Haydn once remarked, "My language is spoken throughout the world," which shows he was aware that his music had universal appeal.

Haydn also was known for his good sense of humor and for taking pleasure in practical jokes. Even his music reflected this playfulness; his Symphony No. 94 in G Major is nicknamed the *Surprise* Symphony because Haydn used it to play a joke on audiences in London. The second movement is the andante and opens softly; the "surprise" is a sudden loud chord that crashes into the piece in the sixteenth measure.

Haydn is considered to be part of the First Viennese School and the founder of the Viennese school of composition. He is recognized as the composer who helped standardize the symphony and as one of the originators of the string quartet. He was able to mold his themes into the new symphonic style; he could construct an entire movement out of one main theme. In 1781 Haydn met the twenty-five-year-old Mozart, and the two composers established a friendship. Mozart had been very interested in Haydn's work, especially his string quartets. Mozart was fascinated by Haydn's forms and structures. In turn, Haydn gained ideas for orchestration from his friend. Mozart wrote a set of string quartets that he dedicated to Haydn. Their friendship was unusual in a time when rivalry and fierce competition were common between artists.

Haydn's instrumental compositions include more than 100 symphonies, dozens of concertos, trios, and string quartets, and over 300 compositions for wind and string instruments. His 17 operas never reached the heights of his 2 great oratorios. His Symphony No. 88 in G Major begins with an opening theme first presented by strings, then repeated by the full orchestra. Two more themes appear in this movement. The second movement has the oboes and cellos introduce a melody. The third movement is a minuet with brass and timpani added, and the fourth movement is a rondo.

The composer returned to Austria with honors and a good deal of money. A few years later a performance of his oratorio *The Creation* was planned in his honor by leading Viennese musicians and sponsored by many aristocrats. During the performance Haydn became so tense and nervous that he had to be taken home. Beethoven, who had for a short time studied with Haydn, kissed his hands as he was carried from the hall. Haydn died a year later, in 1809, after twice dictating his recollections and preparing a catalog of his works.

WOLFGANG AMADEUS MOZART

I pay no attention whatever to anybody's praise or blame. I simply follow my own feelings.

WOLFGANG AMADEUS MOZART,
COMPOSER (1756–1791)

Wolfgang Amadeus
Mozart, posthumous
portrait

Wolfgang Amadeus Mozart (1756–1791) wrote, "Music, even in situations of the greatest horror, should never be painful to the ear but should flatter and charm it, and thereby always remain music." Mozart composed astounding music; he attained a beauty and perfection that often moved his audiences so deeply that they cried. His father wrote to Mozart's sister that when the Piano Concerto in D Major, K. 175, was performed, many of the listeners were moved to tears, and the applause was deafening.

Mozart was born in Salzburg, Austria, the son of a violinist and composer who was deputy Kapellmeister to the court orchestra of the archbishop of Salzburg. Leopold Mozart (1719–1787) was a music teacher who wrote a well-known textbook on playing the violin the year Mozart was born. His parents had several children, but most of them died in infancy. Two youngsters survived, a girl and a boy. The son showed outstanding musical ability: at the age of three he was playing tunes by ear at the piano, and at the age of five he began composing. The young Mozart received comprehensive musical training from his father. Mozart's older sister, named Maria Anna but nicknamed Nannerl, was born in 1751 and even as a child was an accomplished keyboard player.

When he was six years old the boy performed for the Empress Maria Theresa; Leopold quickly realized that he could earn a sizable income by featuring his very talented children as performers throughout the European courts. During the years 1763 to 1766 the family journeyed to Munich, to the court of Versailles in France, to Holland, to Switzerland, and to London, where the young Mozart amazed the audiences. He had the ability to sight-read music; he was also skilled on the violin and viola. Given any theme, he could improvise on it or play it in the style of other composers. The family presented a very exciting show, and Leopold tried to book as many concerts as possible. The children would first perform at court and then go on to play at private concerts. Whenever it was practical, they would also provide a show for the public. Each presentation lasted from one and one half to three hours, and frequently there were two performances each day.

Mozart's initial patron was the prince and archbishop of Salzburg; at first he seemed to be understanding about Mozart's frequent trips, but eventually he became annoyed with Mozart's numerous absences and stubborn personality. Mozart was not satisfied with his position in the court. He wrote to his father that he believed that he was being held in low esteem by his patron: his place at the dining table was just above that of the cook. After several disputes the archbishop dismissed Mozart from his service with the words, "Let him leave, I don't need him!"

In 1777 Mozart traveled with his mother, Anna Maria (instead of his father, because the archbishop had refused to allow Leopold to accompany his son), on a trip to Germany and France to hunt for a job. In 1778, while they were in Paris, Anna Maria became unwell and died. Unable to obtain a job in either country, Mozart returned to Salzburg and spent 1779 and 1780 composing and performing in the cathedral and at court. Now opera became his primary objective, and he eventually received a commission to write a serious opera for a court carnival in Munich, the capital of Bavaria in the southern part of Germany. His *Idomeneo, re di Creta* (Idomeneo, King of Crete) is an opera seria (serious opera) in three acts. The music moves seamlessly from the overture into the first act, and it is filled with passion and strength. The work was an absolute victory for the composer. The amazing thing was that Mozart was pleased with the end result, since in his letters to his father he had complained about the singing, the acting, and just about everything that was happening while the opera was being written and prepared.

At the age of twenty-five, Mozart moved to Vienna to establish himself as a freelance artist until he could attract another patron to sponsor him financially. He supported himself by teaching, publishing his music, performing in public or in the salons of patrons, and, finally, by receiving a commission to compose. This is the time period that he met Joseph Haydn and the two men developed a supportive friendship. Emperor Joseph II requested that Mozart compose some dances for the court balls. This commission offended the young composer, because he believed his talent was too magnificent for such work.

Although Mozart earned a good salary in Vienna, he was often broke. He was known as a wasteful spender and a poor money manager. Even though his father did not approve of the match, in 1782 Mozart married Constanze Weber. His overbearing father, who had dominated his son's life and career, resentfully gave his consent, but father and son developed bitter feelings toward each other. Some people believe that Mozart had a love/hate relationship with his father that kept him from growing into a responsible adult. Also, owing to his fame as a child prodigy, Mozart had a hard time relating to other people, especially those whom he viewed as having little talent. His rude and arrogant behavior caused him to make many enemies. Leopold's letters to his son were filled with fatherly advice about how to control his temper as well as his need to limit his spending.

Mozart was a resourceful composer who wrote in most of the major genres. His works are perfect examples of the classical era. An outstanding pianist, Mozart favored this instrument and composed solo works for it. His Concerto for Piano and Orchestra in D Minor, K. 466, composed in 1785, has an astonishing story attached to it. Mozart was famous for his memory and skill as a pianist; he wrote the concerto and performed the premiere of it the following day without any rehearsal.

The opera *Le nozze di Figaro* (The Marriage of Figaro) was a great triumph for Mozart in 1786. The work created a sensation both in Vienna and in Prague, Czechoslovakia. Mozart was immediately commissioned to compose another opera, so *Don Giovanni* (based on the legend of Don Juan) was written and performed the following year. It met with great acclaim in Prague, where it was premiered, but was not as well received by the Austrian audiences. Today it is considered to be one of the greatest operas ever composed.

Financial problems arose for Mozart once again, so he agreed to compose *Die Zauberflöte* (The Magic Flute) for a minor stage company that usually performed lighter entertainment. The opera was written shortly after the French Revolution and was based on Mozart's involvement with the Freemasons, to which Haydn had introduced him. This is an organization of men that promotes the brotherhood of man. The opera is bursting with the rituals, ideals, and symbols of the Freemasons, who were very influential in eighteenth-century Europe. Comic scenes and spectacular stage effects with mystical representations and great music combined to create a new inspiration for the stage. With this work, modern German opera was born.

Around the same time as *Die Zauberflöte*, an unidentified patron requested a requiem mass from Mozart. As he worked on this piece, he convinced himself that this mass for the dead was actually intended for his own funeral, and that he would not live long enough to complete it. He began to compete against time, expecting that his own death was at hand. *Die Zauberflöte* was doing well, but Mozart's physical and mental health was swiftly declining. It is believed that he wrote in a letter summing up his fear: "I have come to the end without having had the enjoyment of my talent. Life was so beautiful; my career began under such fortunate auspices. But no one can change his destiny. No one can measure his days. One must resign oneself; it will be as providence wills. I must close. Here is my death song. I must not leave it incomplete."

Mozart did not finish the Requiem; later it was completed by a friend. Not long before his thirty-sixth birthday, Mozart died. A strong storm kept his friends from going to the gravesite. He was buried in a common grave with the poorest of the city; the location of his grave is unknown.

LUDWIG VAN BEETHOVEN

Music should strike fire from the
heart of man, and bring tears from
the eyes of woman.

LUDWIG VAN BEETHOVEN,
COMPOSER (1770–1827)

Ludwig van Beethoven (1770–1827) was born into
the first generation to witness the full impact of the
American and French Revolutions, which promoted
the principles of freedom and human dignity.

Ludwig van Beethoven

Beethoven is considered to be one of the most superb composers in the history
of music. His family was actually Flemish in origin. They had settled in Bonn,
Germany, where his grandfather and namesake had been a singer in the court and
where his father, Johann, was now a singer and an instrumentalist. Beethoven's
father was an alcoholic with a terrible temper. His mother, Magdalena, was a
widow when Johann married her in 1767; she was known as an attractive woman
with a gentle personality.

Johann and his wife had seven children; only the composer and two others
survived childhood. He was his son's first music teacher, but his addiction to
drink made him unpredictable as a teacher and as a provider for his family. In
1778, when he was eight years old, Beethoven gave his first public concert on
the keyboard. At this performance his father claimed that Beethoven was only six
years old in order to link him to another child prodigy, the famous Mozart.

Since the father could not be relied upon financially, eleven-year-old Ludwig
began to help support his mother and his two younger brothers as an assistant
organist in the court chapel. At the age of twelve Beethoven published his first
work: Nine Variations for Piano in C Minor. In 1784 the fourteen-year-old
was appointed organist to the court of Prince Maximilian Franz, the Elector of
Cologne. The teen now became the main source of income for his family.

Beethoven went to Vienna to study; in 1787, during his first trip to this city,
it is believed that he met and performed for Mozart. The story continues that
the seventeen-year-old Beethoven improvised on a theme that Mozart suggested
to him; Mozart was so impressed with the brilliant improvisation that he said to
a friend, "Keep an eye on him—this young man will make a noise in the world
someday." The plan was for Beethoven to stay in Vienna and study with Mozart,
however, he was called back to Bonn with the news that his mother was very
ill. Magdalena suffered from tuberculosis and died soon after her eldest son had
returned home. Beethoven remained in Bonn for the next five years, continuing

his duties as an organist, playing the viola in the theater orchestra, giving music lessons, and composing.

Five years later Beethoven returned to Vienna to study composition with Haydn, since Mozart had passed away the previous year. The aging Haydn and the twenty-two-year-old Beethoven did not get along well. Haydn felt that Beethoven was too independent and hot-tempered. Beethoven was considered a virtuoso on the piano because of his mastery of the instrument and his excellent improvisational talent. The aristocrats liked to host competitions between the musicians they admired; often the competition was based on improvisation, and Beethoven won every contest he entered. His performances were praised by the aristocracy, and he was well received by the patrons of music.

His first works to be assigned opus numbers were three piano trios published in 1795. Beethoven was the first composer who did not have to rely on the goodwill of wealthy patrons; instead, he was able to make a living by selling his music. The public attended his concerts and purchased the scores of his pieces, an arrangement that suited the composer perfectly. Beethoven did not wish to be employed in the court of a patron; he did not want someone dictating what he could compose. He was deeply affected by the spirit of equality that was spreading throughout Europe. He had the courage to stand up for his principles, which resulted in his gaining the respect of the aristocracy. He often received their sponsorship, but he remained fiercely independent. His music echoed the belief that man was in charge of his own destiny, and his fame stretched throughout Europe.

In his late twenties, as the composer was being acknowledged for his great talent, he began to realize that he was losing his hearing. This was a tremendous blow to him and caused him to feel distant from others. His doctor suggested that he go to a quiet place to rest. This isolation in a small town created a terrible loneliness that is described in a letter to his brothers known as the Heiligenstadt Testament, written in 1802 from Heiligenstadt, Germany:

> But just consider that for six years I have been inflicted with an incurable condition which has been aggravated by incapable physicians. From year to year, hoping for recovery, I am finally forced to the realization of a long-lasting affliction (the cure of which may take years or even prove impossible). I was born with a heated, lively temperament.... I had to isolate myself early and spend my life in loneliness.... Forgive me when you see me draw back when I would happily mingle with you. I am doubly hurt by my misfortune as it will lead to my being misjudged because of it. For me there can be no relaxation in human company; refined conversation, mutual exchange of thought, cannot take place; almost completely isolated, I may only venture into society when dire necessity requires it. I have to live in exile.

The dread of not being able to hear his own music was overwhelming to the composer. He also feared the reaction of the public when they became aware of his deafness. When he realized that he could not hide his handicap any longer, he acknowledged and accepted it. Beethoven began communicating with others by writing notes on sheets of paper in a notebook. After a huge internal struggle, Beethoven decided that his talent had to provide him with the happiness that would sustain him and give him the will to go on. The themes of his music reflect his inner conflict; they progress from conflict to calm, from calm to joyfulness. Now Beethoven composed what he heard within himself. This allowed him to create a new music that expressed his own ideals and inner struggle.

Beethoven's work is usually grouped into three style periods: early, middle, and late. In his early period his works are often similar in style to the pieces written by Haydn and Mozart; it is considered a period of imitation. These pieces include the Piano Sonata No. 14, known as the *Moonlight* Sonata, and his first and second symphonies.

The middle period begins in 1802, after Beethoven's struggle with his deafness began; it is also known as his "heroic style" era. At this stage in his life, Beethoven was aware that he was setting out on a different path. The music of this period reflects his personal crisis: he composed large-scale, heroic works, including his only opera, *Fidelio*. The opera was strongly influenced by the French Revolution as well as by Beethoven's own inner battles. *Fidelio*'s themes are about unselfish love, courage, loyalty, and self-sacrifice. These themes were deeply felt by the composer and sensed by the people of Europe, who had recently lived through an era that emphasized these ideals.

On November 20, 1805, during *Fidelio*'s premiere, Vienna was occupied by Napoleon's military forces, and most of the audience consisted of French military officers. In May 1804 Napoleon had declared himself emperor of France, and Austria had allied itself with Britain in expectation of an invasion of England by Napoleon's army. Russia also joined this coalition, and a combined Russian and Austrian army was marching on France to stop this invasion. Napoleon was able to smash this force. The Russian army retreated, and the Austrians signed a treaty which gave Napoleon even more Austrian territory. Many Austrians fled Vienna to avoid Napoleon's invasion.

It was under these circumstances that *Fidelio* was premiered. Because of its great length and poor organization, the opera was not well received by the few members of the public in attendance or by the French military men in the audience. Beethoven withdrew the work after three performances. Later, he shortened the opera to two acts and made some other changes; the opera was produced again the following spring before a Viennese audience. It was loved by the people who attended but rated poorly by the music critics. After only a few performances, the composer again withdrew the work. In 1814 the libretto was rewritten; Beethoven worked on other revisions, and this version was a success. Although the second version of *Fidelio* was well received by audiences and began to be performed all over Europe, it was not until the third and final version that the work was considered an operatic masterpiece.

Fidelio is a unique opera. The music bears the imprint of Beethoven's idealism and his passion to compose flawless works. One aria was reworked at least eighteen times before the composer was satisfied; the overture was also recomposed four times. The number of revisions testifies to Beethoven's constant effort to perfect his music. He did not compose comfortably like Mozart; each work was a mighty struggle and a great effort. The opera has been published in all three versions as Beethoven's Opus 72.

The story behind the dedication of the Symphony in E-flat Major, Op. 55, contains a Beethoven legend. The work was originally dedicated to Napoleon Bonaparte, since Beethoven was a passionate believer in the ideals of the French Revolution and he thought Napoleon represented these standards. But Beethoven supposedly flew into a rage upon learning that Napoleon had declared himself emperor of France and exclaimed, "Now, he too will tread under foot all the rights of man, indulge only his own ambition; now he will think of himself as greater than all men and become a tyrant!" Beethoven then removed the title page and retitled the work the *Eroica* (Heroic) Symphony. The *Eroica* is regarded as a turning point in musical history. Its record length, extreme technical difficulties, and strikingly beautiful passages brought it well beyond the normal expectations of the symphonic genre in the classical era. It caused other composers to reconsider what a symphony could be.

Beethoven has been called the supreme architect in music. He was unmatched at handling instrumental forms. His late period dates from about 1815, when he was almost totally deaf; it is known as his "isolated era." At this point, he reached fulfillment in his compositions. The symphonies and sonatas written during this time were experiments in structure, form, and tonal qualities. Symphony No. 9 in D Minor, Op. 125, written in 1824, was the last complete symphony that Beethoven composed. This choral symphony exhibits the composer's genius. The first three movements are pure absolute music, and the fourth movement is a choral finale. Using the poet Friedrich Schiller's *An die Freude* (Ode to Joy), the dramatic conclusion of this work is an example of Beethoven's daring and spectacular thinking.

Schiller's *An die Freude* had interested Beethoven for many years. The composer used about a third of the poem's lines to compose eight 12-line stanzas in which a chorus proclaims that in joy all men are brothers. This great ceremonial work is Beethoven's invitation to the world to sing together. The chorale is often viewed as an anthem proclaiming the unity of all humanity.

Beethoven's life spanned the end of the eighteenth century and the beginning of the nineteenth. His music was a transition from the old society into the new one; he was the most influential composer in history. He developed the classical genres into powerful structures and set the standards for the composers that came after him. His ideals were formed by the Enlightenment, and his message was the freedom of humanity and the victory of the spirit. Beethoven expanded both the orchestra and the development of the symphony. He was also one of the first composers to include a chorale in a symphony. Beethoven died in March 1827, and it was reported that more than twenty thousand people attended his funeral. In 1888 his remains were moved to another cemetery in Vienna and placed next to the grave of Franz Schubert.

FRANZ SCHUBERT

No one feels another's grief; no one understands another's joy. People imagine that they can reach one another. In reality they only pass each other by.

FRANZ SCHUBERT, COMPOSER (1797–1828)

Franz Schubert

Beethoven was a transitional composer—his life and work overlapped the classical and romantic eras. Another composer who fits into that category is Franz Schubert (1797–1828), born in a suburb of Vienna. Schubert's life followed a pattern similar to that of other composers: he was poor, was unappreciated during his lifetime, and died young. It has been stated that there is no equal to Schubert's melodies. He was the son of a schoolmaster with fourteen children, most of whom died while they were still infants.

At the age of five Schubert's father started to teach him how to play the violin, and an older brother gave him piano lessons. Schubert exhibited great talent and became a member of the Vienna Boys' Choir. In 1808 he received a scholarship to attend a music school; the director of the school, Antonio Salieri, also taught Beethoven and Liszt. After he completed his education, Schubert became an assistant teacher in his father's school, but teaching did not suit him. Schubert composed after he finished his teaching duties for the day. He wrote the first of his lieder (art songs), *Gretchen am Spinnrade* (Gretchen at the Spinning Wheel), based on a poem by Goethe, in one afternoon. He also composed his Mass in F Major, and the following year, when he was eighteen, he penned *Der Erlkönig* (The Elf King), which also took him only a few hours.

Schubert's friends were his strongest supporters. They were some of the artists and musicians who led up to the romantic period. One friend offered to share his university room and board money with the composer in order to get him out of a job that he really disliked and to give him the freedom to spend his time on his music. After three years of teaching, Schubert left the classroom and roomed with this friend while giving music lessons and selling some of his compositions to a publisher, but he did not earn much money. Soon Schubert had to find other lodgings.

Schubert had no steady income and no definite place to live for any length of time. In 1818 he obtained employment as a music teacher for the daughters of the Hungarian nobleman Count Eszterházy. The position lasted only for the summer, and then Schubert returned to a life filled with composing, moving in with different friends and going out for enjoyment once in a while. In 1818 Schubert was commissioned to compose two operas by two Viennese opera houses. The results were *Die Zwillingsbrüder* (The Twin Brothers) and *Die Zauberharfe* (The Magic Harp). Both operas were unsuccessful. *Die Zwillingsbrüder* was not performed for two years, which caused Schubert a great deal of grief. It was finally produced in 1820. At the opening Schubert hid himself in the theater and did not take a bow because he felt that his clothes were too worn out to be seen by the public. After the performance the critics declared that the work showed originality and contained some lovely music but was too serious. The work was performed seven times. Two months later *Die Zauberharfe* had its premiere. The critics did not care very much for this opera either.

Schubert never managed to attract a wealthy patron or to earn more than a small amount of money at a time. His publishers either refused to print his work or paid him very little. At one point he had planned to marry, but the law required Schubert to submit a petition and to provide documentation proving that he could support a family, and because he could not declare a source of income, Schubert's request was denied. In 1823 ill health also began to affect him; it is believed that he wrote the twenty lieder for *Die schöne Müllerin* (The Pretty Maid of the Mill) while he was hospitalized. Schubert stated, "My music is the production of my genius and my misery."

In the summer of 1825 Schubert took a five-month tour of Austria, where he spent most of the time composing. He lived in poverty and distress; everything he tried seemed to end in failure. As time passed, the composer became more depressed by his monetary problems. Out of this despair, in 1827, arose a brilliant song cycle: *Die Winterreise* (The Winter Journey). Based on the poems of Wilhelm Müller, these lieder depict the state of Schubert's mind. The cycle contains twenty-four songs that emphasize loneliness, being an outsider, and feeling lost in a cold winter setting. The cycle is very different from anything that was expected in this genre, since there is no enchanting scene and nothing really happens besides a description of the winter. The brook is frozen, the trees are bare, and the harmonies are harsh. While writing this work, the composer, who usually spent so much time with others, withdrew from his friends.

In 1828 a public concert of his works was performed in Vienna on the first anniversary of Beethoven's death. The performance was a success, and Schubert was thrilled. His publisher began printing more of his pieces, and the composer was finally being compensated for his work. Schubert continued working on a symphony, a string quartet, piano sonatas, several lieder, and other projects. His Symphony No. 9 in C Major was completed in March 1828 but was not performed until 1839, when it was conducted by Felix Mendelssohn.

In the beginning of November 1828 Schubert's health declined, and on November 19 he died, just thirty-one years old. He was buried in the village cemetery of Währing. His last wish was to be buried near his idol, Beethoven, and he was: in 1888 both men were reburied in Vienna's Central Cemetery.

His music extends from the classical to the romantic era. Schubert's symphonies are in the style of the great classical composers, yet his lieder and piano pieces definitely reflect the mood of the romantic period. His chamber music is lyrical and in the classical Viennese style. Schubert established the German lied as a new art form. He penned over six hundred songs; the accompaniment perfectly suits the poems, and the melodies are unforgettable. His individuality was expressed through his music; the treatment and form may be traditional, but the composer's personality comes through to the listener. A Schubert quote says it all: "Some people come into our lives, leave footprints on our hearts, and we are never the same."

16 The Great Composers of the Romantic Era

Talent works, genius creates.

ROBERT SCHUMANN,
COMPOSER, PIANIST, AND CRITIC (1810–1856)

Masters of the Romantic Era

The outlook and attitude of composers during the romantic era created music that was more daring, less structured, and far more emotional. They wished to move away from the traditions and standards of those who preceded them. In the beginning of the romantic period even the symphony lost its central position. The romantic composers were annoyed by the restraints that the genres of the past demanded. They wanted freer, more flexible musical genres that lent themselves to being shaped by the will and taste of the designer of the work and that would also appeal to their audiences. They looked for new materials and innovative methods to present this vision. Fresh sources of musical inspiration were to be incorporated into their work. As the middle class grew, so did composers' audiences. The romantic composers realized that they needed to please their public's tastes.

CARL MARIA VON WEBER

An artist's sphere of influence is the world.

CARL MARIA VON WEBER, COMPOSER (1786–1826)

Carl Maria von Weber (1786–1826), the father of German romantic opera, played a critical part in the development of romantic style. He was born in the north German town of Eutin. His father, Franz Anton von Weber, was a former military man who had founded a theater group in Hamburg. His mother had worked as a singer and actress and was her husband's second wife; Carl was her first-

Carl Maria
von Weber

born. He also was a cousin of Mozart's wife, Constanze. Plagued from birth by a disorder of the hip joint, the child could not walk until he was four years old. The family often moved around with the father's traveling theater troupe. The youngster grew up surrounded by the theatrical world and felt comfortable in that atmosphere.

Weber was provided with an excellent education. After his mother died in 1798, the boy was sent to Salzburg, where he studied with Michael Haydn, a composer and the younger brother of Joseph Haydn. In that same year Weber's first work, consisting of six fugues for piano, was published. Weber then went to Munich to learn from other musicians. At the age of fourteen he composed his first opera, *Das stumme Waldmädchen* (The Silent Girl of the Forest). Shortly after his debut as a composer, Weber began to write articles as a music critic for a newspaper in Leipzig, Germany. He was also recognized as a concert pianist.

Weber was appointed Kapellmeister in Breslau, a job he held until 1806. He was then granted a position at the court of the duke of Württemberg, in Stuttgart, from 1807 to 1810. Weber lost this post when he was accused of stealing money (it is probable that his father was the actual thief), and he and his father were ordered to leave the country.

Together with other musicians, Weber formed a Harmonic Society for the advancement of art and music. They were the first composers to actively advance their own careers. This background and the intellectual circles in which Weber was involved led his music toward the romantic conceptions of what music should embrace. Although Weber was a contemporary of Beethoven and Schubert, his work was responsive to the changing point of view and was more typically romantic in style and emotion.

Weber believed that a composer of opera should bind voices, action, and music together into a single unit. In 1817 the king of Saxony appointed him Royal Saxon Kapellmeister. Weber became a major advocate for the creation of a true

German opera. He spent years urging others to help him create a genuine German art form. *Der Freischütz* (The Marksman) is considered the first German romantic opera. It is set in Bohemia after the Thirty Years' War, which had raged through central Europe in the early seventeenth century. *Der Freischütz* was premiered in Berlin in 1821, and audiences were delighted with it. The work helped to bring about a rejection of Italian opera in Germany, thus ushering in the dawn of German opera.

Much of the music in *Der Freischütz* was inspired by German folk tunes. The libretto contained all of the elements that the romantic style required: settings in nature, an innocent heroine, a misguided hero, an evil villain who is finally ensnared in his own trap, and the involvement of the supernatural. The work spoke to the German soul; it embodied all of the characteristics of the German national spirit. In the audience was young Richard Wagner, who eventually took German opera to another level.

Weber, suffering from tuberculosis, was growing weaker and weaker. Defeated by his illness, the composer was buried in London; eighteen years later his coffin was brought back to Germany. Weber once said, "What love is to man, music is to the arts and to mankind." His aim was to shape a genuine German musical genre. His works incorporate the major trends in romantic music; however, his real legacy is his contribution to the creation of a clearly German genre, which was well received by his public during this time of increasing German nationalism.

HECTOR BERLIOZ

Love cannot express the idea of music,
while music may give an idea of love.

HECTOR BERLIOZ, COMPOSER (1803–1869)

Hector Berlioz (1803–1869) was the son of a doctor; his middle-class family lived in a small town near Grenoble, France. As a youngster he learned to play the flute and the guitar. His father was determined that Hector become a physician and sent him to a medical school in Paris. After

Hector Berlioz

two miserable years, the young man left the medical school and entered a music school. His disappointed and angry parents rejected this decision and withdrew their financial support.

While at school Berlioz earned money by giving lessons, singing in a chorus, and writing music criticism. As he studied, he discovered that he had a deep passion for Beethoven's work. The friends he made in Paris were very involved in transforming the arts; they included the great writers Victor Hugo and Honoré de Balzac. The young Berlioz also was an admirer of Shakespeare.

At the age of twenty-seven, Berlioz composed his most famous work, the *Symphonie fantastique* (Fantastic Symphony), Op. 14. This symphony is program music and tells a story about a gifted artist who is madly in love. The music represents the artist's dreams while in a deep sleep. The basic theme of the piece, which symbolizes the object of his love, is carried throughout the five movements and serves to unify the entire work. Other composers had used this concept of a repeating theme, but Berlioz named it an idée fixe (fixed idea; pronounced "EE-day FEEKS"). The use of a motif or melody to represent a certain character or mood became a standard technique of composers. Each movement of the *Symphonie fantastique* expresses a different mood and weaves images that portray the artist's dream.

To earn a steady income Berlioz became a music critic; this cut down the time he had for writing music. His symphony for chorus and orchestra, *Roméo et Juliette* (Romeo and Juliet), was based on the tragedy of the same title by his favorite playwright, Shakespeare. The symphony also expressed Berlioz's admiration for Beethoven, who had impressed Berlioz with his Symphony No. 9. During his last years Berlioz became bitter and disillusioned. He no longer composed. All of the extended concert tours had exhausted him, and his lack of an approving audience harmed him emotionally. In 1868 Berlioz suffered a stroke; he died on March 4, 1869.

Berlioz is famous for his remarkable innovations and his unique approach to everything that he wrote. Berlioz's music was mainly influenced by the composers Beethoven, Gluck, and Weber, yet the sounds he created were definitely original. He dramatized the symphony with theatrical settings and his amazing imagination. Because Berlioz had to organize and pay for his own concerts, the financial and emotional strain was crushing at times. His music was unconventional, but he had a large group of followers who attended these concerts, therefore, they were often profitable.

FELIX MENDELSSOHN

What a divine calling is music!

FELIX MENDELSSOHN, COMPOSER (1809–1847)

Felix Mendelssohn (1809–1847) was one of the most gifted composers of the romantic era. Mendelssohn grew up in a prosperous German family. He was the grandson of the distinguished rabbi and Jewish philosopher Moses Mendelssohn. When Felix Mendelssohn was a young boy,

Felix Mendelssohn

his parents converted and became Lutherans in an attempt to avoid the anti-Semitism that was widespread in Europe at that time. His parents added the last name of Bartholdy, but Felix preferred to use their original last name. His father, Abraham, was a banker, and his mother, Leah Salomon, was regarded as very well read and an intellectual. The family hosted many musical gatherings and cultural events.

Three years after Felix Mendelssohn's birth, Hamburg was invaded by the French. The family fled to Berlin, where his parents decided to remain, as they felt the educational advantages were greater there. The Mendelssohns eventually had four children, and each one received an outstanding education. Fanny Mendelssohn (after she married she was known as Fanny Hensel), the oldest of the children, became a pianist and also a composer. Fanny was believed to be as gifted as her brother, but women of that era did not usually pursue a career.

Mendelssohn began studying the piano with his mother when he was six years old; he also played the violin and painted. He gave his first public performance as a pianist at the age of nine. Mendelssohn was fascinated by the works of Bach, Beethoven, and Mozart: the creations of these composers inspired many of his own pieces. Young Felix and Fanny enjoyed reading translations of Shakespeare's plays, and when Mendelssohn was seventeen he composed an overture based on one of Shakespeare's comedies. He conducted this overture to *A Midsummer Night's Dream*, Op. 21, at a musical gathering in his parent's home. The people assembled to hear the piece were stunned by the young man's talent. The overture had achieved the magic of the Shakespeare play and displayed Mendelssohn's mastery of orchestration.

The overture was first written as a piano duet but was later orchestrated. It opens with four of the most suggestive chords in music, played by the woodwinds; they invite the listener to enter the forest. The violins introduce the music of the fairies on staccato strings. In this enchanted-forest setting Mendelssohn composed a splendid score; it is probably the most famous incidental music ever written. The overture had its premiere for the public in 1827, a concert that turned the eighteen-year-old musician into a sensational celebrity.

The revival of interest in Johann Sebastian Bach can be credited to Mendelssohn. He had created a choir to present Bach's choral works, which at that time were unknown to the public. Mendelssohn organized and conducted the first performance of Bach's *St. Matthew Passion* since the great baroque composer's death eighty years before and prompted a renewed awareness of his work.

In 1843 King Frederick William commissioned Mendelssohn to add to his overture for *A Midsummer Night's Dream*. He used the themes found in the overture to write a complete score for the play. The intermezzo between acts 4 and 5 has become the famous "Wedding March," which is still used today and is possibly the most popular piece ever composed by Mendelssohn.

Mendelssohn's last composition was the oratorio *Elijah*. It was performed in 1846 at the Birmingham Festival in England. The work clearly was influenced by the baroque composers, but it also displayed the concepts of the romantic-era composers. Mendelssohn conducted a choir of 271 singers and a 125-piece orchestra. In a letter to his brother, Paul, the composer wrote, "No work of mine went so admirably the first time of execution, or was received with such enthusiasm by both the musicians and the audience."

Mendelssohn returned to Germany feeling tired and nervous. There he learned of the sudden death of his sister Fanny. His health had been failing, and this news was a final blow to his mental well-being. The composer became extremely depressed; he took a brief trip to Switzerland to rest, but the vacation did not aid his recovery. Six months after Fanny's death, Mendelssohn suffered a series of strokes and died at the age of thirty-eight. Huge crowds attended the funeral.

Mendelssohn's music was carefully crafted and well polished. Mendelssohn continued to compose in the classical style during the romantic era; he enjoyed the orderliness and organization of the classical genres. Some of this was due to his deep admiration for Bach, Mozart, and Handel. Mendelssohn did not exhibit the nationalist yearnings of so many other romantic composers. The composer did not like to give programmatic titles to his works; rather, he wanted the listener to interpret the music for himself or herself. Like his contemporaries, he did reveal his great interest in literature through his music.

ROBERT AND CLARA SCHUMANN

Nothing right can be accomplished in art without enthusiasm.

ROBERT SCHUMANN,
COMPOSER, PIANIST, AND CRITIC (1810–1856)

Robert Schumann

Art is a fine gift! What, indeed, is finer than to clothe one's feelings in music, what a comfort in time of trouble, what a pleasure, what an exquisite feeling to give happy hours to so many people!

CLARA SCHUMANN,
PIANIST AND COMPOSER (1816–1896)

Clara Schumann

Robert Schumann (1810–1856) and Clara Schumann (1816–1896) were married in 1840. Born Clara Wieck, she was the daughter of the music teacher Friedrich Wieck, who had come to the conclusion that his child would be a great musician even before she was born. Until she was four or five years old the child did not speak, and her parents thought that she might be deaf. Once she began to speak, her father started giving her piano lessons.

Clara's first recital took place when she was nine, and by eleven she was performing solo piano recitals at private concerts. In 1828, at the age of twelve, she had her official public debut. The young girl and her father began concert tours in various cities throughout Europe with great success. Clara was a pianist of amazing virtuosity; by 1837 she was recognized as one of the leading performers in Europe. Her career as a composer was also promising, for she had already published several popular piano pieces.

In 1828 Robert Schumann came to Leipzig to be trained by Clara's father. He left to spend a year at the University of Heidelberg to take some law courses but later returned to his music studies in Leipzig. Schumann resided in the Wieck home; this allowed the young people to see a great deal of each other. Wieck noticed that his daughter liked his pupil and warned her not to continue this friendship. Even though her father strongly objected, the couple became secretly engaged. Schumann did try to obtain the father's consent to wed his daughter, but Wieck remained opposed to the match and did everything he could to end the relationship. He was concerned about many things: Schumann had a history of depression and had no income to support a wife and family. Wieck also knew that Schumann had been engaged to marry another woman. The dispute between the couple and her father continued until just one day before Clara's twenty-first birthday, when the couple got married.

Schumann was the youngest of five children; he was born in Zwickau, a town in the German province of Saxony. His father, Friedrich August, was a bookseller and introduced his son to literature. Schumann hoped at one time to be a poet. The youngster demonstrated his musical gift at an early age, and he began composing at the age of seven; however, his mother, Johanna, wanted him to study law. His father had encouraged the young man to continue with his music, but he passed away in 1826 when his son was sixteen.

At the age of nine Schumann attended a concert, which gave him the motivation to apply himself to learning more about music. In 1828 Schumann left his home to go to Leipzig and then to Heidelberg to pursue a degree in law, something his mother insisted upon because she believed it would provide her son with a more secure future. Schumann's letters to his mother displayed his unhappiness with his legal studies. In 1830, with her permission, he returned to Leipzig to resume his music lessons with Wieck.

At one point Schumann sustained a permanent injury to his right hand. Some speculate that it was caused by a device he invented to strengthen his fingers. Others claim the injury resulted from some hand surgery. No matter what caused the damage to his hand, it ended his career as a pianist and pushed him into composition. In April 1834 Schumann helped to produce a music journal, *Die neue Zeitschrift für Musik* (The New Journal for Music). He took over as the editor in 1835 and was also the music critic, reviewing the latest developments. Schumann contributed more than three hundred articles to this journal, which contained his opinions of various composers and performances.

Schumann wanted to have the brilliant but, at this time, neglected works of earlier composers presented to the public, and he sought to give his readers an understanding of what the current romantic composers were writing. Through his articles, he succeeded in making his readers aware of many talented new composers. His own all-time favorite was Mendelssohn. Under his leadership this magazine became important in the world of European music.

Schumann composed his most important pieces for the piano while he was still in his twenties. His *Carnaval* (Carnival), Op. 9, was written during the years 1834 and 1835. The piece demonstrates Schumann's interest in literary themes; it consists of twenty-one pieces for piano that are connected by a returning motif. The title refers to the masked balls that were popular at the time of Carnival (just before Lent), and each piece depicts one character at a ball. The characters either are from literature or are real people, including Frédéric Chopin and Clara Wieck. Schumann wrote the story that the work illustrates. *Carnaval* reflects Schumann's literary leanings and the romantic composer's objective of painting a picture with music. Schumann composed music easily, almost effortlessly. He remarked, "In order to compose, all you need to do is remember a tune that nobody else has thought of."

As a composer of art songs, Schumann was second only to Franz Schubert. His 140 songs are overflowing with emotion, and the accompaniments are extremely responsive to the text. Schumann gave the piano accompaniment equal importance with the voice. Like Schubert, Schumann composed song cycles, and his most frequent theme is love.

In 1841 Schumann turned his attentions from lieder to orchestral music. His instrumental pieces demonstrate his ability to convert an image or a mood into music. The Concerto for Piano and Orchestra in A Minor, Op. 54, took four years to complete. During that time Schumann composed constantly even when he was on tour or writing for the magazine. His health suffered from the strain of the hectic pace he set for himself. This concerto contains a special liveliness. The composer's melodic inventiveness is evident in this piece, which also demonstrates Schumann's technical and artistic abilities. The work had been written in separate sections and at different times; later Schumann edited it together into a concerto. He revised it several more times and changed the titles of the movements. His wife was the soloist when Mendelssohn conducted the work in its second performance in Leipzig.

In 1844, while accompanying his wife on a concert tour to Russia, Schumann suffered a nervous breakdown. His doctors suggested that changing their lives could be helpful. Therefore the family moved to Dresden, and for a short period of time Schumann appeared to recover. Six years later they moved to Düsseldorf because the composer had received his first official appointment as municipal director of music. At first Schumann was contented and productive in this new position. Eventually, though, his ability to function in these circumstances was limited by his mental state; he had memory lapses while conducting that forced him to resign from the job. Through the years, eight children were born to Robert and Clara, of whom seven survived.

As time passed Schumann grew more and more tormented by his illness. He reported hearing a single tone in his head that drove him mad; Schumann had always feared the possibility that he was losing his mind. In 1854 he suffered a severe mental breakdown and spent two years in a clinic for treatment. He died there at the age of forty-six.

Schumann is one of the greatest of German romantic composers. Early in his career he broke with the traditional classical genres, which he believed were limiting; yet he admired the work of the classical composers. His major contribution was to piano music and art song. His piano works were highly original; full of unusual harmonies and spirited rhythms, these pieces make Schumann's music stand out. He followed Schubert's design in his lieder, but his accompaniments brought them to new heights. Schumann also is credited with sparking a renewed interest in Schubert's work. His journal articles elevated the level of appreciation for past and present composers. As a music critic, he stands in the forefront of the nineteenth century.

After the death of her husband, Clara Schumann moved to Berlin in 1857, where she performed, taught, and edited his works and letters. In March 1896 Clara suffered a stroke. She died on May 20, 1896. During most of her marriage she had set her music aside in order to take care of her husband and children. Her own attitude about women attempting to build a career reflects the negative outlook of the time. She wrote, "I once believed that I possessed creative talent, but I have given up this idea; a woman must not desire to compose—there has never yet been one able to do it. Should I expect to be that one?"

Clara Schumann's compositions were representative of the early romantic era, consisting of preludes and single-movement pieces. She wrote most of her pieces for her own piano concerts. She also composed a number of songs, some choral pieces, and a piano trio. An entry in her diary expresses her love of composition: "Composing gives me great pleasure… there is nothing that can surpass the joy of creation, if only because through it one gains hours of self-forgetfulness while one lives in a world of sound."

FRÉDÉRIC CHOPIN

Every difficulty slurred over will be a ghost to disturb your repose later on.

FRÉDÉRIC CHOPIN,
COMPOSER AND PIANIST (1810–1849)

Frédéric Chopin

Known as the "Poet of the Piano," Frédéric Chopin (1810–1849) wrote music that has been described as daring, romantic, fantastic, brilliant, tragic, majestic, and dreamy. Chopin was born in Żelazowa Wola, Poland, a town thirty-five miles west of Warsaw. His father, originally from France, was employed as a French-language tutor in the household of a Polish count. Chopin's mother was born in Poland and was employed as a housekeeper for the same count. The couple had four children, three daughters and a son, who was the second-born. The father moved the family to Warsaw, Poland, shortly after the birth of their son to take a teaching job in the Warsaw Lyceum (high school).

Chopin's musical gift was evident early in his childhood. He began composing at seven, writing two polonaises (Polish dances). In 1818 the eight-year-old gave his first concert. He was instantly hailed as a child prodigy. Written up in the newspapers, the brilliance of his performances caused him to acquire a reputation as a "second Mozart." He attended the school in which his father was a teacher. At the age of sixteen Chopin started lessons at the new conservatory in Warsaw. During the graduation ceremony a note from one of his professors was handed to Chopin with his diploma; it read, "Particular skills: music genius."

In 1829 Chopin fell in love with a vocal student at the conservatory. He stated that she inspired his Concerto in F Minor, Op. 21. In 1830 Chopin performed his farewell concert in the Warsaw National Theater. His friends gave him a silver container filled with Polish soil. The composer was described as the "Poet of the Piano." Chopin knew that he had to get to the center of the new romanticism, which was in Paris, in order to be involved with the leading intellectuals of the times.

Chopin planned first to go to Austria and then on to Italy. In Vienna, after a concert, he learned that a Polish uprising against the Russian czar had begun. By the time Chopin reached the German city of Dresden, he heard that the Russians had recaptured Warsaw. His Étude in C Minor, called the *Revolutionary Etude* (Op. 19 No. 12), was composed in 1831; it expressed the pain and sorrow caused by this news. Anxious about the outcome of this rebellion for his family and his country, Chopin was not certain how to plan his future.

In 1832 a debut concert for Chopin was organized in Paris. The young man was a sensational hit. In his letters he noted that he had met ambassadors, princes, and important ministers. The composer penned variations for the piano based on "Là ci darem la mano," a well-known aria from Mozart's opera *Don Giovanni*. Robert Schumann reviewed this piece, entitled *Variations in B-flat Major on "Là ci darem la mano" from Mozart's "Don Giovanni,"* Op. 2. Schumann's article, titled "An Opus 2," was published in the *Allgemeine musikalische Zeitung* (General Music Journal) of Leipzig. In this review he raved about Chopin: "Hats off, gentlemen, a genius!"

Paris in the 1830s was a major European cultural hub. It was also the center of a circle of romantic writers and artists, and Chopin was now a part of that gifted group. The young composer presented several concert tours outside of Paris and performed occasionally in the city, but he felt his music was too personal for a crowded concert hall. He preferred the salons and living rooms of the nobility over the public-concert audiences. He also gave private music lessons to the Polish and French aristocracy. Chopin enjoyed being around the aristocracy and the life that he was able to lead in their company.

Chopin was a slim and delicate man who suffered from a chronic disease, which may have been tuberculosis, a common illness in the nineteenth century. His letters often mention his poor health. In 1826, at the age of sixteen, he had breathing problems and severe headaches for six months. Chopin was often so weak that he was unable to climb stairs; at times he had to be carried out after his performances, if not forced to cancel them altogether.

Through his friend Franz Liszt, Chopin was introduced to a French novelist, Aurore Dupin, the Baroness Dudevant, who was better known by her pen name: George Sand. Chopin spent the winter of 1838 on the Spanish island of Majorca, where he became quite ill. He left the island and went to the French port of Marseille to recover. The composer was still in poor health when he moved to Sand's estate in Nohant, in central France, in the spring of 1839. For the next eight years Chopin spent his summers on that estate, returning to Paris in the winters. George Sand's house was usually filled with well-known artists and writers. Here Chopin wrote a great many of his compositions, although his health continued to decline.

In 1847 Chopin, his strength still failing, came back to Paris. In 1848 he presented his last concert in Paris; he then went to London, where he became severely ill. In 1849 he returned to Paris, where he died. Almost three thousand people came to the funeral service. The Polish soil that his friends had given to him when he left his homeland was strewn over his grave.

Chopin's music is very original and had a powerful influence on the work of many later composers. His etudes were generally meant to be used as teaching pieces but are also appreciated for their artistic merit. His piano pieces explore the full expressive range of the instrument and display his brilliance both as a composer and as a pianist. These works and his performances made others aware of the real power and capability of this instrument. Felix Mendelssohn expressed his thoughts about Chopin's talent at the keyboard, saying, "There is something fundamentally personal and at the same time so very masterly in his playing that he may be called a really perfect virtuoso."

In all of Chopin's works the melodies are fascinating and the harmonic innovations bold. Chopin was a superb craftsman; his compositions encompass many genres, including national dances such as polonaises and mazurkas. Each piece is exceptionally lyrical, and his inclusion of Polish folk music in these pieces is very evident. He was one of the first nationalist composers who brought to his music the themes and dances of his native country. Although Chopin spent most of his life in France, he is often considered the national composer of Poland, since his music incorporates so much of the folk music of the country he left behind. With the death of Chopin, the early period of romantic composers came to an end. Chopin, Schumann, and Mendelssohn all reflected the musical ideals of the romantic period.

FRANZ LISZT

Sorrowful and great is the artist's destiny.

FRANZ LISZT,
COMPOSER AND PIANIST (1811–1886)

Franz Liszt

Franz Liszt (1811–1886) was born in the village of Doborján (now called Raiding), Hungary. His father was employed by the Esterházy family; his mother was born in Austria. His father, who played both the cello and piano, was his first music teacher. Liszt's public debut was held in 1820 when he was nine years old. The child had an amazing talent that was noticed by the nobility; they provided the funds that allowed the family to move to Vienna so that the youngster could further his studies.

The boy was recognized as a virtuoso on the piano and traveled to Paris and London for concerts. In 1823 Ádám Liszt resigned from his service to the Esterházy family so that he could dedicate himself to his son's career. The family moved to Paris when Liszt was a teenager. He was hoping to attend the Paris Conservatory, but it did not admit foreigners, and so he was not accepted.

While living in Paris, Liszt became fascinated by the French romantic movement and made friends with its leaders. At the age of nineteen Liszt attended a violin concert; the virtuoso's performance impressed him so greatly that he was motivated to practice piano for about ten hours a day. The young man was also impressed by Chopin's mastery of the piano. Liszt and Chopin were friends until feelings of competition between the virtuosos led to a rivalry between them.

From 1839 to 1847 Liszt toured all over Europe. His amazing ability and masterful presentations revolutionized the technical aspects of piano playing. Liszt had become the ultimate showman; he charmed the audience with expressive interpretations and theatrical moves. He instituted the solo recital, where he presented his own piano compositions. Until this time, it had been the custom for the performer to have his back facing the audience. Liszt turned the piano to the side and gave the audience a view of his profile as he performed. His magnetic appeal and the excitement of his performances made the women attending his concerts feel faint; he became the first music superstar, much like the rock icons of today. His reputation rapidly spread across the European continent, and he was constantly in demand.

In 1848, at the peak of his fame, Liszt decided that he now needed to concentrate on his composition, and he became the musical director for the duke of Weimar. As the court conductor, he developed an excellent orchestra and experimented with orchestral genres. Liszt supported the work of many contemporary composers; this sometimes got him into disagreements with the members of the court. His promotion of Wagner's work caused some friction, since Wagner, owing to his political activities, had been exiled from Germany. Liszt's open-door policy attracted musicians and pianists from throughout Europe who came there to learn from this master of the instrument.

In 1861 Liszt moved to Rome. He had always had a religious outlook, and now he sought to fulfill these emotions with action. He took minor vows and became a part of the secular clergy in 1865; he was now known as Abbé Liszt. In this period of his life he also began to compose his major religious pieces. Liszt lived in Rome but spent time visiting Weimar and also Budapest, Hungary. While on a visit in 1886 to his daughter Cosima in Bayreuth, Germany, to attend a festival of operas composed by his son-in-law, Richard Wagner, Liszt became ill with pneumonia. He died on July 31, 1886.

During the years he spent in Weimar, Liszt composed and produced his major orchestral pieces, including two piano concertos and his *Hungarian Rhapsodies*, which were originally written for the piano and later orchestrated. The Piano

Concerto No. 1 in E-flat Major is in a single movement made up of four contrasting sections performed without a break between them. In each section the same basic themes reappear, altered but still identifiable; this is called cyclic form.

Liszt enjoyed program music and was the first to write a symphonic poem (a one-movement piece of program music for orchestra that evokes imagery). He believed that the loose construction of this genre gave his music the correct setting; he held the work together by continuously transforming a few themes. His symphonic poems were inspired by the program music of Beethoven and Mendelssohn, but Liszt coined the term to explain his new works. They were a romantic approach to theme and variations based on a literary idea, a historical event, or a work of art. His twelve symphonic poems inspired other composers in the nineteenth century.

Liszt is most famous for his fantastic performances on the piano; he set new standards for future piano players. People came to hear his music but also to see him perform; he became a charming celebrity during his recitals. Mendelssohn declared: "I have heard no performer whose musical feelings, like Liszt's, extended to the very tips of his fingers."

RICHARD WAGNER

I write music with an exclamation point!

RICHARD WAGNER,
OPERA COMPOSER (1813–1883)

Richard Wagner (1813–1883) had a tremendous impact on the music of the nineteenth century. He was the ninth child born to Carl Friedrich Wagner in Leipzig, Germany. Carl Wagner was a clerk in the office of the Leipzig police department; he died soon after this child was born. His

Richard Wagner

widow remarried one year later. Her new husband, Ludwig Geyer, was an actor, artist, and playwright. In 1814 the family moved to Dresden. Wagner was known as Wilhelm Richard Geyer until he was fourteen years old.

Wagner's stepfather encouraged the youngster to engage in artistic pursuits. The only formal musical training Wagner had during this time was about six months of music theory lessons, but he also tried to teach himself as much as he could. Geyer died in 1821 when Wagner was eight.

Wagner was fascinated by the theater. In 1827 his family returned to Leipzig. Wagner began lessons in composition with a local musician and then attended the University at Leipzig to further his studies in music. At the age of twenty he decided to leave school and take a position as a chorus trainer in a small opera house; there he became more familiar with the current opera repertoire. That year he composed his first opera, *Die Feen* (The Fairies), a lengthy work that followed the traditional operatic style of Beethoven and Weber. But this first attempt actually was not performed until shortly after his death in 1883. For the next six years Wagner conducted orchestras in small theaters.

Wagner was strongly influenced by the operas of Carl Maria von Weber, Gaetano Donizetti, and Giacomo Meyerbeer; he also believed that Beethoven was the ultimate musical genius. The twenty-three-year-old Wagner fell in love with an actress, Christine Wilhelmine Planer, who went by the nickname Minna; they soon married. When he was twenty-four, his second opera, *Das Liebesverbot* (Forbidden Love), based on Shakespeare's play *Measure for Measure*, was performed, but it was not appreciated by the audience. Wagner usually wrote his own librettos; he wanted to achieve complete accord between the text and the music.

The young couple moved to Riga after Wagner was offered a position as a chief conductor at a theater there. At this point he started to work on another opera; in 1839, after completing the first two acts, Wagner and his wife suddenly decided to go to Paris—a few steps ahead of the debt collectors, who were constantly after him. Arriving after a rough sea voyage, Wagner hoped to be recognized for his music. The Wagners lived in Paris from 1839 until 1842, spending far more money than they earned; they were always moving in an attempt to avoid their creditors. Wagner held several jobs, including writing articles and arranging operas by various other composers; however, he did not achieve the admiration that he eagerly sought in Paris. They were penniless and faced debtors' prison.

Der fliegende Holländer (The Flying Dutchman) was Wagner's latest undertaking. Wagner said that this opera was inspired by his and Minna's stormy North Sea voyage from Riga to London. Wagner originally wanted this work to be performed without an intermission; it is sometimes presented that way, but more often it is divided into three acts. In *Der fliegende Holländer* Wagner composed musical themes that reflected the dramatic ones; the themes are unique in their harmonies and in the qualities that they were meant to represent.

Giacomo Meyerbeer was considered one of the world's greatest and most successful composers of nineteenth-century opera. His relationship with Wagner began in friendship; Meyerbeer was a financial supporter as well as an influential musician who helped Wagner. The controversy about Wagner's anti-Semitism can be seen in what happened to this friendship. Meyerbeer had been born into a wealthy Jewish family in Germany. He changed his first name from Jacob to the Italian form, Giacomo, after studying opera in Italy. He was a well-known, successful opera composer and personally tried to help the struggling Wagner. In 1850 Wagner launched a spiteful attack on Jewish musicians. He wanted all Jewish composers, conductors, and performers banned from working in Germany. Anti-Semitic feelings were widespread in Europe, and Wagner used these attitudes to stir up even more hatred and anger. Historians have concluded that Wagner was extremely jealous of Meyerbeer's wealth and accomplishments. Published under a false name, Wagner's essay "Das Judenthum in der Musik" (Jewishness in Music), appearing in *Die neue Zeitschrift für Musik* (The New Journal for Music), attacked Jews in general, and the composers Meyerbeer and Mendelssohn in particular. In 1868 Wagner expanded this essay and had it published under his real name. Meyerbeer never publicly responded to Wagner's malicious attack.

What makes this all quite confusing is that in reality Wagner worked with many Jews. He had learned a great deal from Meyerbeer, who also had helped him get his start. In addition to Meyerbeer, the man who was in charge of Wagner's public relations and who often conducted Wagner's works, his longtime friend Hermann Levi, was Jewish. Another Jewish musician named Rubenstein completed the orchestration of some of his operas.

Wagner stayed in Dresden for six years. This is considered the middle period of Wagner's compositions. At the onset of this period he composed two more operas: *Tannhäuser* in 1845 and *Lohengrin* in 1848. The quest for the perfect German romantic opera reached its goals in these works. All of the required ingredients are included in these operas: the stories were taken from German folk tales, there are supernatural events, and there is admiration for the common people. The "Bridal Chorus," which is traditionally used as a wedding processional, comes from *Lohengrin*. Franz Liszt oversaw the first production of this opera in 1850. It also proved to be successful, even though the composer had been identified as a revolutionary and banished from the country. Eventually, the opera was performed by many German opera companies.

Changes in European society were swiftly taking place. The February Revolution in Paris and revolutions in Munich, Berlin, Prague, and Vienna began in 1848. German nationalist feelings were inflamed by the events in France. Wagner was disenchanted with his life in an aristocratic court; he was pleased with the measures being taken to change the social structure. He became involved with a revolutionary movement and wrote articles for a newspaper stressing the need for a new society that would give people their rights. Soon a warrant was issued for Wagner's arrest, and he had to run away. Wagner escaped to Weimar, where he stayed with his friend Franz Liszt. Then further arrangements were made so that Wagner could cross the border into Zurich, Switzerland. Because of his political activities, Wagner was not allowed to return to Germany until 1862.

Over the next four years, from 1849 to 1852, Wagner published a number of books and essays, but no music. Wagner believed that opera was on the wrong course, since it highlighted the performers rather than the drama. He stated that myths were eternal, so that was what he would base his operas on. He developed the systematic use of the leitmotif (leading motif), which would remind the listeners of a previous situation and provide them with a foreshadowing of what was to come.

During this time, though, he was working on an enormous four-opera cycle. He titled it *Der Ring des Nibelungen* (The Ring of the Nibelungs). Known as the *Ring* cycle, these operas were based on ancient Germanic and Icelandic literature. Considered Wagner's masterwork, the operas in the Ring cycle are *Das Rheingold* (The Gold of the Rhine), *Die Walküre* (The Valkyrie), *Siegfried*, and *Götterdämmerung* (Twilight of the Gods). They were composed over a period of twenty-six years starting in 1848 and were not completed until the composer was sixty-one.

Wagner's *Ring* cycle put into practice the standards that he had determined to be his ideal in his books. Wagner wrote the entire poem first and then composed the music. (He actually began by writing the last epic poem first.) These tales are told through each chord of the music as well as by each word of the poem; this is what the composer believed a music drama must achieve. The operas are about mythological gods and heroes and are quite lengthy. Although he intended the operas to be staged as a series, each one can stand on its own.

Taking a break from composing the *Ring* cycle, Wagner worked on two other operas: *Tristan und Isolde* (Tristan and Isolde), completed in 1859, and *Die Meistersinger von Nürnberg* (The Mastersingers of Nuremberg), finished in 1887. In 1858 the Wagners' marriage fell apart. After eleven years in exile, Wagner was granted a partial pardon in 1860 and allowed to travel in most of Germany; this was extended to a full pardon in 1862. The composer then moved to a town in Austria.

A theater for the purpose of presenting Wagner's music dramas was planned and eventually resulted in the Bayreuth Festival Theater. Wagner societies throughout Europe raised money to fund the construction of the new opera house in Bayreuth, Bavaria, in southern Germany. To assist in the fund-raising, Wagner began touring and conducting concerts. Four years later, in 1876, after nine weeks of rehearsal, the first Bayreuth Festival featured the premiere of the *Ring* cycle. It was a financial disaster, and Wagner had to struggle to overcome his losses.

In 1877 Wagner was composing *Parsifal*, his final opera. Wagner decided that this work could not be described as an opera or even as one of his music dramas and invented his own word to describe it: *Bühnenweihfestspiel*, which, loosely translated, means "consecrated festival play." Wagner had never cared for the term "opera" and had described his work as dramas or festival plays. Perhaps because his dramas were so lengthy (*Parsifal* runs for five hours), he believed that audiences needed to have a great deal of time available to attend instead of an afternoon or an evening. Wagner intended for *Parsifal* to be presented only at Bayreuth, believing that the music would consecrate, or bless, that theater.

Wagner had been experiencing heart problems for several years. In 1882 the composer's health began to fail. As soon as the second Bayreuth Festival was over, Wagner went to Venice, Italy, to spend the winter. In February 1883 he suffered a heart attack and died. He was buried at Bayreuth. His second wife, Cosima (a daughter of Franz Liszt), continued as artistic director of the Bayreuth Festival for the next thirty-one years, until 1908, when their son, Siegfried, who also composed operas, took over this position.

Wagner's contributions have been the cause of his popularity and of the severest critical attacks on his music. Wagner transformed opera. He was capable of writing powerful and intense works that had a lasting influence on music. He insisted that every detail in the text and music have a direct connection to the work's dramatic purpose. He believed that every bar of the music had to be justified by an explanation of something in the action or in the characters. His music flows in a continuous line without the breaks found in other operas; Wagner called this "unending melody." In his music dramas there are no arias, recitatives, or ensembles, since the composer believed they would halt the flow of the action.

The orchestra was a focal point of Wagner's changes; he integrated the use of the orchestra more than any other composer had in the past. At Bayreuth, even though the orchestra was hidden in a sunken pit, its sound was so powerful that only very strong voices could perform with it. The use of leitmotifs, which recur every time a principal character appears, allows the orchestra to convey specific meaning and permits the themes to weave themselves into a thick and compact dramatic fabric. Through modulation or an instrumental transformation, the leitmotif tracks the direction of the opera. The orchestra in Wagner's music dramas tells much about the story.

Wagner often employed the most dissonant chordal sounds to portray the inner feelings of the characters in his dramas. He used chromatic harmonies and tones to create emotion and tension. His intention was to combine all of the arts—music, literature, drama, and the visual arts—into one all-encompassing experience. In his own words, "True drama can be conceived only as resulting from the collective impulse of all the arts to communicate in the most immediate way with a collective public."

In Wagner's view, the ideals of a people had to be reflected in their culture, and his works mirrored these beliefs. Because of his political outlook and his prejudices, he remains a controversial figure. During his lifetime Wagner was either adored or hated, and more than ten thousand books and articles have been written about him. Although Wagner died before the birth of Nazism, his influence on the

German National Socialist movement was huge. His spiteful anti-Semitism plus the ultranationalistic nature of his operas matched the Nazi ideology perfectly; his music became a powerful symbol of that regime.

It is perhaps ironic that Wagner's great-grandson, Gottfried Wagner, has spent his career writing and giving lectures about the anti-Semitism of Richard Wagner and how it was applied to German politics and culture. Gottfried Wagner is a cofounder, with Abraham Peck, of the Post-Holocaust Dialogue Group, which brings Germans and Jews together for discussions. His book *Twilight of the Wagners* examines the intolerance and racism that caused his family members to associate with the leaders of the Nazi Party.

GIUSEPPE VERDI

The artist must yield himself to his own inspiration.... I should compose with utter confidence a subject that set my musical blood going, even though it were condemned by all other artists as antimusical.

GIUSEPPE VERDI, OPERA COMPOSER (1813–1901)

Giuseppe Verdi

For fifty years Italian opera was dominated by one man, Giuseppe Verdi (1813–1901). He built on the rich traditions of the composers who had come before him and brought the genre to its summit. Verdi was born in the village of Le Roncole, in northern Italy. His father realized that he had a very talented child and bought him a piano; by the age of seven the youngster was apprenticed to the town organist at the local Catholic church. Over the next eight years Verdi penned a number of liturgical pieces for his church and others. In 1823 the family moved to Busseto, where a local grocer, Antonio Barezzi, noticed his talent. This merchant paid Verdi's tuition in a music school run by Antonio Provesi, who was the conductor of the Busseto Orchestra. Provesi appointed Verdi assistant conductor when the boy was only thirteen.

In 1833, when Verdi completed his studies at the music school, he applied for admission to the Milan Conservatory. The conservatory rejected his application, stating that he was over the age limit. It is rumored that Verdi actually did not pass the examinations required for admission, as his skills on the keyboard were not up to the standards of the school. Verdi was troubled by this rejection for the rest of his life. In 1836 Verdi got a job as an organist in Busseto. That same year, at the age of twenty-three, he married the sixteen-year-old daughter of the merchant who had sponsored his musical education. They settled in Busseto, where Verdi began directing and composing for the local Philharmonic Society and giving private lessons.

When Verdi returned to Milan three years later, he brought his wife and two young children. His first opera, *Oberto, Conte di San Bonifacio* (Oberto, Count of San Bonifacio), was presented at La Scala in 1839. Although the opera had some obvious flaws, the audience appeared to enjoy it, and Verdi received a contract to write three more. Unfortunately in 1840, shortly after the premiere of his first operatic work, both of his children died; this tragedy was quickly followed by the death of his wife. *Un giorno di regno* (A One-Day Reign) was a comic opera that Verdi had been commissioned to compose just when this disaster struck his family. The opera was a total failure. Verdi was devastated by his loss and the disappointment. He returned to Busseto vowing that he would no longer compose.

Two years later Verdi met Bartolomeo Merelli, the impresario at Milan's famed opera theater La Scala. He convinced the composer to take a look at a libretto for *Nabucco* (Nebuchadnezzar). In this work, set during biblical times, King Nebuchadnezzar of Babylon has defeated the Jewish nation and destroyed Jerusalem. The captive Hebrews are enslaved and sent to Babylon. The libretto immediately appealed to the nationalist feelings of the composer, since at the time the northern portion of Italy was under Austrian rule. The Italians wanted to liberate northern Italy from the foreign power and unite the country.

The opera, with its depiction of tyranny, was sensed as a political statement about Italy by the audience, which assumed that the ancient Jews represented present-day Italy. The chorus "Va, pensiero" (Fly, Thoughts) became a famous anthem of the revolution for Italian patriots. The composer was now strongly identified with the movement to free and unify Italy. Verdi had also always personally identified with this national objective, and his operas supported the goals of the Italian people. Although his operas were set in other places and other times, the audiences viewed the scenes and characters as expressions of sympathy with the revolutionary wave that was flooding Italy.

After the great success of *Nabucco* the shout "Viva Verdi!" was heard throughout Italy. This expression had a double meaning. The Austrian authorities realized that it was a nationalistic acronym (shortening of words): "Viva *V*ittorio *E*manuele, *R*e *D'I*talia" (Long live Vittorio Emanuele, King of Italy). The letters of Verdi's name happened to correspond with the nationalistic slogan. When people were arrested by the Austrians for shouting those words, they replied that they only were referring to their favorite composer, Verdi, and therefore the Austrians had to release them.

Another conflict placed Verdi in the center of controversy: the cause of Italian opera against the growing enthusiasm for German opera as typified by

Wagner. The cultural battle between the two styles was hard fought. During the seventeenth and eighteenth centuries, Italian opera had dominated the European scene. Now German composers were serious competitors and rivals. Verdi, as Italy's most famous composer, and the German Wagner were locked into this rivalry. Although their music and subjects were completely different, both composers revolutionized the opera.

Verdi's use of the orchestra was never as effective as Wagner's, but as he composed, the more his orchestration became imaginative and original. He had a true gift for creating dramatic music that touched the hearts of the Italian public. The focal point of Verdi's operas was the expression of human passion and emotion in song; his arias have tremendous emotional power, and his music has a dynamic force that was new in Italian opera. Verdi sought librettos that were appropriate for his musical style. His popularity expanded throughout the Western musical world.

By 1844 Verdi was becoming a prosperous man. He began to purchase property in the Busseto area. In 1859 Verdi married the opera singer Giuseppina Strepponi, and they lived on an estate that the composer had bought in 1848. Verdi became involved in politics, first as the representative of Busseto in the provincial parliament. Eventually he was elected to the national parliament.

The viceroy of Egypt commissioned Verdi to write an opera for the 1869 opening of a new opera house in Cairo. The composer began work on *Aida*, which is set in Egypt at the time of the pharaohs. Owing to the Franco-Prussian War, the premiere was delayed until 1871. The opera contains huge spectacles, grand ballets, magnificent choruses, and dramatic color. With *Aida* the composer reached beyond anything he had written before. The opera incorporated all of the elements of traditional Italian lyric opera and the bold sweep of French grand opera. Verdi's use of recurring themes and the exotic locale gave the work a continuity that the composer had not wholly achieved in his other operas. The fifty-eight-year-old composer became a worldwide celebrity as the great master of Italian opera.

A requiem that Verdi wrote in memory of the Italian poet, novelist, and national hero Alessandro Manzoni premiered in 1874. Verdi conducted the chorus and orchestra with solo performers from La Scala on the first anniversary of Manzoni's death. The Requiem is one of Verdi's most important non-operatic works and was enthusiastically received throughout Europe. The composer planned to retire and thought that this would be his concluding performance. After the Requiem Verdi returned to the countryside and did not write for thirteen years.

While in retirement Verdi became increasingly depressed by the political situation in Italy and the growth of the Wagnerian musical philosophy in Europe. Verdi believed that the inroads made by the people who supported Wagner's music were undermining the basis of Italian art. He wanted to ensure that the traditions of Italian opera continued, so sixteen years after composing *Aida*, the almost seventy-year-old Verdi wrote *Otello*. This was his response to the threat he felt from German opera. *Otello*, based on the play *Othello* by William Shakespeare, is considered the greatest Italian tragic opera of the nineteenth century. The Italian public buzzed with rumors that their favorite operatic composer was working again.

On January 4, 1887, Verdi arrived in Milan to begin rehearsing *Otello*. The music was a complete change in style for the composer. Instead of breaks in the music that were typical in his earlier works, *Otello* blurs the boundaries between aria and recitative, and the music is continuous. Verdi shaped his music to this text in a flexible and responsive manner. The opera took the music world by surprise and was a huge success; it is considered to be the greatest triumph of Italian opera. The composer was certain that *Otello* would be his last work.

Six years later Verdi, now close to the age of eighty, produced another masterpiece. Once again the original source was Shakespeare: *Falstaff* was based on the playwright's *The Merry Wives of Windsor* and *Henry IV*. This new opera was the finale of Verdi's career and amazed the music world. *Falstaff* is a comic opera that stands out from Verdi's earlier works. The orchestration, the melodic appeal, the unity of the text with the music, and the technical brilliance with which the composer put it all together created a glorious masterwork. The opera does not have an overture; instead, the curtain rises, and the audience is immediately involved in the story. Verdi utilized all of his talents to create a work that sparkles with amusement from beginning to end. The opera ends with a fugue and a chorus declaring, "All the world is a joke."

In 1879 his second wife had passed away, and Verdi moved into the Grand Hotel in Milan. In 1901 Verdi suffered a stroke; he died at the age of eighty-eight. His funeral was attended by over two hundred thousand people. Italy, which had greatly honored the composer during his lifetime, provided Verdi with a state funeral. At the funeral, the great conductor Arturo Toscanini, then a young man, led a chorus of more than 800 in a performance of "Va, pensiero," the Chorus of the Hebrew Slaves from *Nabucco*.

Verdi's greatest skill was melody, which he used to express human feelings. In his scores, the characters reside in his melodic phrases, which flesh them out. He sought passion in his works. His concern that Italian opera preserve its traditions is evident in his statement, "Opera is opera and symphony is symphony. Our music differs from German music. Their symphonies can live in halls, their chamber music can live in the home. Our music, I say, lives mainly in the theater."

By the age of eighty Verdi had written twenty-eight operas, several sacred pieces, a string quartet, and some anthems. Verdi's work monopolized Italian operatic stages for most of the nineteenth century. Few composers have equaled Verdi in melodic quality; he captured the essence of what Italian opera was meant to be. His works were singer's operas: the orchestra was evident, but its basic function was to support the vocalists. Verdi's operas were about the human drama; there is no arcane symbolism or hidden meaning in them. *Otello* was the peak of serious, tragic opera, and *Falstaff* reached a high point in opera buffa. These works were the climax of Verdi's career. He was quoted as saying, "You may have the universe if I may have Italy." Verdi's works are frequently performed in opera houses throughout the world.

JOHANNES BRAHMS

It is not hard to compose, but what is fabulously hard is to leave the superfluous notes under the table.

JOHANNES BRAHMS, COMPOSER (1833–1897)

Although he always was humble about his own musical abilities, the amazing talents of Johannes Brahms (1833–1897) were obvious from the time he was young. Born in Hamburg, Germany, the son of a musician by the name of Jakob Brahms, the boy grew

Johannes Brahms

up surrounded by music. His father was his first teacher and encouraged his child to pursue his gift. The family did not have much money, but the youngster took lessons in piano, theory, and composition starting at the age of seven. By the time he was ten, Brahms was playing the piano in the local restaurants, taverns, and dance halls to earn some money. Brahms also arranged the music for his father's orchestra.

His first performance as a solo pianist was in 1848, and in a few years he was accomplished enough to be asked to accompany the Hungarian violinist Edouard Reményi on a concert tour. Joseph Joachim, a celebrated violinist, composer, and conductor, met Brahms during this 1853 tour and was impressed by his compositions. Joachim introduced the composer to Robert Schumann, who, through his essay "New Paths" in *Die neue Zeitschrift für Musik* (The Journal for New Music), made the public aware of this new "young eagle." Brahms was surprised to discover that he was considered an up-and-coming musician.

The Schumanns introduced the young man to their circle of friends. Suddenly, a few months after their friendship began, Schumann had a mental breakdown. Brahms was very distressed by Schumann's condition and wished to assist his wife and her seven children. It is believed that Brahms was in love with Clara, even though she was fourteen years older than he, and that this was why he never married. Brahms remained a lifelong friend of the entire Schumann family.

The Piano Concerto No. 1 in D Minor, Op. 15, premiered in 1859 in Leipzig; Brahms was the piano soloist, and his friend Joachim conducted. At first Brahms had designed this piece as a symphony; then he rewrote it as a sonata for two pianos. The final concerto version was poorly received by the audience, not only at this first performance but also at two subsequent ones. This response upset the composer and undermined his confidence. Four years later, Brahms returned to Hamburg, where he spent his time composing and hoping for an appointment in his native city. The music establishment in Hamburg did not make any offers to him; therefore, in 1863 he went to Vienna, where he remained for thirty-five years.

Brahms was very self-critical and was also known for his sarcastic humor. He had a coarse quality about him and would often respond to people bitingly when he was annoyed. A typical Brahms remark was widely circulated: "If there is anyone here whom I have not insulted, I beg his pardon." Liszt and Wagner also angered the composer by criticizing his work: they stated that Brahms was living in the past and could not move forward with the new innovations in music. Some people responded that Brahms, who preferred to compose in the classical genres, was following in the footsteps of Beethoven and Mozart. Others joined Liszt and Wagner in their belief that Brahms's music was outdated and too conservative. The conflict caused a serious division in musical circles. Clara Schumann, Joseph Joachim, and the influential music critic Eduard Hanslick took the side of Brahms and rejected the views of Wagner's followers. This episode is known as the War of the Romantics; it was basically a debate between the supporters of program music and those who advocated absolute music.

In 1863 Brahms was appointed director of the Vienna Singakademie; he also toured parts of Europe. Schumann's death in 1856 and the 1865 death of the composer's mother were memorialized in Brahms's *Ein deutsches Requiem* (A German Requiem, Op. 45), which is based on biblical texts rather than on the Roman Catholic requiem mass. The opening three movements of this large-scale choral work were first performed at a private concert in memory of Franz Schubert in Vienna in 1867. This premiere became the subject of a critical debate in the Brahms-versus-Wagner camps because the timpanist misread the score, causing many in the audience to become upset over the loud and unexpected noise. Some Wagner supporters used the error to criticize the entire work. In the Brahms group however, the review by Hanslick (who disliked Wagner) called *Ein deutsches Requiem* "a work of unusual significance and great mastery. It seems to us one of the ripest fruits to have emerged from the style of the late Beethoven in the field of sacred music."

Brahms carefully rewrote the orchestration to make sure that the mistake would not happen again. The original six movements of *Ein deutsches Requiem* premiered in 1868. (A seventh was added later.) The piece was conducted by Brahms at the Bremen Cathedral with over two thousand people in the audience. After this, Brahms was regarded as one of the leading composers of his time. The work had taken Brahms eleven years to compose and is considered to be his magnum opus (greatest work).

In 1872 Brahms was appointed the conductor of the Viennese Gesellschaft der Musikfreunde (Society for the Friends of Music). He resigned this post in 1875 and did not accept another position, instead dedicating his time to compositions. Brahms enjoyed his privacy, and by 1890 Brahms wished to retire, since he had accumulated a large amount of money from the publication and sale of his music. Friends convinced him to continue to compose, and some of his finest works were produced in his later years. Ten months after the death of Clara Schumann, Brahms succumbed to cancer; he died in 1897. He was buried in the central cemetery of Vienna near the graves of Beethoven and Schubert.

Brahms's music was traditional; he purposely followed in the steps of the great masters of the classical era and saw his role as one preserving the traditions. Brahms believed that innovative and important music could be written in the time-honored genres that had been passed down to him, and he studied the compositions of earlier composers to gain an understanding of their concepts so that he could use them in his own. His works revived the appeal of absolute music. Perhaps he would be gladdened to discover that posterity has placed him among the "three great Bs"—Bach, Beethoven, and Brahms.

GEORGES BIZET

I want to do nothing chic; I want to have ideas before beginning a piece.

GEORGES BIZET,
COMPOSER AND CRITIC (1838–1875)

Georges Bizet

Best known for his opera *Carmen*, Georges Bizet (1838–1875) was born in Paris. His mother was a pianist, and his father was a composer who also taught voice students. The boy was given his first music lessons by his parents. Remarkably, he was accepted at the Paris Conservatory prior to his tenth birthday; this was most unusual, since the conservatory had an age requirement. The young man became a highly accomplished pianist.

Bizet's opera *Les pêcheurs de perles* (The Pearl Fishers) was set in exotic Ceylon. It was first performed in 1863 in Paris, where it received a cool reception. In 1865 the opera *Ivan IV* was commissioned. The work, based on the Russian czar known as Ivan the Terrible, faced many problems and postponements. Frustrated by the difficulties he encountered, the composer gave up his attempts to get the opera staged. Next, Bizet wrote *La jolie fille de Perth* (The Fair Maid of Perth), based on the novel by Sir Walter Scott. The premiere took place in Paris in 1867, but the opera was performed for only twenty-one nights.

His next work was also a failure. Bizet felt that it was the Wagnerian influence that ruined the appreciation of his works. Disappointed by the unprofitability of his operas and the lack of audience acclaim, Bizet repeatedly experienced periods of self-doubt and depression. In spite of his failure to please the public and the lack of financial success, Bizet pressed on. To support himself, he gave piano lessons, arranged music for several composers, and accompanied other musicians.

His next commissioned opera was based on one of Prosper Mérimée's stories, *Carmen*. The libretto was written by the dramatist Henri Meilhac and the author Ludovic Halévy, a cousin of Bizet's wife. The story of *Carmen* presented the realities of life in art, which was one of the romantic era's ideals. By the end of the nineteenth century, the distinctions between comic opera and serious opera were disappearing, yet it was still customary for serious works to be staged only at certain theaters, and comic works only at others.

Set in Spain, *Carmen* relates the dramatic story of some rather unsavory characters: the main character, Carmen, is a Gypsy beauty working in a cigarette factory when she meets Don José, a soldier who becomes obsessed with Carmen and gives up his career in the army to join her. When she spurns him for a handsome bullfighter, Don José goes mad with jealousy and stabs her to death. The other characters are an assortment of questionable types, including smugglers and thieves. The themes of the tale are love, fate, and death. In March 1875 *Carmen* was performed at a theater that normally presented comic operas to families. The violence displayed in the opera and its tragic ending certainly were not what was normally presented in this type of theater; Carmen and her criminal companions were not what respectable nineteenth-century audiences expected to see. The gripping force of the music overwhelmed the audience, while the realism of the subject matter caused a major scandal. The opera ran for only forty-eight performances.

Bizet was extremely upset by this new failure. The composer had been hopeful that *Carmen* would finally be a success with the audiences and critics. Three months after the premiere, Bizet had a heart attack and died; he was thirty-seven years old. Within a few years, *Carmen* had been performed in London, Brussels, Vienna, and New York. Its 1880 return performance in Paris was a triumph. Today

Carmen is the most popular and significant French opera of the late nineteenth century.

Bizet was one of the composers who advanced the verismo (an Italian word meaning realistic) style of opera. The literary verismo movement began in Italy in about 1875. The movement attempted to have the writer portray his character's perspective rather than the writer's own personal views and thoughts. In opera this style contains continuous music, without the "numbers" that had previously been popular. Bizet wanted his characters to exhibit natural behavior on stage and had placed spoken dialogue in *Carmen*, which, after his death, was changed to recitative by one of his friends so that the work could be performed in grand opera houses. The scenes and characters in Bizet's operas come to life through his music. He evokes the faraway places that he never actually saw with melodies that had their origins in his French vision.

Great Nineteenth-Century Nationalist and Russian Composers

17

The romantic movement included many composers who reflected the growing feelings of nationalism that was so important to nineteenth-century Europe's political developments. These composers wrote music to celebrate their people and homelands; many were considered national heroes. They expressed the sentiments of their countrymen in their struggle for independence or their love of country. Composers often used a national champion, a historical event, or a local landscape as their subject. Some, like Verdi, wrote music that mirrored events that were currently taking place; others, like Wagner, reached back into the history, literature, or mythology of their country. National pride was encouraged by these musical outpourings.

Eastern European and Scandinavian Masters

BEDŘICH SMETANA, ANTONÍN DVOŘÁK, AND EDVARD GRIEG

Two Czech composers, Bedřich Smetana (1824–1884) and Antonín Dvořák (1841–1904), were a part of the movement to support Bohemian culture and

Bedřich Smetana   Antonín Dvořák   Edvard Grieg

make it flourish. There is a deep awareness of his homeland in all the works of Smetana, who is considered the father of Czech opera. His melodious and comic *The Bartered Bride* abounds with the rhythms and tunes of his native land. Dvořák also used themes from his native folk music throughout his symphonies and chamber works; the best examples are his two sets of *Slavonic Dances*, Op. 46 and Op. 72. The *Norwegian Dances* of Edvard Grieg (1843–1907) also reflect this musical nationalism. Grieg was the most important Norwegian composer of the later nineteenth century; he created a typical Norwegian style of music by employing the unique melodies and harmonies of the local folk music.

Russian Masters

Czar Peter the Great (1672–1725) started a drive to modernize his country and introduce vast reforms to remove Russia from the isolation of its past. The Russian czar toured Europe to become familiar with Western science and culture; he brought back ideas to set his country on a path toward becoming part of the West. During the middle of the nineteenth century, there was a sharp disagreement between two schools of thought in the Russian music scene. The first group of mainly foreign-trained musicians believed that Russian music should follow the same paths as the rest of European music, while the other side argued that Russia's music had to be uniquely Russian.

ANTON RUBINSTEIN

Anton Rubinstein (1829–1894) was a famous concert pianist and composer. He was at the forefront of the people who saw Russia as a partner in the art and culture of Europe; this group maintained that nationalism was not the right foundation upon which to base the future of Russian music. This group assumed that only full-time musicians who were well educated and professional could bring Russian music into the modern world. Rubinstein was the director of the Imperial Conservatory in St. Petersburg, and his ideas carried considerable weight.

Several musicians with the opposite viewpoint formed the Russian national school. Their intention was to define their country's music using entirely Russian culture and traditions. These composers applied their native resources, including folk melodies and the chant of the Greek Orthodox church, to provide a definite Russian flavor in their compositions. Mikhail Glinka, Alexander Borodin, Modest Musorgsky, Nikolai Rimsky-Korsakov, Pyotr Ilyich Tchaikovsky, and Sergei Rachmaninoff were among the musicians who agreed with this point of view. Russian nationalism is reflected in the works of all these men.

MIKHAIL GLINKA

The year 1836 brought Mikhail Glinka's (1804–1857) *Ivan Susanin* (also known as *A Life for the Czar*) to the stage. Until the premiere of this tale about a Russian peasant who sacrifices his life for the czar, there was no genuinely Russian opera. Glinka was the first composer from Russia to be recognized internationally, and he helped to establish the Russian national school.

His work inspired a group of other composers. Known as the Five, they included Mily Balakirev, César Cui,

Mikhail Glinka

Modest Musorgsky, Nikolai Rimsky-Korsakov, and Alexander Borodin. Balakirev and Cui were amateurs, and their compositions are rarely performed today. Balakirev was a self-taught musician who convinced the others to join together to fashion a distinctly Russian style of music in 1856. Their aim was to write music that was free of Western European influences. In 1862 the group founded the Free School of Music to further their goals. The Five began to fall apart in the 1870s because of financial problems, the withdrawal of Balakirev, and disputes among its members. Nonetheless, it had a tremendous influence on the direction of Russian music.

ALEXANDER BORODIN

Alexander Borodin (1833–1887) was trained as a research chemist and held a doctorate in medicine. He was internationally recognized for his scientific contributions. Music was his hobby; he studied chemistry and languages while he learned to play the cello, piano, and flute. Borodin enjoyed performing with string quartets and playing piano duets with his wife, Ekaterina Protopopova, who also was a fine musician. In 1864 he joined the Five, whose members encouraged him to compose.

Alexander Borodin

He worked on his opera *Prince Igor* for eighteen years, yet it was still incomplete at his death in 1887. His friends Nikolai Rimsky-Korsakov and Alexander Glazunov finished the orchestration and some parts of the third act using Borodin's themes. Franz Liszt made arrangements for a performance of Borodin's Symphony in E-flat Major in Germany. *In the Steppes of Central Asia*, a symphonic tone poem he was commissioned to write in 1880 to celebrate the silver jubilee of Czar Alexander II, is a concert favorite. The work combines themes depicting Russians and Central Asian nomads on a Russian geographical plain called the Caucasus. His works are full of Russian images and folk melodies.

MODEST MUSORGSKY

While preparing for a career in the military Modest Musorgsky (1839–1881) became friendly with several Russian composers who fired up his interest in music. Except for piano lessons, he had never had any serious musical training. Aware that he had a splendid talent, he was attracted to the idea of composing. At the age of twenty-two he withdrew from his military duties and joined his musical friends. He worked in the St. Petersburg Ministry of Transport while composing part-time.

Modest
Musorgsky

Musorgsky's opera *Boris Godunov*, which he began to compose in 1868, underwent many revisions before it was performed. At its premiere, the opera was disliked by the music critics, but the public adored it. The Russian royal family was nervous about an opera that depicted an uprising against a czar, and Musorgsky had to make several changes prior to its being performed during the next opera season. Thereafter the opera was dropped from the repertoire.

Musorgsky was very depressed by this turn of events. His alcoholism had caused even some of his closest friends to abandon him. The composer began to drink even more heavily; as his former friends became recognized for their music, his spirits sank. In 1874 he wrote a suite of ten piano pieces entitled *Pictures at an Exhibition*, but it was not published until five years later. He worked on another historical opera, *Khovanshchina*, a tale of a revolt against Peter the Great. But this work was never finished. By 1880, Musorgsky had lost his job; his health declined further, and he was hospitalized. He died in 1881.

NIKOLAI RIMSKY-KORSAKOV

Nikolai Rimsky-Korsakov (1844–1908) believed that it was his responsibility to complete Musorgsky's opera *Khovanshchina*. He took the piano score and orchestrated it for his friend. Rimsky-Korsakov had attended the Naval School at St. Petersburg and, like his older brother, was a career naval officer. He had taken piano lessons in his childhood and had shown promise, but his parents discouraged this interest because the family traditionally served in the Russian navy. At first Rimsky-Korsakov accepted this career choice. In 1861, however, he met Mily Balakirev, who encouraged him to spend time composing even though his musical background was incomplete.

Nikolai Rimsky-Korsakov

The young man began writing a symphony during the last year of his studies at the naval academy. In 1862 his squadron left Russia to embark on an extended voyage; they docked in Germany, England, France, Spain, Brazil, and the United States. Rimsky-Korsakov was impressed by what he saw during this three-year journey. When he returned to Russia he brought his almost-complete Symphony No. 1, which had been composed during the voyage even though there had been no piano on board the ship. His friends urged him to finish the piece, and it was performed in 1865, with Balakirev conducting. Excited by the excellent reception of this first work and having received an offer to teach at the St. Petersburg Conservatory, the twenty-seven-year-old Rimsky-Korsakov started to consider a career change. In 1871 he accepted the teaching position. Since he had to continue to earn an income, he remained in the navy for another two years.

Acknowledging his lack of musical training, Rimsky-Korsakov enrolled in harmony and counterpoint classes, joining some of his own composition and orchestration students, who included Sergei Prokofiev and Igor Stravinsky. His respected textbook *The Principles of Orchestration* is still in use today. Rimsky-Korsakov wrote fifteen operas, most of them based on Russian history or folk tales. His orchestral pieces, which are his most famous works, are outstanding examples of orchestration.

Shéhérazade is a symphonic suite that displays Rimsky-Korsakov's great skills in orchestration. Although *Shéhérazade* is based on the narrative *A Thousand and One Arabian Nights*, the work is definitely Russian in feeling. The composer had intended to write individual, unconnected episodes portraying various scenes from the *Arabian Nights*, but on the advice of friends he labeled the movements descriptively. The voice of the storyteller Shéhérazade, presented by a solo violin, is the link between the movements. Rimsky-Korsakov wanted the listener to sense the atmosphere of the Orient in this work. He stated that it was not his intention to interpret the stories through music, but simply to set up hints that let the listener paint his or her own scene. The composer shied away from the idea of classifying *Shéhérazade* as program music and directed the listener to view the work in terms of absolute music.

In 1905 Rimsky-Korsakov lost his professorship in St. Petersburg due to some political statements he made protesting the Russian people's horrid living conditions. After a number of other faculty members resigned in protest, the composer was reinstated. He began to work on a new opera, *Le coq d'or* (The Golden Cockerel), based on a poem by Alexander Pushkin. This is a tale about a weak and foolish king who takes the advice of an astrologer and leads his country into battle against a neighboring country. The opera was a satire intending to tease the czar and to express disapproval of the Russo-Japanese War, which had a terrible effect on the lives of the Russian people. Immediately upon its completion, the czarist regime banned the opera and would not allow a performance. Rimsky-Korsakov died before the premiere of *Le coq d'or*.

PYOTR ILYICH TCHAIKOVSKY

The creative process is like music which takes root with extraordinary force and rapidity.

PYOTR ILYICH TCHAIKOVSKY, COMPOSER (1840–1893)

Pyotr Ilyich Tchaikovsky (1840–1893) grew up in a prosperous, upper-class family that was not particularly musical. His father, Ilya Petrovich, was a government official in Votinsk, a remote Russian town. Tchaikovsky's parents expected him to also have a career in government.

Pyotr Ilyich Tchaikovsky

In 1854 his mother died of cholera and the fourteen-year-old composed a waltz in her memory. While he was preparing for a degree in law and working for the Ministry of Justice, he was also taking music classes at the St. Petersburg Conservatory. The director of the conservatory, the pianist, composer, and conductor Anton Rubinstein, commented that Tchaikovsky was very talented. This type of confirmation of his talent led Tchaikovsky to decide to study music and give up his other pursuits. The young man completed his courses in three years. In 1865 he was appointed to teach composition and harmony in the new Moscow Conservatory, where he remained for twelve years.

Tchaikovsky often experienced bouts of depression; he was a sensitive man and was putting in many hours teaching. In 1877 Tchaikovsky had a breakdown and took a leave of absence from his teaching position for a year. He spent time in Switzerland and then on an estate in Kiev. He tried to return to the Moscow Conservatory, but the stresses caused by teaching made it no longer an option for him.

At this point an important patron entered the composer's life. Nadezhda von Meck was the widow of an industrialist and the mother of eleven children; she was also a recluse, living on her estates outside of Moscow, from which she conducted her business. Very impressed by Tchaikovsky's music, she wished to be his benefactor, but because the limits imposed on women by the conventions of that era and her own worries of being seen as more interested in the man than in his music, she agreed to offer her patronage on the condition that they were never to meet. Their correspondence was conducted by letters, and for thirteen years von Meck provided for the composer and was a keen supporter of his works. They might have accidentally caught sight of each other before or after a performance, but they stuck to the agreement and never formally met.

Tchaikovsky dedicated his Symphony No. 4 in F Minor, Op. 36, to Nadezhda von Meck. It is filled with brilliant orchestral sound. Although the first two movements are melancholy, the final movement starts with a blast of brass and percussion. It is often said that this symphony illustrates the composer's personal progress out of depression into contentment.

Tchaikovsky's music combines Russian folk melodies, European elements, and intensely emotional passages, all written with rich harmonies and magnificent melodies. He composed in many genres, and his output includes operas, symphonies, concertos, and overtures. His ballets are exceptional and are performed frequently; *Swan Lake*, *Sleeping Beauty*, and *The Nutcracker* have an ageless and enduring appeal. He was the first Russian composer whose music was admired in the West, and in 1891 he was invited to come to America for the opening of Carnegie Hall in New York. In a discussion about Tchaikovsky, the composer Igor Stravinsky once stated, "He was the most Russian of us all!" After Tchaikovsky, Russian composers and performers quickly came to prominence on the international scene.

SERGEI RACHMANINOFF

Music is enough for a lifetime,
but a lifetime is not enough for music.

SERGEI RACHMANINOFF,
COMPOSER AND PIANIST (1873–1943)

Sergei Rachmaninoff (1873–1943) composed intensely Slavic pieces that reflected the mood of the Russian people prior to the Russian Revolution of 1905. He was the last

Sergei
Rachmaninoff

composer to write in the tradition of Russian romanticism. Rachmaninoff began to study piano with his mother at the age of four and became a virtuoso pianist. He attended St. Petersburg Conservatory until a diphtheria epidemic raged through the city, killing his sister. He then moved to Moscow to study piano and entered the Moscow Conservatory.

The 1896 premiere of Rachmaninoff's Symphony No. 1 in D Minor was a disaster. The conductor had been drinking heavily prior to the performance, and the music suffered. The critics gave the work terrible reviews; Rachmaninoff became depressed and could not compose for three years. It took sessions with a hypnotist to the draw the young man out of his miserable frame of mind. His mental state improved after he married.

Rachmaninoff was a famous pianist as well, and the piano is central to most of his instrumental works. He admired and was influenced by the work of Pyotr Ilyich Tchaikovsky. Russian Orthodox chants are also evident in his music. Although Rachmaninoff composed mostly in the twentieth century, his music retained the expressions and traditions of nineteenth-century romanticism. After the Russian Revolution of 1917, the composer and his family left Russia and settled in the United States.

Rachmaninoff's choral symphony *The Bells* was based on a poem by Edgar Allan Poe. Heard throughout the work are Russian church bells. The composer said, "The sound of church bells dominated all the cities of the Russia I used to know: Novgorod, Kiev, and Moscow. They accompanied every Russian from infancy to the grave, and no composer could escape from their influence." In his poem, Poe described sleigh bells, wedding bells, alarm bells, and funeral bells to represent the different phases of life. Rachmaninoff employed all four sections of the poem, writing four movements in the style of a classical symphony; the work is orchestrated for three soloists, a chorus, and a large orchestra. This was the composer's favorite piece.

Three years before his death from cancer in 1943, Rachmaninoff wrote the *Symphonic Dances*, Op. 45, which suggest Russian Orthodox chants. First written for two pianos, the piece became a dramatic work for orchestra, using the alto saxophone as a solo instrument. Rachmaninoff was aware that his music reflected his Russian heritage. In *The New Book of Modern Composers*, by David Ewen, the composer is quoted as saying:

I am a Russian composer, and the land of my birth has inevitably influenced my temperament and outlook. My music is the product of my temperament, and so it is Russian music. I never consciously attempt to write Russian music, or any other kind of music, for that matter. I have been strongly influenced by Tchaikovsky and Rimsky-Korsakov, but I have never consciously imitated anybody. I try to make my music speak simply and directly that which is in my heart at the time I am composing.

❧

The Nationalist and Russian composers created styles and genres that often were related to their national folk cultures. Some of them had truly nationalistic objectives, wanting to establish their national identity during a time of disorder or oppression. Composers who resided in countries that did not have a tradition of their own art music had to devise ways of giving voice to their works. They had to find their own musical paths to join the nations with older musical cultures so that they could be recognized as a part of the international musical scene.

18 Great Composers of the Post-Romantic Period

The real composer thinks about his work the whole time; he is not always conscious of this, but he is aware of it later when he suddenly knows what he will do.

IGOR STRAVINSKY, COMPOSER (1882–1971)

Toward the end of the nineteenth century the standards and concepts of the romantic composers had run their course. New trends, such as neoclassicism (new classicism) and atonal (without a tonal center) music, challenged the romantic style. Neoclassicism retained some elements from the classical period, but it was also a reaction to the emotionality of the romantic era. The experimentation with atonal and serial music (a system of tone relationships not centered on any one tone) led many composers to return to more traditional concepts, although they often added modern components to their pieces.

Many composers born in the later years of the nineteenth century felt that they needed to create more current and original musical customs as they entered the new century; yet, numerous others who were composing at that time continued to create works in the romantic style well into the next century. Some composers were more comfortable writing pieces that followed the accepted standards of the past, while others constructed imaginative pathways that led to innovative works for musicians and their listeners. Several of these composers are described as "modernists" even though a portion of their work is in the romantic fashion. Throughout the Western musical world, composers attempted to bridge the opening between the traditions of the past and the music of the future.

Masters of the Post-Romantic Period

GIACOMO PUCCINI

Inspiration is an awakening, a quickening of all man's faculties, and it is manifested in all high artistic achievements.

GIACOMO PUCCINI, OPERA COMPOSER (1858–1924)

In general, Italian opera lovers of the late nineteenth century did not care for the Wagnerian style. There was much discussion of what was happening in the operatic world and how these changes would challenge the future of Italian opera. These people were concerned about the continuation of the methods and traditions of Italian composers and did not want any radical changes or experiments in their operas. Of course, what occurred in German opera had some influence on the Italian traditions, but this effect was limited and minimal.

The leading composer of Italian opera at the end of the nineteenth century was Giacomo Puccini (1858–1924). Called the "King of Verismo" (King of Realism), Puccini was able to write works that followed the great traditions of Italian opera and yet provide his audiences with the latest trends. He was born into an Italian family that was long involved in music. His father, Michele, was a church choirmaster and organist whose ancestors had held this position since 1739. Sadly, his father died when Giacomo was five years old, leaving his pregnant wife, his young son, and five daughters. Puccini's mother, Albina, sent him to study with his uncle at the Institute of Music. The uncle reported that the youngster was restless and not a good pupil. Assigned to another teacher, the boy was exposed to the operatic works of Giuseppe Verdi. Under the guidance of this new teacher the young man's musical gifts became clear.

By the age of fourteen Puccini had been hired at several local churches as an organist. In 1876 he hiked almost twenty miles to the city of Pisa to attend a performance of Verdi's *Aida*. It is believed that this experience was the turning point that caused the eighteen-year-old to decide to compose opera. In 1880 Puccini was able, with a scholarship and the aid of an uncle, to enroll in the Milan Conservatory.

Puccini's third opera, *Manon Lescaut*, set him on his rapid rise to fame. With the money he earned from this work Puccini built a house on a lake in the small town of Torre del Lago. His next three operas, *La Bohème* (Bohemian Life, 1896), *Tosca* (1900), and *Madama Butterfly* (Madam Butterfly, 1904), gained international recognition for him. *La Bohème* is an emotional and romantic work with some realism: the opera takes place in the Latin Quarter of Paris, where starving artists lived while seeking fame and fortune. *Tosca* was Puccini's first tragic opera that can be labeled as verismo. The composer was concerned about presenting realistic detail in his opera, and Puccini researched every aspect of the text and even the costumes for historical accuracy. *Madama Butterfly* is set in Japan; it is a tale of love and betrayal in an exotic location. When it premiered at La Scala, the audience reacted with hostility. Historians report that this negative response to the opera was caused by Puccini's rivals. After the premiere, Puccini reworked the original two-act opera into a three-act version, which was a rousing success.

Puccini spent a great deal of time painstakingly revising and improving his music. He focused on every detail until he was satisfied. Many of Puccini's operas follow a pattern—the characters fall in love and then one of them dies—so they have been accused of having a restricted emotional range. This pattern established the fate of his heroines: they are women who are completely devoted to the men they love but in the end are punished for their love. The composer was most comfortable remaining within the boundaries he set for his music, and these romantic and heartbreaking stories were best suited to his work. Puccini crafted dramatic pieces rich in gorgeous melody; certainly he was aware of the heroic Wagnerian epic dramas, but he felt that this style would not work for him.

In 1907 Puccini went to New York to oversee performances of his operas at the Metropolitan Opera Company. He also began to write *La fanciulla del West* (The Girl of the Golden West) for the Metropolitan Opera; it premiered in December 1910 with the famous Arturo Toscanini conducting. The premiere was a major event, and the composer believed that this opera was his finest work. The setting is a mining town during the California Gold Rush. Puccini incorporated the rough behavior of the men of that era, including fistfights and gunfire. Minnie, the heroine, enters shooting her gun. Yet this is not a tragic opera where the heroine dies after completing her aria at the end; instead, *La fanciulla del West* has comic moments and is very upbeat.

Turandot, Puccini's final work, is set in China; this opera is the tale of a beautiful but cruel Chinese princess. Puccini worked on the piece for four years before going to see a specialist in Brussels, Belgium, for cancer treatment. He brought the unfinished score with him but died before completing the final scenes. Puccini's friend finished the work based on Puccini's outline. *Turandot* was the last Italian opera to attain worldwide fame.

Upon Puccini's death a national state of mourning was declared in Italy. When *Turandot* was performed at La Scala on April 25, 1926, with Arturo Toscanini conducting, Toscanini conducted the score up to the point Puccini had reached before dying; then, turning toward the audience, the conductor said, "Here ends the master's work."

Puccini, like Verdi, understood what Italian opera audiences wanted to see. He had a real sense of what would work on the stage: his flair for drama, his ability to match a theme to a dramatic situation, his portrayal of memorable romantic characters, and his skilled orchestration combined to shape each opera into a work that would please his listeners. Attentive to every detail, Puccini drove his librettists and himself to revise and reconsider every aspect of each work. His music flows with rich harmonies and color. He was a romantic composer entering a new century as an ambassador for the Italian operatic tradition. His music brings a great era to an end.

RICHARD STRAUSS

Never look at the trombones,
it only encourages them.

RICHARD STRAUSS,
COMPOSER AND CONDUCTOR (1864–1949)

Richard Strauss

Famous for his symphonic poems and his operas, Richard Strauss (1864–1949) is associated with the work of Wagner, Liszt, and Berlioz. Strauss was born in Munich, Germany; his father was a horn player in the court opera orchestra. At the age of four he began taking piano lessons, and by the age of six he had composed his first pieces. His father was very traditional in his musical tastes, and even though he allowed his son to attend Wagner's operas, he made it clear to him that he was forbidden to study the scores. Strauss's first compositions were quite conventional and written in the classical genres.

In 1882 Strauss attended the University of Munich, studying philosophy, but he left a year later to go to Berlin. There Strauss met the composer and violinist Alexander Ritter, who was the husband of one of Richard Wagner's nieces. Ritter convinced Strauss to give up working in the classical traditions favored by his father and to look toward the "New German Movement" in the style of Liszt and Wagner.

At the age of twenty-one Strauss discovered his fondness for program music and wrote his first tone poem, *Macbeth*, Op. 23. It was a defining moment for the young man; this work displays the composer's move from his conservative style to his progressive style. A series of tone poems written in the 1890s, among them *Till Eulenspiegels lustige Streiche* (Till Eulenspiegel's Merry Pranks, Op. 28), identified Strauss as the successor to Wagner and Liszt and led to international recognition of his music. Employing a huge orchestra, dissonance, and complex harmonies, these tone poems surprised the music establishment. Later in his life Strauss said, "Thirty years ago I was regarded as a rebel. I have lived long enough to find myself a classic."

As a conductor Strauss toured throughout Europe. Toward the end of the nineteenth century he developed an interest in composing operas, and he entered the twentieth century focused on this interest. Although his first two attempts were not well received, his third attempt, *Salome*, which premiered in 1905, attracted worldwide attention. The opera was written in Wagnerian style, with the orchestra taking an important role and a system of leitmotifs. It was a shocking work for its time; in Dresden a famous diva refused to perform the title character's Dance of the Seven Veils because she felt it was vulgar and indecent. The Metropolitan Opera House in New York ran only one performance of *Salome* before a hostile audience shut it down. All of this disapproval added to the lure of the opera, and it later drew in audiences that were curious to see it.

Strauss reached the peak of his career in 1911 with the success of *Der Rosenkavalier* (The Knight of the Rose) on the eve of World War I. This comic work contains speedily moving scenes and is considered to be his best and most popular opera. The score requires 114 instruments, with 17 of them onstage.

When the Nazis came to power in 1933, they appointed Strauss president of the Reichsmusikkammer (State Music Bureau). It is unclear whether Strauss was consulted about this appointment, but he did accept the position. Strauss continued to write operas; in 1934 he worked with the Austrian writer Stefan Zweig to compose *Die schweigsame Frau* (The Silent Woman). In 1935 the Nazis banned the opera because Zweig was Jewish. Many artists and intellectuals began leaving Germany after the Nazi Party gained control. Strauss decided to remain; he wrote and conducted the *Olympic Hymn* for the 1936 Olympics, which were held in Berlin. He was forced to resign from the Reichsmusikkammer when he refused to remove Zweig's name from the playbill for *Die schweigsame Frau*. Strauss also did not support the Nazi plan to ban the music of Mendelssohn. He completed a one-act opera (which he had begun with Zweig), entitled *Friedenstag* (Peace Day), with a new librettist; it was premiered in 1938. *Friedenstag* was banned by the Nazis after the outbreak of World War II because of its antimilitary ideas.

Strauss was criticized for his behavior during the Nazi regime by several well-known musicians. The conductor Arturo Toscanini remarked, "To Strauss the composer, I take off my hat; to Strauss the man, I put it back on." Since he had acted as a government official, Strauss was later tried for his Nazi ties and affiliations; he was cleared of all charges. In 1945, when the war ended, the composer was eighty-one years old. He had moved to Austria and, after the war, to Switzerland;

now he returned to his house in Germany. He continued to write music. In 1949, on the occasion of his eighty-fifth birthday, there was a celebration at the Bavarian Academy of Arts; shortly afterward Strauss died.

Strauss's symphonic poems are tied to literature. They incorporate realistic sounds in order to tell a story: the bleating of sheep, the clanging of pots, the pounding of hoofbeats, and the fury of a storm are all found in his music. He enlarged the orchestra and utilized all of the instruments to achieve the effects that he wanted. His music is full of surprises and fiery rhythms. His operas are steady stretches of music combining powerful, emotional expressions and startling theater. Strauss dominated the scene with his shockingly dissonant and tense works. Then, with *Der Rosenkavalier*, the innovator returned to his early musical style.

GUSTAV MAHLER

If a composer could say what he had to say in words he would not bother trying to say it in music.

GUSTAV MAHLER,
COMPOSER AND CONDUCTOR (1860–1911)

Gustav Mahler

Gustav Mahler (1860–1911) was once quoted as saying, "What's best in music is not to be found in the notes." This composer is considered to be the last in the line of great Viennese symphony composers. Mahler was born in Bohemia, which was then part of the Austro-Hungarian Empire; he was the second of fourteen children. Soon afterward his family moved to Moravia, in what is today a part of the Czech Republic. His father was a brewer and probably a tavern owner. Mahler began his piano instruction at the age of six. He was not yet ten when he held his first recital, and soon after that he started composing his own music. Mahler went on to study at the Vienna Conservatory when he was fifteen. By the time he was twenty, Mahler had only one goal in his life: to become a composer.

In 1880 the young Mahler took a summer job as a conductor at a theater. His reputation grew as he conducted in opera houses over the next few years. His Symphony No. 1 was completed in 1888; however, the composer could not convince any orchestra to premiere the work. He finally had to conduct the first performance himself in 1889, and the only reason they allowed him to present it was that he was the director of the Hungarian Opera. The audience was stunned into total silence by the aggressive finale. Finally a bit of applause was heard, but more people began booing. The music critics also responded with hostility toward the work; they stated that Mahler's symphony was bizarre, vulgar, and filled with noise. Mahler conducted this symphony every two or three years until the end of his life, and it always seemed to upset and dissatisfy the audiences. Nowadays it is performed and enjoyed often. The composer stated, "All that is not perfect down to the smallest detail is doomed to perish." Mahler paid attention to those smallest details: his reputation as a perfectionist grew as he held his performers to higher and higher artistic standards and reformed the concertgoing experience.

In 1902 Mahler married Alma Schindler. The couple had two daughters, but the older one died at the age of four. The death of his child had a profound affect on the composer. Mahler had to resign his position as director of the opera house in Vienna due to the rise of anti-Semitism; ultimately, this anti-Semitism drove him out of Europe in 1907. In one year Mahler lost both his daughter and his position as director of the Vienna Opera, and he also learned he had a serious heart condition that the doctors believed would ultimately kill him.

The composer moved to the United States, where he was employed as a conductor for the Metropolitan Opera and later on for the New York Philharmonic. While he was working as a conductor, Mahler composed eight symphonies and seven song cycles. His symphonies are massive and very lyrical. Mahler expanded the orchestra for his works, and four of his symphonies contain choral or solo voices. His Symphony No. 8 is also known as the *Symphony of a Thousand* because of the gigantic performing forces it requires. Mahler viewed the human voice as an instrument to be included in orchestral music. This work is divided into two very different parts: part 1, in Latin, is derived from a ninth-century religious source, the hymn *Veni creator spiritus* (Come, creator spirit); and part 2, in German, is based on an eighteenth-century secular source, Wolfgang Goethe's poem *Faust*. Mahler draws it all together using the thematic material to create unity. The 1910 premiere of his Symphony No. 8 was a defining moment in the history of music. Mahler's work had great impact on many later composers, especially Schoenberg.

His masterpiece, *Das Lied von der Erde* (The Song of the Earth), is a symphonic song cycle of six songs. Mahler died before he could hear it performed. The genre of this piece is unique; it has been called a "song-symphony." The score of *Das Lied von der Erde* calls for two solo voices and orchestra. The work premiered in 1911, six months after Mahler's death, with his friend Bruno Walter conducting. It has often been said that Mahler did not want to designate this work as a symphony, since that would make it his ninth, and he was superstitious that he would die shortly afterward—a superstition based on the fact that many composers, including Beethoven, Schubert, and Dvořák, died after writing nine symphonies.

Mahler is acknowledged as one of the last great romantic composers, and yet he embodied many of the new ideas of modernism. Mahler's style is lyrical; his music overflows with a wide collection of melodies and powerful emotions. He was one of the first composers to envision what music in the modern era would become.

JEAN SIBELIUS

Pay no attention to what the critics say. A statue has never been erected in honor of a critic.

JEAN SIBELIUS, COMPOSER (1865–1957)

In Finland, Jean Sibelius (1865–1957) is considered a national hero. At first Finland was under Swedish rule, then Russia conquered Finland in a war with Sweden. At the time of the composer's birth, Finland was a province of Russia. During this period, a Finnish

Jean Sibelius

national movement arose that was attempting to break Finland away so it could become an independent nation. Sibelius became a major symbol of this national desire for self-determination.

Sibelius was born in a small town north of Helsinki. At the time Finland was a self-governing grand duchy controlled by czarist Russia. His father was a medical doctor who died from typhoid fever when the boy was two years old. The family went to live in the home of his maternal grandmother. He was born with the name Johan, but Sibelius began using the French form of his name, Jean, while he was still a very young man. He began composing before he had any real musical education by picking out notes on a piano. Sibelius's sister played the piano, and his brother played the cello; the three formed their own ensemble, performing music composed by Jean. Although the family was Swedish-speaking, Sibelius attended a Finnish school, which introduced him to the culture of Finland. He graduated from high school in 1885 and went to Helsinki to study law. He also enrolled in the Helsinki Music Institute. Soon Sibelius left the university and devoted his studies to music; he learned to play the violin and worked on composition. He continued his music education in Berlin and then in Vienna before returning to Helsinki in 1891.

Sibelius's symphonic poem *Finlandia* illustrates events in the history of the Finnish people. The composer later reworked the melody from the last section of this piece, and the Finnish poet V. A. Koskenniemi supplied the text for the *Finlandia* hymn. His five-movement choral symphony, *Kullervo*, Op. 7, premiered in 1892, with the twenty-six-year-old composer conducting. The work was an immediate success; the influence of its Finnish heritage was obvious to all. Sibelius withdrew the work shortly after the premiere and revised it many years later.

In 1892 Sibelius married Aino Järnefelt; they later moved into a home that they named Ainola. Sibelius enjoyed living in the countryside, where he could compose without many distractions. He loved the landscape of Finland, with its thick forests and ice-cold lakes. The surroundings had a strong effect on his music and led him to compose pieces that reflected the spirit and energy of Finland. The Finnish people proclaimed him a national artist. When Sibelius was thirty-two, the government of Finland provided him a yearly salary so that he could concentrate on his music.

Wagner's ideas influenced Sibelius for a while after a trip he took to see *Parsifal* at the Bayreuth Festival. He studied the scores of Wagner's operas and began to write an opera of his own; however, Sibelius concluded that using a leitmotif system was artificial and did not suit his purpose and, furthermore, that finding great opera singers who could sing in Finnish could be a problem. Sibelius's seven symphonies are his claim to fame. The first two are traditional romantic works, but the next five change course. The works swell with energy and contain modern elements while still reflecting the traditions of the past. His themes are brilliantly structured, and the clarity of his orchestration makes every detail stand out.

Sibelius wanted to have his work heard as absolute music. In 1914 he conducted his symphonic poem *Aallottaret* (The Oceanides, or Sea Nymphs, Op. 73) at the Norfolk Festival in Connecticut. This tone poem provides impressions of all of the characteristics of the sea, from relaxed waves gently moving onto the shore to the raging intensity of a storm. The concert was very well received, and the composer's work was hailed as a distinctive piece.

In some of his compositions the orchestration was quite sparse, since he selected only those instruments that were required instead of using complete string or brass sections. His Symphony No. 5 in E-flat Major, Op. 82, was begun during the opening months of World War I. Sibelius revised the symphony three times before he was satisfied with it, and the work reached its final form in 1919 after five years of rewrites. Breaking from the tradition of the four-movement symphony, Sibelius's Fifth contains three movements. Sibelius wrote in his diary, "Today at ten to 11 I saw sixteen swans. One of my greatest experiences! Lord God, that beauty! They circled over me for a long time and then disappeared into the solar haze like a gleaming, silver ribbon." The finale of the symphony features a theme presented by the trumpets and horns that rises and falls melodiously like the call of swans.

Sibelius planned his Symphony No. 7, Op. 105, for ten years. He actually worked on three symphonies at the same time, always refining and revising each one until he felt it was exactly as he wanted it. The premiere of his last symphony took place in Stockholm, Sweden, in 1924, with Sibelius conducting. After completing his Symphony No. 7 and the tone poem *Tapiola*, Op. 112, he did not produce any more music. He was aware that the public expected an eighth symphony from him. It is said that Sibelius worked on this anticipated eighth symphony for many years but, never satisfied with it, burned it in the 1940s. All of Finland mourned when he died in 1957. Sibelius was buried at Ainola.

CLAUDE DEBUSSY

Music is the silence between the notes.

CLAUDE DEBUSSY, COMPOSER (1862–1918)

Claude Debussy

Claude Debussy (1862–1918) was the most important composer of the post-romantic period. He stated, "I love music passionately. And because I love it I try to free it from barren traditions that stifle it." He was born in St. Germain-en-Laye, a small town near Paris; his father was a salesman, and his mother was a seamstress. His piano teacher, a former student of Chopin, discovered his talent.

At the age of eleven Debussy was accepted at the Paris Conservatory. He attended the conservatory for ten years, wanting at first to become a pianist. After attending composition classes, Debussy found he was more interested in composing. By the age of sixteen he was engaged in debates with his teachers about musical principles. He shocked them with harmonies that they found so unusual, some considered them bizarre.

In 1885 Debussy won the Prix de Rome for his cantata *L'enfant prodigue* (The Prodigal Son) and was sent to study for three years in Italy. However, Debussy was very unhappy in Rome, and he returned to Paris two years later without completing his course of study.

Trips to Bayreuth in 1888 and 1889 introduced Debussy to Wagner's work. Initially Debussy was an enthusiastic supporter of Wagner and viewed his compositions as the future of music, especially in opera. Later on he considered Wagner's music "a beautiful sunset mistaken for a dawn." In 1889 Debussy attended the Paris Exhibition and heard Far Eastern music. Now Debussy wished to go beyond what Wagner had offered, and he found a place for himself among the impressionists, a group of Parisian writers and artists who were exploring new venues of expression. This movement developed during the late nineteenth and early twentieth centuries. Impressionists emphasized tonal color and mood over the traditional structures. These concepts suited Debussy, who went on to develop a combination of new and old methods in his music. He replaced the traditional genres and forms with his own ideas of what music should be. His music was imaginative and painted pictures; borrowing the names of his works from artists created a frame and established the atmosphere for his compositions.

Debussy's *Prélude à l'après-midi d'un faune* (Prelude to the Afternoon of a Faun, 1894) was the composer's first major work for orchestra and a totally new kind of tone poem. At the premiere the audience was so enthusiastic about the piece that the conductor repeated it. In this decade Debussy also composed the opera *Pelléas et Mélisande* (Pelléas and Mélisande), which was perceived as a revolutionary work. Debussy used musical understatement, imagery, and hints to suggest moods. The opera earned the composer the highest French cultural award, the Legion of Honor, and a secure income.

In October 1899 Debussy married and started working as a music critic. The marriage ended in divorce. In 1908 Debussy married the singer Emma Bardac, and they had a daughter whom they called Chou-Chou. In her honor Debussy wrote a suite for solo piano entitled *Children's Corner*. The suite is divided into six pieces, and each one has an English-language title. Debussy often traveled abroad to conduct his works and present piano concerts.

For eight years Debussy concentrated on pieces mainly for the piano. An exception to this was *La mer* (The Sea), composed between 1903 and 1905. The three movements are entitled "De l'aube à midi sur la mer" (From Dawn to Midday at Sea), "Jeu de vagues" (Game of the Waves), and "Dialogue du vent et de la mer" (Dialogue of the Wind and the Sea). This portrait of the sea altered the way symphonies were envisioned by future composers. The piece is full of pure tonal color, but without the blending favored in the past. Debussy suggests the movement of the water in the swell of thematic development. With Debussy's whole-tone scale and subtle textures, the music flows in waves of sound and holds together as a unit. *La mer* stirred up great controversy. Music critics were in disagreement over the work; some found it to be a fascinating piece, while others were baffled by its unusual harmonies and form.

The outbreak of war depressed the composer, and for a while he could not write any music. He died in 1918, during World War I, while Paris was being blasted by German artillery. Because of the war, Debussy did not receive the honors of a large state funeral. In 1904 he wrote, "The primary aim of French music is to give pleasure." His concepts moved away from the restrictions of traditional Western theory, harmony, and form. He experimented with different harmonies and scales, and he freed music from the confines imposed by traditional harmony. Debussy was the first composer to successfully exploit the whole-tone scale. He used orchestral instruments to produce sounds and effects that were unique for the time. His musical language also included pentatonic scales, with five pitches per octave. Debussy wrote in abstract genres that were flexible in structure. He was an important transitional figure between the romantic and modern eras of music, inspiring inventive ways to define musical principles.

MAURICE RAVEL

I begin by considering an effect.

MAURICE RAVEL, COMPOSER (1875–1937)

Maurice Ravel

Critics of Maurice Ravel (1875–1937) claimed that he was an imitator of Debussy. In response to this accusation Ravel said, "And if I have been influenced by Debussy, it has been deliberately, knowing that I could leave him whenever I chose." Ravel was born in Ciboure, France, a village near the Spanish border. His mother was Basque, and his father was an engineer and inventor from Switzerland. Because of this background, the composer was attracted to the Spanish and Basque cultures.

The family moved to Paris when Ravel was an infant. His introduction to music was through piano lessons at the age of seven. At the age of fourteen he began his musical training at the Paris Conservatory, which he attended from 1899 until 1905. While at the conservatory Ravel tried five times to win the Prix de Rome, but he was never successful. He left school and began to compose.

Ravel is known for his craftsmanship. He stated, "I did my work slowly, drop by drop. I tore it out of me by pieces." He never married and was always very concerned about his privacy. Ravel preferred to live in the French countryside at his forest retreat. He joined a group of young writers, artists, and musicians who were known as "Les Apaches" (the Apaches), a nickname given to them because of their wild behavior and unconventional thinking. Ravel enjoyed their meetings, where they talked about ideas and cooperated on projects.

Ravel shared Debussy's interest in medieval musical scales, impressionism, and music of the Far East, and to this he added his own attraction to Spanish rhythms and styles. Also, like Debussy, Ravel did not care for Wagner's influence and believed that music itself should be the sole object of a composition. He wished to move away from the romantic ideals and into a new era. Ravel's works differ from Debussy's in many ways; he employs more traditional genres, and the texture of his music is contrapuntal. His orchestration is also more conventional.

The composer appreciated the art of the Russian ballet. In 1912 his ballet *Daphnis et Chloé* (Daphnis and Chloe) premiered. It was adapted from an ancient Greek tale. The composer described the ballet as "a choreographic symphony in three parts." Ravel's genius for orchestration is very evident in this work. It is scored for a large orchestra that includes a wind machine and a wordless chorus. Ravel pulled out music from this ballet to create two orchestral suites; the Suite No. 2 from *Daphnis et Chloé* is regarded as his masterpiece.

After World War I Ravel traveled extensively as a conductor. While on a four-month concert tour of the United States, he met George Gershwin and was exposed to American jazz. Jazz musicians in the United States were also attracted to Ravel's music. Jazz harmonies and rhythms are evident in some of Ravel's compositions: for instance, his Sonata for Violin and Piano contains a movement called "The Blues." In 1918 Debussy died, and Ravel's musical style changed. He had always been attracted to classical genres and structures; now he became a neoclassicist, drawing inspiration from the music of the eighteenth century.

The French government wished to offer the Legion of Honor to the composer in 1921 and announced the award before the composer was informed of the government's intention. Angrily, Ravel turned the award down. Some music critics have said that the composer was still angry about not winning the Prix de Rome during his student days and that his declining this new prize was his idea of revenge.

The dancer Ida Rubinstein asked Ravel to write a dance/pantomime with a Spanish flair. His last ballet score, *Boléro*, was the result of this commission. It featured Rubinstein in the lead role when it was produced at the Paris Opéra in 1928. Today this piece is often performed as a one-movement orchestral work, but it is actually based on an eighteenth-century Spanish dance called the bolero. The work was instantly successful. *Boléro* repeats the same theme and countertheme over and over as they make their way through the orchestra, from one instrument to another. The dynamic level rises as the music builds to its climax. Ravel considered this piece unimportant, yet *Boléro* is Ravel's most popular work.

In 1927 Ravel began to have severe problems with his health. A car accident added to these troubles; he began to have difficulty with his daily activities and could not write or speak. During the last five years of his life he could no longer compose. Ravel died in Paris on December 28, 1937. Even in a setting dominated by Claude Debussy's music, Ravel retained his own sense of what he wished to achieve. His interest in writing music as entertainment was shared with Debussy, and he was also inspired by the impressionist movement. However, Ravel's music has more crispness and brightness to it, and his rhythms are sharper. He employs lines of counterpoint in contrast to Debussy's blocks of sound.

The influence of Spanish music is evident in many of Ravel's works. His use of the orchestra remains one of his finest contributions to post-romantic music. He carefully examined the abilities of each instrument so that he could put it to its best use in his pieces. He was a thorough and tireless craftsman, always working to create a variety of sound and tonal color in his pieces. Stravinsky described Ravel as "the Swiss Watchmaker" because of his strict attention to detail. Together Debussy and Ravel created a distinctive French style that would have an impact on music well into the twentieth century.

19 Great Composers of the Modern Era

The first thing that struck me about contemporary music in general had been that there was not much interest in rhythm.

ELLIOTT CARTER, COMPOSER (BORN 1908)

In 1900 music took a huge turn: composers wanted to create something new and original that reflected the vast changes in society. To many listeners it sounded as though composers had gone to extremes, but each novel project led to additional ideas and experiments, and people began to accept the new music. The invention of mechanical means for the reproduction of music also had a great impact. The phonograph, the radio, movies with sound, and the latest technological processes of reproducing music quickly allowed a work to be heard by millions of people worldwide. What had taken years to reach people in the past now became almost instantaneous.

Composers who were considered avant-garde or experimental in the early twentieth century are today called "masters"; but, at the beginning of this transformation, many people thought that the "new music" was very strange indeed. Some purists still do not consider some of the avant-garde works as belonging to the realm of classical music. The movement away from romantic-era standards was obvious in all of the arts. Modern works rejected traditional practices and sought new expressions. Artists believed that there were other ways to present their ideas; they often looked to so-called primitive societies—those that made little use of technology and whose economy was not based on industrialization—for inspiration. The abstract artists used shape and color rather than reproductions of the real world to make their statements. Architects designed buildings that included and made use of technological advances. Musicians also explored harmonies, rhythms, melodies, and technology in unexpected combinations.

Masters of the Modern Era

ARNOLD SCHOENBERG

I owe very, very much to Mozart; and if one studies, for instance, the way in which I write for string quartet, then one cannot deny that I have learned this directly from Mozart. And I am proud of it!

ARNOLD SCHOENBERG, COMPOSER (1874–1950)

Arnold Schoenberg

Arnold Schoenberg (1874–1950) wrote in one of his books, "Every tonal progression, every progression of even two tones, raises a problem which requires a special solution." The composer was born in Vienna, the second child in the family. His mother, Pauline, was a piano teacher, and his father, Samuel, was a businessman. At the age of eight, Schoenberg began to take violin lessons and to compose his own music.

Schoenberg left school in 1891 and began an apprenticeship in a private bank. He composed pieces, learning as he progressed. In his writings he explained how he studied music. "Meyer's *Konversations-Lexikon* (an encyclopedia, which we bought on installments) had reached the long-hoped-for letter 'S,' enabling me to learn under 'Sonate' how a first movement of a string quartet should be constructed. At that time, I was about eighteen years old" ("Introduction to My Four Quartets," 1949). In 1895 he left his job at the bank to seek a career in music. Schoenberg became a conductor and took a position as a chorus master.

Schoenberg composed his string sextet *Verklärte Nacht* (Transfigured Night), Op. 4, in 1899, when he was twenty-five. The piece was written while the composer was on vacation with his friend Alexander Zemlinsky and Zemlinsky's sister Mathilde. Schoenberg later arranged the piece for string orchestra. It consists of five sections in one movement. *Verklärte Nacht* is considered an example of a post-romantic work influenced by Richard Wagner and Franz Liszt and is Schoenberg's best-known piece.

In 1901 the composer married Mathilde Zemlinsky. That year Schoenberg began working on his next composition (which he did not complete for a decade), *Gurre-Lieder* (Songs of Gurre), a huge orchestral song cycle that describes a tragic tale of death and reunion after death. Based on a German translation of poems by the Danish writer Jens Peter Jacobsen about the legendary Danish Castle Gurre, the cycle contains some of the most personal and sensitive music that Schoenberg ever penned. Gustav Mahler's influence on Schoenberg is clearly heard in this music. A massive production, *Gurre-Lieder* requires over three hundred performers, including six vocal soloists, four choirs, and a huge orchestra. Since the work is not written in any particular key, it is sometimes difficult for audience members to pay complete attention to the work during the two hours that it takes to perform.

Schoenberg worked from 1901 to 1903 as a conductor in Berlin. The symphonic poem *Pelleas und Melisande* (Pelleas and Melisande), Op. 5, was completed in 1903. Richard Strauss, who had assisted Schoenberg in obtaining a teaching position in Berlin's Stern Conservatory, suggested that the composer consider this drama as the basis for an opera. Schoenberg decided to use the play as a source of a symphonic poem instead. The premiere was conducted by the composer and caused a riot in the audience. The work also received horrid reviews. The composer exposed audiences to even more innovative creations. In 1912 Schoenberg composed one of his most influential works, *Pierrot lunaire* (Moonstruck Little Pierre), Op. 21, using a technique known as *Sprechstimme* (speech that is sung). The atonal piece presents the poetry with an instrumental background.

Schoenberg spent most of World War I in military service. He had attended a school for reserve officers but his health did not allow him to continue. He was temporarily released from military duty when the Viennese Composers' Union requested it. In 1917 he was recalled to the army but then released a few months later when it was determined that he was physically incapable of performing his duties.

In 1919 Schoenberg founded the Society for Private Musical Performances, which presented music to select, invited audiences in order to avoid the public fights that often had accompanied performances of his work. Schoenberg introduced his "Method of Composing with Twelve Tones Which Are Related Only with One Another," a form of serialism. In this system the twelve pitches of the octave are seen as equal, and no tonality is given the importance that it occupied in classical harmony.

In 1925 Schoenberg was appointed to the Berlin Academy of the Arts. Anti-Semitic remarks about his appointment appeared in the journal *Zeitschrift für Musik* (Music Journal). In 1933, when the Nazis took over the government,

Schoenberg was dismissed from his position at the academy and left Germany. That year the family immigrated to the United States.

Schoenberg had a wonderful sense of humor. When he was told that a soloist would need six fingers to perform his concerto, Schoenberg replied, "I can wait." Schoenberg retired at the age of seventy; he remained in Los Angeles until his death in 1951. Schoenberg was a pioneer. He often ignored the rules of traditional harmony. His prominent use of changing tone colors is most evident in his orchestral works. During the years 1907 to 1916 his music moved into a new system away from the major/minor construction and rhythms that were common.

Pierrot lunaire contains free rhythms and measures that are unequal in a piece that utilizes *Sprechstimme*. This atonal work led to the next step in Schoenberg's experimentation: the twelve-tone method. His Five Piano Pieces, Op. 23, was his first piece composed with the twelve-tone method throughout its five movements. In this system no note can be repeated until all eleven others have been heard. Schoenberg redefined music in the early twentieth century and had a lasting impact on the principles of music.

CHARLES IVES

If a composer has a nice wife and some nice children, how can he let the children starve on his dissonances?

CHARLES IVES, COMPOSER (1874–1954)

Charles Ives

While the Europeans were experimenting with new musical ideas, the American musician Charles Ives (1874–1954) was working on some extremely novel and challenging pieces of music. Born in Danbury, Connecticut, he was the son of George Ives, leader of a town band; he had been a bandmaster during the Civil War. George Ives had his own concepts about music theory and enjoyed experimenting with sounds; he was his son's first music teacher. The youngster played the drum in his father's town band. At the age of thirteen Ives worked as a church organist and composed several hymns and compositions for religious services. His early works include an organ piece containing unusual sounds entitled *Variations on "America"*; composed in 1891, this piece employs "My Country 'Tis of Thee" in many variations.

In 1894 the young Charles Ives began his studies at Yale University. The head of the school's music department, who was considered an exceptional composer at the time, taught his composition class. This department head was frequently unhappy with Ives's harmonic experiments and tried to make his student write more traditionally. Ives quickly understood that he would have to keep his more extreme musical ideas to himself. Shortly after Ives started his classes, his father passed away. Musical historians have stated that Charles Ives accomplished what his father had begun.

After graduating from Yale, Ives began working for an insurance company in New York. He continued working as a church organist and composed when he had free time. In 1907 Ives and a friend opened their own insurance agency. In June 1908 the composer married Harmony Twichell, a minister's daughter who was trained as a nurse. His insurance business was doing well, and he continued to compose after his work day ended.

Since the pieces he wrote were so non-traditional, Ives feared that his music would not be accepted well enough to allow him to support a family; therefore, he remained in the business world while he continued composing. He did not attempt to have his music performed, and only a few pieces were published.

The Ives family purchased farmland and constructed a home in Connecticut so that they could spend time in the countryside as well as in New York City. In 1918 Ives suffered a heart attack from which he never fully recovered. At that point Ives began to compile his music so that it could be printed. His book *114 Songs* had never before been available; it included pieces that were composed in his teen years as well as much later pieces. The book therefore represented the span of his work. Ives paid for the printing of it and gave out copies without charge.

Because of his poor health, by 1930 Ives had stopped composing; however, he did continue to revise his earlier works. Surprisingly, once Ives could not write any more music, his works began to be performed, and his reputation started to grow. In 1945 Ives was elected to the National Institute of Arts and Letters, and in 1947 he received the Pulitzer Prize for his Symphony No. 3 (subtitled *The Camp Meeting*). Ives gave away the money associated with this impressive award. He had earned enough through his insurance agency and was a charitable man. Charles Ives died in May 1954.

"Every great inspiration is but an experiment," Ives told himself as he composed. In the beginning of the 1920s American musicians were becoming involved in the modernist movement, and Ives's compositions were right in line with their thinking. His *Scherzo: Over the Pavements*, which imitates the rhythms of people walking as they passed Ives's Manhattan apartment, was no longer considered unusual.

Ives's *Three Places in New England* is an orchestral piece in three movements. The first movement is entitled "The 'St. Gaudens' in Boston Common (Col. Shaw and His Colored Regiment)"; the music was inspired by a sculpture found in the Boston Common Park in Massachusetts that depicts the first African American corps of soldiers who fought in the Civil War. The second movement is entitled "Putnam's Camp" and is based on a remembrance of General Israel Putnam's soldiers, who fought at the Battle of Bunker Hill during the American Revolutionary War. The last movement, called "The Housatonic at Stockbridge," is based on the composer's memory of seeing the Housatonic River. Each movement is about a specific New England location and also contains a reflection of American ideals and patriotism. The piece was begun in 1908 and completed in 1912 when Ives scored it for orchestra. *Three Places in New England* was revised for performance and premiered in 1931 in a concert funded by the composer himself. It was the first complete presentation of any of Ives's major orchestral works.

Ives took themes from hymns, marches, classical compositions, and folk songs and incorporated them into his music. He did not care for "pretty sounds" and had no tolerance for classical genres and strict forms. Ives created music that reflected his vision of America; he constructed images of hardy, individualistic Yankee types in an expansive land. His works predicted many twentieth-century musical techniques. He experimented with polytonality (the simultaneous use of more than one key), polyrhythms (the simultaneous use of two or more independent rhythms), and atonality. Ives's unusual approaches to rhythm and harmony were not appreciated until much later. His compositions were stamped with American images and the impressions of his New England childhood. Ives explained how he wrote: "In 'thinking up' music I usually have some kind of a brass band with wings on it in back of my mind."

ERNEST BLOCH

I have hearkened to an inner voice,
deep, sacred, insistent, burning....

ERNEST BLOCH, COMPOSER (1880–1959)

Ernest Bloch (1880–1959) was born in Geneva, Switzerland; his musical style was strongly influenced by what he called "the Hebraic spirit." Although Bloch's Jewish works actually are a small portion of his entire output, it is these works by which he is best known and on which his reputation is based. He was the third child in his family; his father was a manufacturer of Swiss watches and clocks. At the age of ten Bloch made a pledge that he would become a composer. As a young man, he studied the violin and composition while working as a bookkeeper and salesman in his father's business. He attended the Brussels Conservatory and then the Hoch Conservatory in Frankfurt, Germany.

In 1904 Bloch married; he and his wife had three children. His opera based on Shakespeare's tragedy *Macbeth*, which Bloch composed in 1903, premiered in 1910. The audience appeared to be confused by the work; it was criticized for its modern harmonies and rhythms. Even though *Macbeth* received favorable reviews from the music critics, it was dropped from the repertoire.

At about this time, Bloch began writing music with specifically Jewish subject matter. His music also employed Jewish worship chants and folk music. *Schelomo* (Solomon) was written in 1916, during a time that is now known as Bloch's "Jewish Period." A composition for cello and orchestra, *Schelomo* is both a tone poem and a cello concerto. The work is based on the biblical poet King Solomon, whom the cello represents in the music. *Schelomo* is a single-movement virtuoso cello piece that evokes a biblical landscape. The cello and the orchestra are equal partners in this piece; it is at times hard to tell the accompanist from the soloist.

Soon after composing *Schelomo*, Bloch traveled to the United States as an accompanist for the Maud Allan Dance Troupe. Unfortunately, before long the troupe was bankrupt, and Bloch was stranded in Ohio. Penniless, he somehow got to New York and rented a room in Manhattan. In 1917 he obtained a teaching position at the David Mannes School of Music (now the Mannes College of Music) in New York City. Later, after moving to Ohio, he helped to found the Cleveland Institute of Music and served as its director until 1925. In 1924 Bloch became an American citizen.

Bloch became the director of the San Francisco Conservatory. His work *America* won first prize in a 1927 contest sponsored by a magazine. The competition required a symphonic work by an American composer on an American theme. Bloch had planned a work to celebrate America when he first saw the New York Harbor, and this appeared to be the perfect time to write this piece. The three movements of *America*, which Bloch called an "epic rhapsody," consist of a musical collection containing melodies that signify the historical development of the country. The first movement incorporates Native American themes; these lead to themes representing the landing of the *Mayflower*, which brought the Pilgrims from England. The second movement uses tunes from American ballads and songs from the Civil War. In the final movement, Bloch integrates the sounds of a city, utilizing car horns, sounds of industry, and jazzy rhythms. The work is tied together with a theme that becomes the foundation for a hymn at the end, which Bloch hoped would be sung by the audience along with the chorus onstage.

After 1927 Bloch returned to writing in a neoclassical style. He returned to Switzerland for most of the 1930s, but the worsening conditions in Europe leading up to World War II caused him to return to the United States. In 1939 the composer moved to Agate Beach, Oregon. In 1942 Bloch became the first musician to be awarded the gold medal of the American Academy of Arts and Letters. Until he retired in 1952, he taught summer courses at the University of California at Berkeley. Ernest Bloch died in 1959.

Bloch was a unique composer and had tremendous influence as a teacher. His works contained enough of the classical structures and sounds to allow listeners to become accustomed to the new developments that were also present in them. His music displays individuality and emotional intensity. Bloch's music helped twentieth-century music gain the approval of audiences.

BÉLA BARTÓK

I cannot conceive of music that
expresses absolutely nothing.

BÉLA BARTÓK,
COMPOSER AND ETHNOMUSICOLOGIST (1881–1945)

Béla Bartók

Albert Einstein stated, "Béla Bartók (1881–1945) is perhaps the only man who has achieved a synthesis of the primitive and artistic languages of music." Bartók was born in a village in Hungary. His father was director of the school of agriculture in that community, and his mother was a schoolteacher. A smallpox vaccination gave the child a rash that lasted until he was five years old; due to this he was not allowed to play with other children. At the age of six he began taking piano lessons from his mother. His father died when the boy was seven years old, and the family moved, first to the Ukraine and then to Bratislava, in Slovakia. The youngster started composing when he was nine years old, and at the age of ten he gave his first public performance.

In 1895 Bartók met the composer and pianist Ernő Dohnányi, who convinced Bartók to attend the Royal Academy in Budapest, Hungary, even though Bartók had been accepted by the Vienna Conservatory. At the Royal Academy he took classes in piano and composition, but his teachers did not understand Bartók's goal of utilizing only Hungarian sounds in his music, and the student and his teachers often clashed. For a while illness prevented Bartók from continuing his studies; he had to go to a warmer climate to recover.

Bartók became involved with a nationalist organization that wanted to eliminate German influences in music. His symphonic poem *Kossuth*, honoring one of the heroes of the Hungarian Revolution of 1848, was written in 1903. This was a period of nationalist pride in Hungary, so *Kossuth* was well received.

In 1905 Bartók entered the Rubenstein Music Competition in Paris, but another pianist won. Bartók was extremely disappointed and decided that he would no longer attempt to make a living as a pianist. Instead, he turned to composing. Bartók had a great interest in Hungarian folklore, and this led him to understand that the music that had been represented by Liszt and Brahms as "Hungarian" was in reality Gypsy music, not Hungarian folk music. This awareness caused him to begin collecting Hungarian folk melodies, and they became great inspirations for his music.

With another composer, Zoltán Kodály, Bartók toured remote villages throughout Hungary in order to collect as many authentic folk tunes as possible. The men traveled around the country asking peasants to sing in order to record their folk tunes on a wax cylinder that had been developed by Thomas Edison. They were amazed to learn that traditional Hungarian folk tunes were based on a pentatonic (five-pitch) musical scale. Bartók and Kodály began to incorporate elements of this Hungarian peasant music into their own compositions. In 1906 they published *Hungarian Folk Songs for Voice and Piano*. Bartók later did further research and became an authority on the folk music of Slovakia, Turkey, and Romania.

In 1907 Bartók accepted a position as a professor of piano at the Royal Academy in Budapest. Together with his friend Kodály he tried to establish a New Hungarian Music Society for the presentation of contemporary music. They could not find a conductor or orchestral musicians who understood their musical concepts, and they also encountered hostility from the public, which was not ready for their music. This made Bartók feel resentful, and he withdrew from the concert scene.

He continued his research throughout World War I, looking at military music during the summer months. The discovery of the ancient scales used in Hungarian folk music and the music of Claude Debussy, which Kodály had brought back from a trip to Paris, completely altered the way Bartók composed. His work changed from romantic to neoclassical; by means of the twelve-tone scale he was able to use new harmonies, but his music never became atonal. The piano pieces that he wrote in this period demonstrate that a genuinely Hungarian Bartók was emerging.

In 1913 the composer traveled to Algeria collecting Arab folk music, but his trip was ended by World War I. The influence of Arab folk music can be heard in his String Quartet No. 2 and his ballet *The Miraculous Mandarin*. A one-act opera composed in 1911, *Duke Bluebeard's Castle*, contains only two characters and little dramatic action, and it was rejected by two opera competitions. The opera finally premiered in 1917, at a time when Hungary was experiencing a surge of nationalist feelings due to the downfall of the Austrian regime. At last, in this nationalist mood, Bartók's music found favor, and for the next ten years he was a major figure in Hungarian music.

The Hungarian alliance with Nazi Germany during the 1930s alarmed the composer. Bartók was strongly opposed to the Nazis and refused to have his music performed in German concert halls or on the radio. His friends urged him to leave Europe, because had he made his anti-Nazi sentiments known publicly and they feared for his safety. As life in Hungary became more unbearable, he decided to immigrate to the United States. From 1940 until his death Bartók lived in New York City. His health was failing—he had developed leukemia—and his last five years were hard. He and his wife, a pianist, appeared in some concerts, but as the disease advanced he could no longer perform in public.

In 1943, while confined to a hospital bed, Bartók was visited by the music director of the Boston Symphony Orchestra, Serge Koussevitzky, who commissioned him to write a piece for the orchestra. Bartók was pleased by this tribute. After he left the hospital he composed his *Concerto for Orchestra*, which was completed the year before he died. In this five-movement concerto the composer moves the focus from one section of the orchestra to the other, creating a very interesting effect. A sample of the flavor of Hungarian folk tunes opens four of the movements, and the last movement ends with a stirring brass coda. The work was performed in 1944 at Boston's Symphony Hall, conducted by Koussevitzky. It established an appreciation for Bartók in the United States.

Toward the end of his life Bartók lived in a nursing home, yet the composer continued to compose. He began writing a viola concerto but died before finishing it. Bartók was buried in Hartsdale, New York. Almost immediately after his death there was a renewed interest in his music. Bartók was one of the most significant musicians of the twentieth century and a productive composer. He wrote in the classical forms and genres; classical and romantic elements are found in his works. His rhythms are full of repeated patterns and syncopation. Often Bartók employed dissonant harmonies, yet he did not abandon the use of keys, and his music is not atonal. The influence of Hungarian folk music, which was based on five-note scales and asymmetrical rhythms, presented new concepts in harmony.

IGOR STRAVINSKY

I am an inventor of music.

IGOR STRAVINSKY, COMPOSER (1882–1971)

In 1948 *Time* magazine named Igor Stravinsky (1882–1971) one of the most influential people of the twentieth century. The composer was born in Oranienbaum, a suburb of St. Petersburg, located on the Gulf of Finland. His father sang in the Imperial Opera. In 1890 Stravinsky attended a performance of Tchaikovsky's *Sleeping Beauty* ballet; the performance

Igor Stravinsky

excited and inspired him. At the age of nine he took some piano and theory lessons, but, because he originally intended to study law, he did not receive extensive musical training.

As he grew up, Stravinsky felt himself drawn to a career in music, and he tried to decide whether he wanted to continue as a law student. He entered the University of St. Petersburg in 1901; during his second year there Stravinsky met Nikolai Rimsky-Korsakov. After hearing Stravinsky perform some of his own compositions on the piano, Rimsky-Korsakov recommended that the young man make up his mind. Stravinsky continued pursuing a law degree but began spending more of his time composing. After Stravinsky brought a piano sonata that he had just completed to the older composer, Rimsky-Korsakov acknowledged that the young man had a definite talent and should direct his studies toward music. Stravinsky briefly considered attending the Russian Conservatory to study music, but Rimsky-Korsakov suggested private lessons instead. From 1903 until 1908, Stravinsky studied with the famous Russian composer. They focused on orchestration and composition. This was the extent of Stravinsky's musical education.

In 1908 Stravinsky composed a piece entitled *Feu d'artifice* (Fireworks) as a gift for the wedding of Rimsky-Korsakov's daughter; it was to be performed during the festivities. The music had been sent to Rimsky-Korsakov's home, but the package was returned a few days later marked "Undelivered due to the death of the addressee." His teacher had died, and the young composer, filled with grief, put the piece aside for a while. It was performed some months later in St. Petersburg and heard by Sergei Diaghilev, the founder of the renowned Ballets Russes.

Diaghilev had commissioned a ballet that was to be based on some Russian fairy tales; the composer who had been hired repeatedly delayed writing the work. Desperate for the piece to be composed, Diaghilev asked Stravinsky to create the score for this ballet. *L'oiseau de feu* (The Firebird) premiered in Paris in 1910. The work was a huge success and brought the composer immediate recognition. After the ballet's premiere Stravinsky used the score as the basis for a five-movement concert suite. In 1919 he revised this suite, and in 1945 he created a third suite based on his previous changes. Diaghilev and the Ballets Russes, working in Paris, requested two more works from Stravinsky, so he moved there in 1911.

The ballet *Le sacre du printemps* (The Rite of Spring) caused quite a commotion. Set in ancient pagan Russia, it employs an unusually large orchestra, dissonant harmonies, and complex rhythmic treatments. Furthermore, the choreography turned classical ballet inside-out: on opening night, the curtain rose on dancers standing on the stage pigeon-toed, instead of in the normal heels-together position. At that, some in the audience, convinced that the music was disrespectful of traditional ballet, began to boo, hiss, hoot, and argue with the work's supporters. Some people shouted at the unruly crowd to stop the noise and let the work continue. Diaghilev, distraught, stood up in his box and begged the audience to remain calm. Some audience members started to exchange blows, and these scuffles grew into a larger riot. The police were summoned to restore order, but that proved impossible. Stravinsky left the theater in tears. Although the controversy continued throughout the work's run, the ballet was able to complete its scheduled performances without any further outbursts. In this work Stravinsky had completely ignored traditional harmony and had made use of new and unique tone colors. Many musicians consider *Le sacre du printemps* the beginning of a new era in composition.

In 1914, with the outbreak of World War I and the turmoil in Russia that led to the Revolution, Stravinsky relocated to Switzerland. This move took him away from the mainstream of musical development. When the Russian Revolution began, Stravinsky realized that his exile from his homeland would be permanent. He and his wife resettled in France, where the composer became a citizen in 1934. Eventually Stravinsky left France and settled in Hollywood, California, where he became an American citizen in 1945.

The composer undertook works in many differing styles: he composed the *Circus Polka* for a young elephant act for the Ringling Brothers Circus and a concerto for a swing band. The ballet *Agon* (The Contest), which contains Stravinsky's experimentation with the twelve-tone scale, was composed in 1957. In Greek drama, an *agon* was a time of decision in a contest between two characters or two competing ideas. *Agon* was performed for Stravinsky's seventy-fifth birthday in Los Angeles as a concert performance; several months later, in New York City, the ballet premiered. The work is considered by many dance critics to have created a monumental change in ballet music.

Stravinsky was internationally recognized as the Western world's greatest living composer. He spent his last years conducting and recording his works. He died at the age of eighty-eight and was buried in Venice, Italy. Throughout his composing career, Stravinsky worked toward inventing his own musical voice. His early pieces reflect folk song–inspired melodies and the influences of his Russian background, while his ballets were considerably influenced by Debussy's music. *Le sacre du printemps* introduced Stravinsky's use of polytonality. Toward the end of his composing career his friend and biographer, the conductor and music critic Robert Craft, convinced Stravinsky to consider Schoenberg's twelve-tone concepts. This led to Stravinsky's last stylistic experiments. Stravinsky embraced both the twelve-tone scale and serial composition.

Stravinsky experimented with all of the techniques available to the composers of the twentieth century. He had a fantastic sense of sound that made his orchestrations superb. His daring harmonies, dynamic rhythms, and creative use of tonality altered modern music.

PAUL HINDEMITH

There are only two things worth aiming for, good music and a clean conscience.

PAUL HINDEMITH, COMPOSER (1895–1963)

Paul Hindemith

Born in Hanau, Germany, Paul Hindemith (1895–1963) was the oldest son of working-class parents. Recognizing that their son had talent, his parents made certain that he would receive an education in music, so his family moved to the city of Frankfurt. Hindemith began violin lessons at the age of seven, and by the age of thirteen he was helping support the family by performing in theaters. By fifteen he was giving concerts with his sister, a talented pianist. In 1908 a scholarship allowed Hindemith to attend the Hoch Conservatory. The young man took classes in conducting and composition; Hindemith was skilled at playing the violin, viola, piano, and clarinet.

During his student years, Hindemith performed with various dance bands. Hindemith was awarded the prize for the best composition of the year at the conservatory and was given an award from the Mendelssohn-Bartholdy Foundation for his String Quartet in C Major, Op. 2. Hindemith became the concertmaster of the Frankfurt Opera House orchestra, but in 1917 he was drafted for military service; he was now a drummer in a military band. Hindemith's unit was stationed in Frankfurt, however, so he was able to continue working for the orchestra. After the Armistice in 1918, Hindemith returned to Frankfurt to compose.

In 1919 Hindemith switched instruments from the violin to the viola. The Donaueschingen Festival was founded in 1921 with the aim of presenting new music to the public. Hindemith wished to provide a showcase for avant-garde composers and experimental music, so he joined the festival's directing committee. Soon, as a leading member of the committee, the young man was able to include the music of Igor Stravinsky, Alban Berg, Anton Webern, and Arnold Schoenberg in the events.

Immediately after World War I expressionism became a popular style in German literature, art, and films. This trend reflected the atmosphere of doubt and distrust that was so widespread after Germany's defeat in the war. Kaiser Wilhelm II had given up his throne, and the social structure of the country was shaken. By the end of the war the restraints that bound the German people to their traditions had loosened. The Weimar Republic that had governed Germany from 1919 until 1933 was extremely liberal and open to new ideas. Hindemith's early works were composed within this experimental and liberated atmosphere of the post–World War I years.

The performances of Hindemith's trilogy of one-act operas, which he wrote between 1919 and 1921, caused scandals. The conductor Fritz Busch stated that the libretto of one of them contained shocking subject matter, and he refused to perform it. The new operas outraged the public and the critics, and Hindemith's work was angrily attacked in articles and journals. These works reflected a bitter time period in Germany's history; as the social conditions improved and as the composer matured, though, his music changed too.

In 1922 Hindemith composed his first chamber concerto, entitled *Kammermusik* (Chamber Music), which was in baroque style; this work led to a series of seven chamber concerti written between 1922 and 1927 called the *Kammermusiken* (Chamber Music Works). Throughout this return to tradition Hindemith used a contrapuntal interplay of melodies with a diverse combination of strings and winds. Some of these concerti remind the listener of the old masters, even though they employ an expanded tonal harmony and characteristically modern elements, including jazz. In the *Kammermusiken* Hindemith began his research into a system of harmony based on chords built on the interval of a fourth, rather than the customary third.

In 1927 Hindemith started teaching composition at the Berlin Academy for Music. Here he intended to instruct his students to further the concepts developed by the music of the eighteenth century. His 1926 opera, *Cardillac*, written in a style based on baroque composers, revived the use of separate musical numbers and was written as absolute music, with the orchestra and the dramatic action running parallel to each other.

Hindemith's oratorio/opera *Mathis der Maler* (Matthias the Painter), for which he wrote his own libretto, was composed during 1933 and 1934. This work was full of meaning to the composer, since it mirrored what was happening in his personal life. The opera is based on the life of the sixteenth-century German painter Mathis Nithardt, known as Grünewald, who was involved in the Peasants' War of 1524. This struggle to end serfdom occurred during a time of fierce fighting between Catholics and Lutherans. After a series of events, Grünewald eventually decides that he can best serve mankind by returning to his art. For Hindemith, the painter portrayed in this opera symbolized the predicament of artists who are hindered by political turmoil; it is an examination of the artist's role in society during a time of war. Hindemith created a three-movement symphonic suite from parts of the opera in 1934. Each movement of the symphony represents one of the panels of the altarpiece painting that Grünewald created at Isenheim.

During the 1930s Hindemith made several trips to Ankara, Turkey, at the request of the Turkish government. There he assisted Turkish educators to overhaul their music education system. He also came to the United States on several concert tours. When the Nazi regime came to power in Germany, they promoted what they considered to be "purely German art." Hindemith's music was far too avant-garde for the Nazis. By 1937 Hindemith's works, considered radical by the German officials, were banned from performance in Germany. The attitude of the Nazi regime and the fears they raised caused Hindemith to leave; he first went to Switzerland in 1937 and then to England. In 1940, shortly before the outbreak of World War II, the composer moved to the United States, where he was appointed visiting professor at Yale University in New Haven, Connecticut, to teach composition.

Hindemith had his students perform the music of the Renaissance and medieval eras on the old instruments on which this music would have originally been played. In 1946 Hindemith became an American citizen. Hindemith also taught students at the Berkshire Music Center in Tanglewood, Massachusetts, during the summer months; his students included Leonard Bernstein. In 1953 he accepted a position at the University of Zurich, where he continued to teach until 1955, after which he took a more active role as a conductor.

In his last years Hindemith composed *Die Harmonie der Welt* (The Harmony of the World), a mystical opera about the astronomer John Kepler. In November 1963 Hindemith became ill and was brought to a hospital in Frankfurt, where he died.

In his book *A Composer's World: Horizons and Limitations*, Hindemith expressed his concern about the role of music in society. He believed that music had an ethical and moral responsibility to the public and that music was not an end in itself. He said, "People who make music together cannot be enemies, at least while the music lasts."

Hindemith always had a strong sense of form, especially the contrapuntal forms of the baroque era. Polyphony and dissonant counterpoint provided the basis for his musical thinking. His twelve-tone-based harmonies have a tonal center, and his works have a definite key. The dissonance of his earlier pieces became chromatically melodious in his later works. Hindemith is among the most significant German composers of his time; through his music, his books, and his teaching, he has impacted many of today's musicians.

20 Other Great Modern Composers

Perhaps it is music that will save the world.

PABLO CASALS, CELLIST (1876–1973)

Although music contains universal qualities, every culture imprints its own special identity on its music. Throughout the centuries composers have expressed in their works their individuality and the uniqueness of the society in which they live. Numerous composers in many countries were involved in the transformations that took place in the early part of the twentieth century. Some of them were on the front lines of these changes, while others were influenced by the innovative and novel ideas of others.

Austrian Composers

ALBAN BERG

Music is at once the product of feeling and knowledge,
for it requires from its disciples, composers and
performers alike, not only talent and enthusiasm, but

*also that knowledge and perception which are the result
of protracted study and reflection.*

ALBAN BERG, COMPOSER (1885–1935)

The Austrian composer Alban Berg (1885–1935) was a disciple of Arnold Schoenberg. The three composers together—Schoenberg and his students Berg and Anton Webern—are known as the Second Viennese School. (The First Viennese School was made up of Mozart, Haydn, and Beethoven.) Berg's first pieces were written in a romantic style, but under the guidance of Schoenberg, his music became more atonal. His music mixes romantic elements, such as lush orchestration and tonal harmonies, with modern, atonal aspects.

Berg's opera *Wozzeck*, written while the composer served in the Austrian Army during World War I, is terrifically intense. It was a hit with audiences throughout Europe until it was banned by the Nazis. His instrumental pieces sometimes make use of complex mathematical structures; Berg's *Lyric Suite* for string quartet includes codes and cryptic messages which are woven into the music.

In 1935 Berg was commissioned to compose a violin concerto. This piece became a memorial to the daughter of Gustav Mahler's widow, Alma, and her second husband, Walter Gropius. The young girl died while Berg was working on the composition. The finale of this Violin Concerto employs a chorale that is based on a composition by Johann Sebastian Bach. The work is based on a twelve-tone row, but it ends with a whole-tone scale. The concerto has a mystical and spiritual quality that attracts violinists, who often select it for performance. The composer died before he heard the Violin Concerto performed, and the piece became his own funeral anthem.

ANTON WEBERN

*Your ears will always lead you right,
but you must know why.*

ANTON WEBERN, COMPOSER (1883–1945)

Another Schoenberg pupil was Anton Webern (1883–1945). Born in Vienna into an aristocratic family, Webern was not a good student until college. He entered the University of Vienna in 1902 and received a doctorate in music in 1906. Schoenberg had introduced the young man to his harmonic theories while he was attending the university, and these ideas attracted Webern's attention. Webern and his fellow student Alban Berg formed a lasting friendship with their teacher; both of these men employed their own versions of Schoenberg's technique.

Upon graduation Webern worked as a conductor of theater orchestras in different European countries. He also composed music that was not accepted by audiences due to its unique and novel style. The Nazi regime excluded his music as part of their ban of all atonal works. Webern spent the years during World War II working as a proofreader for a music publisher. His life ended tragically when he was accidentally shot by an American soldier after World War II.

Webern used only the twelve-tone technique in his music; he was also a miniaturist, composing relatively short pieces of music. His music has a tendency to be intense and concentrated; a few of his pieces take but a moment to perform. In the middle of the twentieth century, audiences and critics found his works bewildering and confusing. Webern was unappreciated during his lifetime, but his reputation rose after his death. Many contemporary composers have found great value in his work.

French and Spanish Composers

DARIUS MILHAUD

For a long time I have had the idea of writing a composition fit for high school purposes.

DARIUS MILHAUD, COMPOSER (1892–1974)

Born in France, Darius Milhaud (1892–1974) spent his childhood in Aix-en-Provence. Both of his parents were involved in music; his father was one of the founders of the Musical Society of Aix-en-Provence, and his mother had studied voice in Paris. Milhaud was already an accomplished pianist by the time he was four, and he began to study violin at the age of seven. He also started composing while he was very young. He often performed with his parents and with a local string quartet. In 1909 he entered the Paris Conservatory intending to become a violinist, but then he decided to focus on composition.

He was connected to the composers known as Les Six, a group that sought simplicity in musical ideas and brevity in the expression of themes. The composers belonging to Les Six wanted to overturn customs and conventions; they sought clarity and directness in their work. Additionally, they discarded the idea of composing Impressionist works and any of the romantic-era sentimentality while they explored new materials such as jazz.

Milhaud's memories of the years he spent in Brazil with the French consular mission (from 1917 to 1919) were the source of the Latin rhythms and themes that invaded his music. Upon his return to Paris, in 1921, he composed a suite for piano titled *Saudades do Brazil* (Souvenirs of Brazil, Op. 67), consisting of an overture and a suite of twelve short dance pieces for piano. While he was on a concert tour of the United States, Milhaud encountered jazz and blues in the streets and theaters of Harlem, in New York. His 1923 ballet *La création du monde* (The Creation of the World), Op. 81, contains elements of jazz style. The work is based on an African folk tale of creation. A combination of classical style and the American jazz culture was fashionable in Paris at that time, and *La création du monde* was the first of Milhaud's works to employ this mixture.

Milhaud was afflicted with rheumatoid arthritis, which eventually confined him to a wheelchair. The composer immigrated to the United States in 1940 after receiving a commission from the Chicago Symphony Orchestra. Milhaud obtained a teaching position at Mills College in Oakland, California, and for the next thirty years he composed and lectured throughout California. Failing health forced him to retire, and he died in Geneva, Switzerland, in 1974.

Milhaud developed new rhythmic structures, incorporated elements from many cultures, and used sophisticated dissonant harmonies in his music. He explored polytonality, created when several keys sound at the same time. Milhaud wrote more than four hundred compositions in almost every possible genre, including eighteen string quartets, fifteen operas, over twenty scores for films, twelve symphonies, and nineteen ballets.

LILI BOULANGER AND NADIA BOULANGER

The art of music is so deep and profound that to approach it very seriously only is not enough. One must approach music with a serious rigor and, at the same time, with a great, affectionate joy.

NADIA BOULANGER,
COMPOSER AND TEACHER (1887–1979)

Lili Boulanger

Two French sisters, Lili Boulanger (1893–1918) and Nadia Boulanger (1887–1979), gained worldwide recognition for their accomplishments. Having endured fragile health throughout her life, Lili Boulanger died very young. At the age of eight she had already begun to perform as a pianist and violinist. Trained at the Paris Conservatory, where her father taught vocal students, she won the Prix de

Rome in 1913 for her cantata *Faust et Hélène* (Faust and Helene). She was the first woman in history to be awarded this sought-after prize. The outbreak of World War I and a return of her illness cut down the time she was able to spend in Italy, though, so Boulanger had to return to France.

Once back in Paris, the young woman resumed her composing, aware that death was near and might prevent her from completing her works. Lili Boulanger composed more than fifty pieces during her short life, ranging from choral works to chamber music. *Clairières dans le ciel* (Clearings in the Sky), Boulanger's cycle of thirteen songs, was written in 1914. Her pieces were impressionist in style; she used complex harmonies and chromatic textures to enhance the poetry in this song cycle. The sorrow she felt over the loss of her father and her own illness found its way into many of her pieces. The orchestral work *D'un soir triste* (Of a Sad Evening) employs an inventive use of percussion and brass, and the colorful harmony of the piece hints at the influence of Claude Debussy. Lili Boulanger wrote amazingly mature music for such a young composer. Her untimely passing deeply touched the life of her sister.

Nadia Boulanger

Nadia Boulanger was her sister's first teacher and her foremost supporter. The fact that Lili's music remained in the repertoire was mostly due to her sister's promotion of her works. At the Paris Conservatory Nadia Boulanger studied the organ and composition. Her cantata *La siréna* (The Siren) had won second prize in the Prix de Rome in 1908. She wrote an opera, *La ville morte* (The Dead City), with the pianist and composer Raoul Pugno; in 1914, when Pugno suddenly died, Nadia completed the work. The outbreak of World War I prevented the opera from being produced.

Lili's death caused her older sister to declare that she would never again compose. Instead, she became a teacher and a mentor to young composers and performers until 1979, when she died at the age of ninety-three. Boulanger, who opened a pathway for other women, was considered to be the most important woman involved in music education. She was known for her strictness and her insistence that her students memorize both books of Bach's *Well-Tempered Clavier* so that they would have the ability to improvise fugues. Her pupils included Aaron Copland, Virgil Thomson, Darius Milhaud, Elliot Carter, Leonard Bernstein, Marc Blitzstein, and Philip Glass. Her friends Igor Stravinsky and Darius Milhaud sought her advice; Stravinsky brought his scores to Boulanger for suggestions and comments.

In 1937 Boulanger became the first woman to conduct an entire program of the Royal Philharmonic in London. In 1938 she became the first woman to conduct the New York Philharmonic, the Boston Symphony Orchestra, and the Philadelphia Orchestra. During World War II Boulanger came to the United

States to teach at the Peabody Conservatory in Baltimore, Maryland, and at the Washington (D.C.) College of Music. Returning to France afterward, she resumed teaching at the American Conservatory, where she was appointed director in 1949. She also taught at the Paris Conservatory and gave private lessons. Boulanger's teaching greatly influenced modern classical music. Her life was dedicated to helping musicians become first-class composers and assisting them in their efforts to gain recognition.

MANUEL DE FALLA

Manuel de Falla (1876–1946) was Spain's first major nationalist composer and brought Spanish music into the twentieth century. Born in the seaport town of Cadiz, he moved to Madrid at the age of twenty. Later he went to Paris, where he met Ravel and Debussy. He lived there until World War I began.

His most famous compositions include *Nights in the Gardens of Spain* for piano and orchestra, the ballet *The Three-Cornered Hat*, and the *Pièces espagnoles* (Spanish Pieces) for the piano. Falla brought local folklore and native culture into his music. His one-act opera *La vida breve* (The Short Life) displayed his use of Spanish traditions and customs. The Spanish Civil War (1936–39) caused the composer a great deal of distress and sorrow; he moved to Argentina in 1939, where he lived until his death in 1946.

Composers in the Soviet Union

Modern Russian music is represented by Sergei Prokofiev and Dmitri Shostakovich. The Armenian composer Aram Khachaturian followed the path of Rimsky-Korsakov and other Russian greats of the past. After the Russian Revolution, all of the music that was composed was required to support and be in line with Communist Party guidelines. In 1921 all of the arts were placed under government control. The Union of Soviet Composers was formed in 1932 to oversee the political activities of each composer, and all contemporary Western music was forbidden.

SERGEI PROKOFIEV

My mother had to explain that one couldn't compose a Liszt rhapsody because it was a piece of music that Liszt himself had composed.

SERGEI PROKOFIEV, COMPOSER (1891–1953)

Sergei Prokofiev

Sergei Prokofiev (1891–1953) studied at the St. Petersburg Conservatory with Rimsky-Korsakov. The young man was opinionated and stubborn; he thought that the teachers at the conservatory were boring and old-fashioned, so his time there was not a pleasant experience. By 1911 Prokofiev was publicly performing his works; often the critics were confused by his distinctive combinations of sounds. Prokofiev was very impressed by Igor Stravinsky's ballets and was commissioned by Diaghilev to write for his company. *Chout* (The Buffoons), Op. 21, premiered in Paris in 1921. The ballet contains sudden and unexpected effects, and it blends Russian folk music with jazz. *Chout* was too avant-garde for the conservative Soviet authorities when Prokofiev returned to Russia.

Prokofiev often varied his music with many unusual elements; his *Peter and the Wolf*, Op. 67, was composed in 1936 for a children's theater in Moscow. Each orchestral instrument presents a leitmotif, or recurring musical theme, that symbolizes a character in this story: a bird is represented by the flute, Peter by the string quartet, the grandfather by a bassoon, and the wolf by three horns. Prokofiev wrote the narration, which is read by the conductor in between the musical sections.

Some of Prokofiev's music reflects the neoclassical style, drawing its inspiration from music of the eighteenth century. His Symphony in D Major, Op. 25, is called his *Classical* Symphony and was purposely written to imitate the type of work that Wolfgang Amadeus Mozart or Franz Joseph Haydn would have produced. The composer's works were wide-ranging, from his classical imitations to more modern music that suddenly modulates to another key.

DMITRI SHOSTAKOVICH

A creative artist works on his next composition because he was not satisfied with his previous one.

DMITRI SHOSTAKOVICH, COMPOSER (1906–1975)

Dmitri Shostakovich

Dmitri Shostakovich (1906–1975) was the first Russian composer who was entirely a product of the Soviet Union's music educational system. There was no artistic freedom under the Communist regime in the Soviet Union; the government dictated to all artists what was allowed to be written, painted, or performed. Shostakovich entered the Leningrad Conservatory in 1919, two years after the Russian Revolution; he graduated with a degree in composition in 1925.

By the early 1930s, Shostakovich was viewed as a promising Russian composer both within and outside the Soviet Union. His early works were patriotic and admired by the authorities. But his 1933 opera, *Ledi Makbet Mtsenskovo Ujezda* (Lady Macbeth of the Mtsensk District), caused trouble for him. At first the work was hailed by the Soviet newspaper *Pravda*, which claimed it "could only have been written by a Soviet composer, brought up in the traditions of Soviet culture."

Then, in 1936, the leader of the Soviet Union, Joseph Stalin, saw the opera and became very upset with it. The music critics in the Soviet Union now denounced the work and condemned it in newspapers as "a confused scream of sounds" and "un-Soviet, unwholesome ... tuneless." When, a few days later, Stalin attended a performance of Shostakovich's ballet *Bright Stream*, the composer faced another attack on his work. At this time people were being sent to Siberia for any departure from the Communist viewpoint; being seen as a threat to the government created an extremely dangerous situation for any individual. This is just the position Shostakovich suddenly found himself in, and his music was banned from performance. The authorities condemned any artist who did not meet the standards set by the regime. The year 1936 marked the beginning of the "Great Terror," during which many of Shostakovich's friends and colleagues were arrested or killed.

The 1937 premiere of his Symphony No. 5, Op. 47, which was more conventional harmonically, immediately reestablished the composer's popularity with the Soviet regime until 1948, when his works were again banned. Shostakovich was forced to apologize publicly, and his family lost certain privileges they had enjoyed up till then.

While presenting the composer outside of the Soviet Union as the musical prodigy of the Revolution, the regime regulated what he could produce. Out of fear, Shostakovich joined the Communist Party in 1960; he also had to continue to contain his music within the boundaries approved by the authorities. This is why Shostakovich's music was written using traditional structures and harmonies while other composers outside the Soviet Union were abandoning those elements. The restrictions that the government placed on art led Shostakovich to write more conventional-seeming pieces; however, his harmonies were often harsh.

Like other composers living in a restrictive society, Shostakovich suffered from the stifling atmosphere in which he was forced to exist. In 1962 he had the courage to compose his Symphony No. 13, Op. 113, commemorating the massacre of Jews at Babi Yar, outside of Kiev, during World War II. This was a dangerous subject in view of the anti-Semitism prevalent in the Soviet government. The work was largely ignored by the authorities.

Shostakovich, like Prokofiev, enjoyed using grand musical forms with melodies that evoke the romantic era. He has been considered as the greatest mid-twentieth-century symphonist. Sharp contrasts, fantastic harmonies, and repeated rhythms and melodies are found in his works. Many of his compositions reflect the political values that the Soviets required, yet at a deep level, his music expresses the profound tragedy and sorrow of a great artist forced to work in a repressive society.

ARAM KHACHATURIAN

Aram Khachaturian (1903–1978) celebrated his Armenian culture in his imaginative works. The composer was nineteen years old when he first began to study music, but he quickly made up for lost time. Although he had no background in theory or composition, Khachaturian performed well on his cello at the auditions for the Russian Academy of Music and was accepted as a student. During the same time, the composer took a degree in biology from the Department of Physics and Mathematics at Moscow State University. At the age of twenty-three he transferred to the Moscow Conservatory, where he received a postgraduate degree.

Composed for his graduation, his Piano Concerto in D-flat Major became a favorite in the Soviet Union. The work interwove colorful Armenian folk music into its movements, giving it an oriental flavor. Khachaturian used folk elements from Soviet Georgia, Armenia, Uzbekistan, and Azerbaijan in his compositions. For a short while he added more modern components to his works, but he tended to write in the classical genres and forms, and his music is traditional and romantic in style.

After joining the Soviet Composers' Union in 1937, the young man held several administrative positions. He became a member of the Communist Party in 1943. A symphonic poem, which was renamed Symphony No. 3, employs the orchestra, an organ, and fifteen trumpets; it was written in praise of the Soviet regime. Khachaturian's music was criticized, and, like Shostakovich and Prokofiev, the composer had to make a public apology for it. He also responded to the criticism with more patriotic works, including the 1949 *Ode in Memory of Lenin* and the 1952 *Poem about Stalin*.

In 1950 a long-held dream of Khachaturian's came true: he made his debut as a conductor. The composer began to urge the government to loosen the severe restraints on musicians and artists in the Soviet Union, and in 1958 some the restrictions were removed. Khachaturian's music is known for its variety of variation techniques and "Khachaturian's seconds," a kind of rhythmic ostinato (short, constantly repeated rhythmic patterns).

DMITRY KABALEVSKY

Some Russian-born composers decided to fashion their works to fit the guidelines that were set for musicians by the Soviet government after the czarist monarchy was overthrown. Dmitry Kabalevsky (1904–1987), born in St. Petersburg, was a composer, painter, and poet. He studied piano and composition at the Moscow Conservatory. Kabalevsky made every effort to remain faithful to the musical objectives of the Soviet era. He held important positions in the Composers' Union, of which he was a founder; in this position he was a major advocate and enforcer of what the Soviet government considered appropriate in music.

His vocal works, including his operas and operettas, were very popular in his country; outside of Russia he is famous for his orchestral and piano pieces. Kabalevsky wrote many pieces for children. His Violin Concerto, Cello Concerto No. 1, and Piano Concerto No. 3 were dedicated to Soviet youth. The music he composed was conservative and reflected the traditional forms and harmonies. During the cold war, the fact that Kabalevsky was writing music approved by the Soviets caused his work to be immediately dismissed by musicians in democratic societies; therefore, his music was not frequently performed outside of Russia. Today his lyrical works are being heard more often.

British and American Composers

BENJAMIN BRITTEN

It is cruel, you know, that music should be so beautiful. It has the beauty of loneliness and of pain: of strength and freedom. The beauty of disappointment and never-satisfied love. The cruel beauty of nature and everlasting beauty of monotony.

BENJAMIN BRITTEN, COMPOSER (1913–1976)

The British composer Benjamin Britten (1913–1976) wrote well-crafted music. Britten was the youngest child in a household of four children. His father was a dentist, and his mother was an amateur musician. Britten started composing at the age of six. At sixteen he entered the Royal College of Music, where he studied composition. Britten composed music for the concert hall, the opera, radio, and films. In 1935 he worked as a composer for the General Post Office film unit, which produced documentaries. In 1939, as World War II approached, he moved to the United States, where he wrote his first opera, *Paul Bunyan*.

Britten was opposed to war; this is evident in his choral symphony *War Requiem*, Op. 66. The symphony was dedicated to four of Britten's friends who had died during World War I. The theme of the work is the horror and pointlessness of war and the suffering that it produces. His 1945 three-act opera *Peter Grimes*, Op. 33, heralded a new beginning for English opera. The composer had been born in a seaside town, and his experiences there are evident in *Peter Grimes*, which illustrates how fishermen and the sea are dependent on one another. The music establishes the atmosphere, especially the orchestral "Sea Interludes," which create a sense of the seashore. *Peter Grimes* established Britten as an important composer.

In 1948 Britten founded the Aldeburgh Festival to provide a venue for his operas, but later it was expanded to include art exhibitions, dramas, poetry readings, and lectures. Britten continued to compose operas throughout his life; several of his works were classified as chamber operas, a term that the composer coined to mean an opera that uses a chamber orchestra rather than a full orchestra. These include his *The Turn of the Screw*, a two-act opera. Even though he wrote it in just four months, it is considered one of his best works for the stage. The music distinguishes the human characters from the ghosts, who are provided with eerily disturbing themes. Britten used the twelve-tone method here to create dramatic effects: before each scene there is a variation of the theme that indicates a turning of the screw. The tension builds as the music presents unusual intervals and unconventional sounds.

As Britten matured, his music became more sparing in texture. Britten wished to convey a fresh musical message through various methods that included many avant-garde trends. Suffering is a frequent theme in Britten's works. His music encompassed all genres, and he was noted for his abilities as a conductor and pianist.

As the leading British composer after World War I, Britten received many awards and honors. In 1974 he was presented the French government's Ravel Prize, and in 1976, the year of his death, he was proclaimed a Life Peer in Great Britain. Britten had open-heart surgery in 1973, from which he never fully recovered. He died in Suffolk on December 4, 1976, and was buried in the cemetery of his parish church.

VIRGIL THOMSON

I've never known a musician who regretted being one. Whatever deceptions life may have in store for you, music itself is not going to let you down.

VIRGIL THOMSON, COMPOSER AND CRITIC (1896–1989)

Virgil Thomson (1896–1989) filled his works with material from his American heritage. Born in Kansas City, Missouri, his ancestors had been Scottish and Welsh settlers in Virginia. Thomson was brought up in the midwestern American culture and the traditions of the Southern Baptists. He was drawn to music at an early age and began to improvise on a piano when he was five years old. By his twelfth birthday Thomson was a substitute organist for the Calvary Baptist Church in Kansas City.

When World War I began, Thomson enlisted in the National Guard. He studied radiotelephony and aviation before receiving orders to go overseas in September 1918. The war ended just before Thomson was to leave for France. Thomson graduated from a St. Louis, Missouri, junior college; he then went on to Harvard University, where he was a member of the Glee Club. In 1921 he went on a tour of Europe with this ensemble. After the trip, Thomson remained in Paris for a year and arranged to study the organ and counterpoint with the famous teacher Nadia Boulanger. During this time he also encountered the avant-garde composers of Les Six. These people would have a great influence on his work.

He returned to Harvard until his graduation, when a grant from the Juilliard School of Music gave him the opportunity to go to New York to take composition classes. His experience in Paris drew him back to that city, where he remained, except for some visits to the United States, until 1940. Thomson enjoyed the company of Les Six and became an avid believer in their philosophy, which advocated simplicity and brevity.

In 1928 Thomson and the American writer Gertrude Stein collaborated on the opera buffa *Four Saints in Three Acts*. It was a daring attempt: at the time there was no experimental American opera. *Four Saints in Three Acts* is about two Spanish saints and their followers. Stein's libretto was unusual; she focused not on telling a story, but on using odd language combinations and on how the words of the text sounded together. Her writing style has been compared to cubist paintings, which attempt to depict the many-sided parts of a whole. Thomson's score is also unusual in its simplicity, its suggestion of church hymns, its use of American folk melodies, and its inclusion of ragtime, tangos, fox-trots, and waltzes. But the music is based on traditional harmony, so it is tonal and melodic. *Four Saints in Three Acts* is filled with the sounds of Thomson's childhood in Missouri. First opening in Connecticut, the opera, with an all–African American cast of singers and dancers (which was again highly unusual), then went on to New York's Broadway, where it ran for sixty performances.

Four Saints in Three Acts changed the course of American opera; it was a milestone in modern theatrical history and became Thomson's most famous work. Never before had an all-black cast been used in presenting a work that had nothing to do with race. Never before had an American audience witnessed an opera with vibrant sets made of lace and cellophane as the backdrop to music reminding them of their American heritage. The critics were puzzled by Stein's libretto. Wrote the *New York Daily News* music critic: "Virgil Thomson takes the glory, Gertrude Stein supplies the confusion; Music: 3 stars, Libretto: 0."

In the 1930s Thomson wrote scores for movies, such as the 1936 documentary *The Plow That Broke the Plains*. He also composed the ballet *Filling Station*, which contains some distinctive music with titles such as "The Truck Driver's Dance," "Trooper and Truck Drivers," "The Hold-up," and "The Chase." *Filling Station* was the first classical ballet written for a clearly American subject and set somewhere in rural America. The music contains some familiar American tunes, including some Salvation Army band music and a tune that is noticeably similar to "For He's a Jolly Good Fellow." Thomson also worked on the documentary film *The River*, which depicted the efforts to control the flooding of the mighty Mississippi River. The score includes several traditional American hymns and songs. The efforts to hold back the waters are portrayed in repeated, throbbing rhythms. Aaron Copland stated that this composition is "a lesson in how to treat Americana."

Thomson, inspired by an idea of Gertrude Stein's, composed a series of musical portraits of people that were like the work of an artist or a photographer. He wrote these pieces while the person "sat" for them, attempting to capture the character and personality of the individual in these miniatures. Thomson composed over 150 of these "portraits," which musically described all kinds of people, ranging from the famous, such as the conductor Eugene Ormandy, to the completely unknown, such as Louis Rispoli, Thomson's personal secretary. Thomson died in New York in 1989. He had a tremendous influence on twentieth-century American music.

GEORGE GERSHWIN

True music must repeat the thought and inspirations of the people and the time. My people are Americans and my time is today.

GEORGE GERSHWIN, COMPOSER (1898–1937)

George
Gershwin

The New York City–born George Gershwin (1898–1937) carried American popular music into the concert halls of the world. His parents were poor Jewish immigrants from Russia living in the Lower East Side of Manhattan. George (originally named Jacob) Gershovitz was the second son of the four children born to Morris and Rose; his brother, Israel Gershwin (later renamed Ira), was born in 1896. Their father tried various businesses, and the family moved from one apartment to another many times.

A story that has circulated about Gershwin relates to his hearing a classmate play the piano at a school assembly one day. Listening to another youngster perform made Gershwin interested in "this music stuff." He began to play a friend's piano. When, in 1910, his parents purchased a piano intended for his brother, Ira (who was expected to become the musician in the family), the younger brother took over the instrument. Hearing George play, his parents realized his talent, and he was provided with piano lessons.

Gershwin entered the world of classical music through the musical comedies he saw on Broadway. New York City had become a gathering place of the popular music world; musicians would go to Tin Pan Alley, a street in Manhattan where most popular music publishers and producers had their offices, to audition their work. Gershwin dropped out of school at fifteen to take a job with a music publisher. He began his career as a song salesman, playing and singing the company's latest published music for possible buyers. Before long he was also composing his own piano pieces and songs. In 1916 one of his songs, called "When You Want 'Em You Can't Get 'Em, When You've Got 'Em You Don't Want 'Em," was accepted for publication. Gershwin earned $12 for the piece. In Tin Pan Alley Gershwin also encountered the music of Irving Berlin and Jerome Kern, which inspired him.

In 1917 Gershwin came to Broadway, taking a job as a rehearsal accompanist for a show entitled *Miss 1917*. The year he turned twenty-one, 1919, was a big one for Gershwin. His song "Swanee" was recorded by the top vocalist of the time, Al Jolson; it was the composer's first big hit. He composed his first musical, *La La Lucille*; it ran for one hundred performances. And he composed his first classical piece, *Lullaby*, a string quartet. His one-act jazz opera, *Blue Monday Blues*, followed in 1922. Ira collaborated with George in 1924 to create the show *Lady Be Good!* This cheerful musical comedy, one of their biggest successes, ran for almost a year and featured the song "Fascinating Rhythm."

In 1924 Gershwin's *Rhapsody in Blue*, for solo piano and jazz band, premiered with the composer at the piano. The audience's excitement started the minute the clarinet began to play the wailing glissando that starts the piece. Combining classical and jazz elements, the work was an instant triumph. Gershwin described how he began to compose *Rhapsody in Blue* during a train ride to Boston in 1931:

It was on the train, with its steely rhythms, its rattle-ty bang, that is so often so stimulating to a composer—I frequently hear music in the very heart of the noise....And there I suddenly heard, and even saw on paper—the complete construction of the Rhapsody, from beginning to end....I heard it as a sort of musical kaleidoscope of America, of our vast melting pot, of our unduplicated national pep, of our blues, our metropolitan madness.

A one-movement concerto, *Rhapsody in Blue* is one of the most popular concert works in the repertoire; it is a "crossover" piece, meaning that it moved from the popular genre into the classical. Gershwin was the man who carried jazz into the concert hall. The success of *Rhapsody in Blue* made Gershwin determined to compose more "serious music."

The symphonic poem *An American in Paris* incorporates the composer's impressions of the sounds and atmosphere of that city. It was composed while Gershwin was in Europe seeking additional instruction in composition. He approached Maurice Ravel, who responded, "Why do you want to become a second-rate Ravel when you already are a first-rate Gershwin?" In 1929 Gershwin made his conducting debut with the New York Philharmonic Orchestra, performing *An American in Paris* and *Rhapsody in Blue*.

He continued to compose songs with his brother Ira as the lyricist. Ira Gershwin created memorable song lyrics; he wrote the words to some of the twentieth century's favorite songs. Their Broadway shows were tremendous hits; their 1930 musical, *Girl Crazy*, introduced the song "I Got Rhythm." The musical *Of Thee I Sing* was the first musical comedy to win a Pulitzer Prize and was their longest-running Broadway show.

In 1934 George Gershwin decided to write a show that he had been considering for a long time. This was to be based on a novel by DuBose Heyward entitled *Porgy* that Gershwin had read in 1926. *Porgy* is about a disabled black man who lived in the slums of Charleston, South Carolina. Gershwin traveled to South Carolina several times to learn about the people and to listen to their music and unique speech patterns. Heyward wrote the libretto, and *Porgy and Bess*, billed as a folk opera, opened in 1935, first in Boston and a few weeks later in a New York theater. The show ran for 124 performances but never made back the money spent on the production. The work was criticized by some who felt it had "racist overtones" and portrayed African American life in a negative light. As the first opera about African Americans, *Porgy and Bess* was a daring venture. Today it is viewed as Gershwin's masterpiece and is often performed in opera houses throughout the world.

In 1937 Gershwin began to have headaches and spells of dizziness. The cause turned out to be a brain tumor. He was thirty-eight years old when he died. Gershwin had the gift of song; he wrote memorable tunes in all of his works. He was able to bridge the gap between the worlds of jazz and classical music. The jazzy elements in his work are authentic because he understood and played jazz. His orchestral music is full of melodic vitality and has broad appeal. Today Gershwin's works have an important place in the classical repertoire. In 2007 the Library of Congress named their prize for popular song in honor of the two brothers who had so outstandingly influenced popular music. The Library of Congress Gershwin Prize for Popular Song is awarded annually to a composer or performer whose lifetime contributions embody the standard of excellence associated with the Gershwin brothers.

AARON COPLAND

So long as the human spirit thrives on this planet, music in some living form will accompany and sustain it and give it expressive meaning.

AARON COPLAND, COMPOSER (1900–1990)

Aaron Copland

Aaron Copland (1900–1990) stated, "I don't compose. I assemble materials." Copland was born in the New York City borough of Brooklyn, the youngest of the five children of Harris and Sarah Copland, Jewish immigrants from Lithuania. Copland's older sister, Laurine, was his first piano teacher, and by the age of fifteen he was certain that he wanted to become a composer. In 1914 he started formal piano lessons. At the age of twenty Copland won a scholarship that allowed him to attend the newly founded American Conservatory in Fontainebleau, where his teacher for orchestration and composition was Nadia Boulanger. He was her first full-time American student. That same autumn his first piece for the piano, *Scherzo humoristique: Le chat et la souris* (The Cat and the Mouse), was published. This work employs the whole-tone scale and the alternation of black notes against white notes.

While in Europe, Copland became aware of the styles of national music arising in Europe; he concluded that a uniquely American musical style should be developed. Returning to the United States Copland became involved in promoting American composers by organizing concerts and festivals to showcase their works. He worked to organize a community of composers and became a member of the League of Composers.

Copland once wrote that he had four different styles as a composer: his jazz phase, from 1925 to 1929; his abstract, avant-garde phase, from 1930 to 1936; his populist phase, from 1936 to 1949; and his final phase, serialism. In 1936 Copland, noting the drastic changes in the world, concluded that more appropriate music was needed for the audiences who now listened to the radio, attended films, and bought records—not just for the people who attended concerts. He simplified his music and made it more melodious so that it would reach out to a broader audience. This phase produced scores that increased Copland's popularity and established him as a truly American composer whose music was on a level equal to that of European composers.

Incorporating elements of American folk music in his scores, Copland composed the ballets *Billy the Kid, Rodeo*, and *Appalachian Spring*, for which he was awarded the 1945 Pulitzer Prize. *Rodeo* is one of the best examples of the composer's Americana style; this musical picture of the old west includes tunes from the American square dance tradition. He also composed two works for young students: the opera *The Second Hurricane* and the orchestral piece *An Outdoor Overture*. He composed music for films, including *Of Mice and Men, Our Town*, and *The Heiress*; he won an Oscar for this last score.

Copland's Symphony No. 3, his last symphony, was composed in 1946 and premiered by the Boston Symphony Orchestra. Written at the end of World War II, this piece was intended by the composer as a patriotic American tribute. He employed and developed his brass theme from his 1942 *Fanfare for the Common Man* in the fourth movement. It is Copland's longest orchestral work, with the standard four movements of this genre, and it received the New York Music Critics' Circle Award as the best orchestral work by an American composer performed during the 1946–47 season. The Symphony No. 3 has been labeled difficult because Copland used long themes that recur at various points instead of shorter themes that are developed through variations. In it the composer combined his Americana style with the traditional grand symphonic style; there is nothing of his "popular" music style in it.

In 1953 Copland was summoned to a secret hearing conducted by the House Committee on Un-American Activities at the United States Congress. This was the era of the notorious Joseph McCarthy hearings, which sought to expose American communists. The committee questioned Copland about his past political associations, and he was accused of having socialist political leanings. After the closed hearing, Copland issued a statement: "On late Friday afternoon, I received a telegram from the Senate Permanent Subcommittee on Investigations to appear as a witness. I did. I answered to the best of my ability all of the questions which were asked me. I testified under oath that I have never supported, and am now opposed to the limitations put on freedom by the Soviet Union." Although the charges against him were weak and his career was not critically affected, Copland felt the effects of this incident for some time.

Aaron Copland received the Presidential Medal of Freedom in 1964 and was awarded the Congressional Gold Medal in 1986. In the 1970s Copland stopped composing, but he continued to lecture and conduct until he retired in 1983. By then he was suffering with Alzheimer's disease. He died on December 2, 1990, in Tarrytown, New York. Most of his estate was willed to assist composers of new music: his home was established as a retreat for young composers, and the Aaron Copland Fund was founded to help these composers have their music recorded and performed.

Copland has been described as the most American of the American composers. His music had great clarity and usually had definite tonal centers. He often employed simple harmonies and folk melodies that were familiar to the American public, and many of his pieces employ distinctly American themes. Copland's music evoked the American scene and spirit, but as Igor Stravinsky observed, "Why call Copland a great American composer? He's a great composer."

ELLIOTT CARTER

My musical life started with hearing and being fascinated by contemporary music.

ELLIOTT CARTER, COMPOSER (BORN 1908)

Elliott Carter

Elliott Carter (born 1908) is recognized as the successor to Aaron Copland and today is considered one of the most influential figures in American new music. Carter was born in New York City; his father imported lace. His childhood piano lessons did not inspire him, and he did not display any interest in music until he was exposed to modern music. Charles Ives sold insurance to Carter's parents and encouraged the youngster to explore contemporary trends.

He once stated that it was hearing Stravinsky's *Le sacre du printemps* (The Rite of Spring) that made him wish to be a composer. Carter graduated from the Horace Mann School in the Bronx; one of his teachers there had taken him to hear avant-garde concerts in Greenwich Village. When he began his studies at Harvard in 1926, he was interested only in studying literature and mathematics. Ives encouraged the young man to pursue his love of music, so he enrolled in music classes as well. Carter received his bachelor's degree in English in 1930 and a master's degree in music two years later.

In 1932, against the advice of his parents, he went to Paris for three years to study with Nadia Boulanger. Upon returning to New York, he began to write articles for the journal *Modern Music*, where he was viewed as a capable critic. Carter also applied himself to composing and teaching. Carter has turned his back on many of his early works, including two string quartets that date from 1935 and 1937, since they were the products of a very different way of thinking about composition and what he later decided he wanted his music to convey.

During a part of World War II he was as a consultant in the Office of War Information, which sent music to Europe. *Holiday Overture* is like much other American concert music composed during the war, when Americans were longing for the war to end and composers, in the hope of raising morale, wrote inspiring pieces. The liberation of France in 1944 was particularly meaningful for Carter because of his three years in Paris; it was a critical victory, which led to the final days of World War II the following year. As the overture celebrates the Allied liberation of France, it imparts a sense of triumph.

Carter's Piano Sonata was composed during 1945 and 1946; it is considered to be the start of a new trend in his musical style, since its dissonance and rhythmic complexity are characteristics found in all of his later compositions. The premiere of this work was disastrous. As the composer sought the gradual removal of a definite scheme of tonality, his compositions became less and less understood. The Piano Sonata hovers between two keys that are just a half step apart.

In 1950 Carter won a Guggenheim Fellowship and a grant from the National Institute of Arts and Letters, which allowed him to move to Tucson, Arizona. While there, he pondered what he wished to accomplish. He decided to return to composing the type of music that had caught his attention when he was younger. Carter's next work was his First String Quartet, a piece filled with his rhythmic innovations. In the last movement, every time a theme returns, it is played more rapidly than it the time before. This counterpoint of themes becomes a polyrhythm, with some getting faster at one rate and some getting faster at a different rate. The First String Quartet introduced Carter's concept of metrical modulation, in which variable meters lead from one tempo or pulse to the next. This method allows various layers of rhythms to occur at the same time but at different speeds, so that the music constantly shifts from one speed to another. Despite the difficulties that other musicians found with the score, the First String Quartet was recognized as an exciting piece.

In 1960 Carter received his first Pulitzer Prize for his contributions to the traditions of the string quartet. In 1963 he was made a member of the American Academy of Arts and Letters and was also appointed composer in residence at the American Academy in Rome. He lectured at Cornell University from 1967 until he returned to New York and the Juilliard School in 1972. Since the 1970s Carter's compositions have generally been written for small ensembles or as solo music. Since 1980 Carter has written more than thirty-five new works for a broad variety of instrumental and vocal combinations. Known for his extraordinarily complex rhythms, non-repetitive themes, and atonal music, Carter had at first a greater audience in Europe than in America. In recent years his popularity in the United States has increased tremendously.

SAMUEL BARBER

*Born of what I feel. I am not a
self-conscious composer.*

SAMUEL BARBER, COMPOSER (1910–1981)

Samuel Barber

The romantic era did not come to a close for Samuel Barber (1910–1981). Because he wrote music in a style that was out of fashion in the twentieth century, Barber often referred to himself as "a living dead" American composer. Born in West Chester, Pennsylvania, near Philadelphia, he grew up in a musical environment. His father was a doctor, and his mother was an amateur pianist. Barber began piano and cello lessons at the age of six and composed his first piece at the age of seven. By the time he was nine he had decided to have a career as a composer. He left a note for his mother saying, "I was meant to be a composer and will be I'm sure.... Don't ask me to try to forget this unpleasant thing and go play football—please."

The teenaged Barber worked as a church organist and considered becoming a professional singer. At the age of fourteen Barber was one of the first students at the new Curtis Institute in Philadelphia. Barber was a gifted pianist with a fine baritone voice, but he excelled in composition; when he was eighteen Barber won the 1929 Bearns Prize from Columbia University for his Violin Sonata.

For his graduation work Barber composed a concert overture, *The School for Scandal*, Op. 5, which won a prize in 1933. He won a Pulitzer scholarship and in 1936 was awarded the American Academy's Prix de Rome, which provided a two-year residency in the Italian capital. He spent several years in Europe, composing, performing at recitals, and conducting.

Barber rearranged the slow second movement of his composition the String Quartet in B Minor, Op. 11, for string orchestra as his *Adagio for Strings*. This is probably his most famous piece; it was first performed along with his *First Essay for Orchestra*, Op. 12, on the radio by the NBC Symphony Orchestra under the direction of Arturo Toscanini. The *Adagio* is composed in what is called an arch form: a single lyrical subject beginning in the violins is repeated, reversed, extended, and embellished by the other voices, rising in the high strings to its fortissimo climax before it fades. The piece evokes feelings of sadness and was performed at the funerals of Presidents Franklin D. Roosevelt and John F. Kennedy.

In the 1940s Barber began to include more modern elements of harmony and scoring. His setting of James Agee's *Knoxville: Summer of 1915*, Op. 24, was written at the request of the Metropolitan Opera singer Eleanor Steber, who premiered it with the Boston Symphony Orchestra. Composed for soprano and orchestra, this piece exemplifies Barber's commitment to lyricism; the original prose poem first appeared in an edition of the *New Yorker* magazine as a remembrance of a more uncomplicated America before two world wars. The poem is written through the eyes of a child and recalls a time when people sat on their front porches in rocking chairs, keeping an eye on the street; it then moves to a backyard scene of the family gazing at the stars, "lying, on quilts, on the grass, in a summer evening, among the sounds of the night." Barber's score pictures the tranquil summer evening with the opening woodwind passage; the tranquil night is suddenly interrupted by flashes of street noise but then returns to the calmer mood until the climax of the piece climbs to a steadily higher register. The music of *Knoxville: Summer of 1915* is fused to Americana and captures the memory of that more innocent time.

In 1966 the New York Metropolitan Opera turned to Barber with a commission for an opera to launch their new home at Lincoln Center. His *Antony and Cleopatra* premiered on September 16, 1966. Despite an all-star cast, the opening was a disaster. The opera suffered because the production was supposed to exhibit the complicated onstage machinery and capabilities of the new opera house. Many technological malfunctions and overwhelming sets ruined the performance. Barber believed that the music had barely been heard over the noise made by the machinery. The critics found the music both unoriginal and uninspiring, causing Barber to go into a deep depression and isolate himself. In 1975 Barber revised *Antony and Cleopatra* and presented it at the Juilliard School, where it was much better received. But after the initial failure of this opera, Barber composed very few new pieces. Toward the end of his life Barber had a dreadful time combating his depression and feelings of loneliness, yet through it all he retained his sense of humor.

Barber was a great admirer of Schubert, Brahms, and other nineteenth-century composers. He remained a romantic lyricist, avoiding the experimentation of some other American composers of his generation and preferring to stick to traditional harmonies, genres, and forms. His musical style was in direct contrast to the twelve-tone technique promoted by other American composers. Barber's tuneful works and his melodic approach hold strong emotional appeal for audiences. He occasionally used some atonality and even some jazz in his works, but usually he stayed within the boundaries that made his audiences most comfortable. Stricken with cancer, Barber died in New York City in 1981. He is buried in his hometown.

LEONARD BERNSTEIN

When I am with composers, I say I am a conductor. When I am with conductors, I say I am a composer.

LEONARD BERNSTEIN,
COMPOSER AND CONDUCTOR (1918–1990)

Leonard Bernstein

Born in Lawrence, Massachusetts, Leonard Bernstein (1918–1990) was a composer, conductor, author, lecturer, and teacher. The son of Jewish immigrants from Russia, he believed that music should play a role in the lives of all people. His father, Samuel, was in the beauty products business; his mother, Jennie, was a housewife. The name on his birth certificate was Louis, which had been chosen by his grandmother. His parents did not care for this name and called him Leonard at home; the composer legally changed his name to Leonard on his sixteenth birthday. Throughout his life he was affectionately called Lenny. As a child he suffered from chronic asthma and various allergies. In 1929 Bernstein took the examination for and was admitted to Boston Latin School, the oldest public school in America.

Bernstein's aunt stored her piano with Leonard's family, and he began taking piano lessons at the age of ten. By the time he was thirteen he needed a more experienced teacher. His father replaced the original upright piano with a baby grand, signaling that he was now less opposed to his son's interest in music. Although Sam Bernstein feared that the field of music was too risky and uncertain to ensure a secure future, in 1935 he paid $300 to the radio station WBZ in Boston to broadcast a series of piano recitals by his son. That year Bernstein entered Harvard University, majoring in music. He also met Aaron Copland, who remained a close friend throughout his life. Bernstein had planned to become a concert pianist, but after he graduated and began attending the Curtis Institute of Music, he got more involved in orchestration. He also spent the summers of 1940–43 at the Boston Symphony Orchestra's Tanglewood Institute in Massachusetts. In 1942 Koussevitzky invited Bernstein to be an assistant conductor in Tanglewood. In this position, the young man was noticed by many people in classical music circles.

The conductor Arthur Rodzinski had taken over the New York Philharmonic after Toscanini left in 1936. Rodzinski was impressed with Bernstein's performances and style, and in 1943 he offered the twenty-five-year-old a position as his assistant. On November 14, 1943, the conductor Bruno Walter had been scheduled to conduct a live national broadcast of the New York Philharmonic, but he was too unwell, and Rodzinski was away. The assistant to Rodzinski, the unknown Bernstein, was Bruno Walter's last-minute replacement. The night before this concert Bernstein had attended the premiere of his song cycle *I Hate Music* and then later had gone to a party that lasted until dawn. Later that morning Bernstein received the call to conduct; the concert was scheduled for three in the afternoon, so there was no chance for a rehearsal. Bernstein was only able to meet quickly with Walter to review the scores and get to the concert. The program planned for that Sunday afternoon broadcast was very demanding, and this was the first time the Philharmonic was to be led by an American-born and American-trained conductor. Bernstein instantly became famous and appeared on the front page of the *New York Times*. After that concert, his conducting career rapidly advanced. Within two years of his live broadcast from Carnegie Hall, Bernstein became the director of the New York City Symphony Orchestra. In 1951 the composer married Felicia Montealegre Cohn, an actress and pianist from Chile.

In 1944 Bernstein's Symphony No. 1: *Jeremiah* was performed by the Pittsburgh Symphony Orchestra, with the composer conducting. He had begun writing the work in 1939 after graduating from Harvard and decided to complete it in 1942 for a competition sponsored by the New England Conservatory of Music. He completed the piano score just ten days from the day he learned about the competition. He asked his sister, Shirley, and others to complete making a copy of the score while he continued to orchestrate the piece, which took three more days. By the time *Jeremiah* was finished it was too late to mail the score and get it into the judges' hands by the closing date, so Bernstein took a train to Boston and delivered it in person just prior to the deadline. *Jeremiah* did not win the contest, but it won the New York Music Critics' Circle Award for 1944. Dedicated to his father, it was one of Bernstein's many works that use Jewish themes.

The ballet *Fancy Free*, bursting with Bernstein's mixture of classical and jazz components, is about three sailors on leave in New York. The composer later adapted and expanded the ballet to become a Broadway musical titled *On the Town*. The show opened in 1944 and ran for 463 performances. Shakespeare's *Romeo and Juliet* was the source for Bernstein's most famous work, *West Side Story*, composed in 1957. The musical's story involved not Shakespeare's feuding families in Verona, Italy, but rival gangs of white and Puerto Rican youths in a poor New York City neighborhood—a major social issue at the time. *West Side Story* received rave reviews. It ran for two years on Broadway and then toured for a year before returning to Broadway for another run. The movie made of the musical won many Academy Awards in 1961, including the award for Best Picture.

Bernstein believed strongly in bringing classical music to the a broader audience. Starting in 1954 he appeared on the CBS television program *Omnibus* in a concert and lecture series. He was featured on the cover of *Time* magazine in February 1957 and labeled a "Wunderkind" (child wonder). In 1958 Bernstein was appointed director of the New York Philharmonic, a position he held for eleven years. With the Philharmonic he continued to use the medium of television to achieve his goal of reaching the general public. His *Young People's Concerts*, which began in 1958, were broadcast nationwide and in Canada and were syndicated to forty other countries. In this televised series, Bernstein and the orchestra brought classical music into homes across America for fourteen seasons. In 1959 his book *The Joy of Music* was published. His introduction spells out his view of "the public ... [as] an intelligent organism, more often than not longing for insight and knowledge," and his desire to inform them.

Bernstein's 1980 *Divertimento for Orchestra*, which was composed for and dedicated to the Boston Symphony Orchestra on the occasion of its centenary, expresses Bernstein's fond memories of the city. The work is filled with humorous suggestions of the music he heard in his youth. It is unified by a two-note theme: the notes B and C represent Boston and Centennial. The piece also contains two twelve-tone rows, fanfares, and lots of longing for that earlier time.

In 1985, on the fortieth anniversary of the dropping of the atomic bomb on Japan during World War II, Bernstein toured with the European Community Youth Orchestra. He also conducted a concert at the dismantling of the Berlin Wall in 1989 that featured musicians from all the countries that had been involved with the original partitioning of Germany. The concert was broadcast to an audience of around 100 million people in more than twenty countries.

Bernstein conducted his final performance at Tanglewood on August 19, 1990, with the Boston Symphony. He died on October 14, 1990. Bernstein's career opened new vistas for his younger colleagues and for other American conductors who followed him. He championed the works of various composers and received dozens of honorary degrees and awards. Beginning in 1953 and continuing until 1967, Bernstein gave his most important music manuscripts to the Library of Congress.

Bernstein's music evidenced the influences of Jewish liturgical music, jazz, American popular music, and the composers Mahler, Gershwin, and Copland. He is remembered mostly for his wide range of abilities and for his stage and film music. Bernstein was quoted in the *New York Times* as saying, "I don't want to spend my life, as Toscanini did, studying and restudying the same fifty pieces of music. It would bore me to death. I want to conduct. I want to play the piano. I want to write for Hollywood. I want to keep on trying to be, in the full sense of that wonderful word, a musician. I also want to teach. I want to write books and poetry. And I think I can still do justice to them all."

NED ROREM

The current state of music presents a variety of solutions in search of a problem, the problem being to find someone to listen.

NED ROREM, COMPOSER (BORN 1923)

Ned Rorem was born in Richmond, Indiana, on October 23, 1923, the second of two children. His parents were Quakers and pacifists after World War I because his mother's brother had been killed in battle. Rorem also believed in pacifist principles throughout his life. The family moved to Chicago when he was a youngster. His father was a medical economist, and his mother was active in pacifist movements. In Chicago Rorem began piano lessons and attended concerts.

His teachers nurtured his interests in American and French musical traditions. Rorem studied at the American Conservatory before he attended the school of music at Northwestern University. In 1943 he was offered a scholarship from the Curtis Institute in Philadelphia. A year later he moved to New York and got a job as a copyist with Virgil Thomson; Thomson paid him a small salary and provided composition and orchestration lessons. Rorem also took lessons for two summers in 1946 and 1947 from Aaron Copland at the Berkshire Music Center at Tanglewood. Rorem first received a bachelor's degree from the Juilliard School of Music; in 1948 he earned a master's degree from the same school.

Rorem had performed the compositions of Ravel and Debussy and was very impressed with their works. The idea of absorbing the culture of France and the traditions of French musicians drew him there. After completing his master's degree, the young man went to Morocco, where he learned to speak French and penned a number of his early works, including twenty orchestral compositions. In 1950 Rorem traveled to France to study composition; he had initially planned to spend three months in France but ended up staying there from 1949 until 1957. He won several awards and scholarships, including a Fulbright Fellowship in 1951.

Rorem's opera *Miss Julie* is based on a play by the Swedish writer August Strindberg. Commissioned by the New York City Opera, it was premiered in 1965 to poor reviews. The opera was revised by the composer in 1979 into a one-act format that was highly praised by the critics. In 1976 Rorem was awarded the Pulitzer Prize for his orchestral suite *Air Music*.

In 1998 Rorem composed *Evidence of Things Not Seen*, a cycle of thirty-six songs set to the poetry of twenty-four poets, including Elizabeth Barrett Browning, William Wordsworth, Edna St. Vincent Millay, and Oscar Wilde. It was commissioned by the Library of Congress and the New York Festival of Song. The assignment allowed Rorem to realize his dream of composing a piece that would sum up his work in the realm of the art song. It was completed in time for his seventy-fifth birthday. *Evidence of Things Not Seen* is scored for four voices and piano and portrays a person's life cycle, with the songs divided into three sections: Beginnings, Middles, and Ends. This concert-length piece, which was premiered at New York's Carnegie Hall, is the composer's largest work and requires an entire evening for a performance.

Rorem wrote *Aftermath* in 2001 for baritone and a trio including piano, violin, and cello. The composer noted, "I wrote these sketches during the days of watching the horror of the attacks of September 11: the collapse of the World Trade Center, the attack on the Pentagon, the plane crash in Pennsylvania." *Aftermath* is a ten-song cycle about the ugliness of war and mortality. The text was taken from poets from the sixteenth through the twentieth centuries. In the program notes the composer wrote, "In the wake of the September 11th shock, I asked what a thousand other composers must have asked: what is the point of music now? But it soon grew clear that music was the only point. Indeed, the future will judge us, as it always judges the past, by our art more than our armies—by construction more than by destruction."

Rorem's music is romantic in approach, French influenced, definitely tonal, and most often lyrical. His compositions cover a wide range, including chamber and choral music, tone poems, and symphonies, but he is best known for his vocal works. His art songs are based on texts from a broad range of poetry and prose. His lyrical songs are known for their charm and humor; his melodies flow with the text to create a mood.

Besides his operas and songs, Rorem composed orchestral pieces, chamber music, ballets, piano pieces, and some incidental music for plays. His early instrumental works were influenced by twentieth-century French composers; later on he plunged into more adventurous harmonies, even trying some serial techniques. However, Rorem has been a believer in tonality throughout his career.

21 Trends in Experimental and Contemporary Music

My music is best understood by children and animals.

IGOR STRAVINSKY, COMPOSER (1882–1971)

I n the 1930s the term "classical" was employed to distinguish between the popular music that was in fashion and the music that was considered to be older and more serious. In the mid-twentieth century, when composers began to experiment and create avant-garde musical languages, the definition of what was classical was expanded to include new styles, forms, and genres. As each new movement grew, it became more complex in variety and more flexible. Western composers were now being influenced by many foreign cultures as well as by the numerous forms of popular music that flourished. Today the term "classical music" appears to have more than one meaning.

Experimental Composers

EDGARD VARÈSE

Everyone is born with genius, but most people only keep it a few minutes.

EDGARD VARÈSE, COMPOSER (1883–1965)

Edgard Varèse

The French composer Edgard Varèse (1883–1965) is called the "Father of Electronic Music." Varèse moved to the United States after the outbreak of World War I Europe; he became a citizen in 1926. *Amériques*, his first orchestral composition in his new country, honored and celebrated his relocation. Working as a conductor, he presented many contemporary composers to the public and cofounded the International Composers' Guild. Varèse understood that new electronic musical instruments would produce novel sounds and offer new musical possibilities. He called his music "organized sound." A tape recorder gave him the opportunity to begin his experimentation in 1937; eventually, as new electronic resources were invented, he incorporated their capabilities into his works.

In 1937 Varèse stopped composing, since he felt that he was not able to find the sounds he believed were necessary for him to continue. Years later, in the 1950s, a tape recorder and the availability of electronic instruments inspired him to return to writing music. *Poème électronique* (Electronic Poem) was written for the 1958 World's Fair in Brussels, Belgium. It is a purely electronic work using multimedia, and many sources supply the sound. The piece was very advanced for the time; it employed machines, fragments of music, lights, and even the architecture: the sound was piped over 400 loudspeakers in a pavilion.

Varèse composed only about a dozen pieces, but his concept of organized sound influenced many composers. He is known for his unconventional use of instruments and his interest in new sources of sound. His quite dissonant music features an emphasis on timbre (musical color) and complex rhythms. The composer sought progress in the development of electronic instruments. In 1941 he wrote to Léon Theremin, the inventor one of the first electronic musical instruments, to ask him if he had developed any new instruments. Theremin had returned to the Soviet Union, though, and it is said that he did not know about this letter until he returned to the West in 1989. Varèse integrated all kinds of sounds in his compositions and greatly influenced the avant-garde composers of the mid-twentieth century.

HENRY COWELL

Henry Cowell (1897–1965) wrote music that was influenced by many cultures. His experiments with tone clusters, which consist of three or more adjacent notes sounded at the same time, and simultaneously played complex rhythmic patterns created a whirlwind in modern music. The composer's experiments led him to reach inside the piano to brush his hands across the strings in order to add unexpected sounds to his music.

Cowell's ideas were explained in his book *New Musical Resources*; his aim was to "find the universal elements in all music. … Welcome and explore and inquire into everything, new or old, that comes your way, and then build your own music on whatever your inner life has been able to take in and offer you back again." His String Quartet No. 3, known as the *Mosaic* Quartet, allows the performers to determine the order and the variation of the movements. *Twenty-Six Simultaneous Mosaics*, written in 1963, lets the performers make even more decisions about the outcome of the pieces, including where they stop and start. Many of his ideas were embraced by composers who had very dissimilar styles, ranging from John Cage to George Gershwin.

JOHN CAGE

Sound and rhythm have too long been submissive to the restrictions of nineteenth century music. Today we are fighting for their emancipation. Tomorrow, with electronic music in our ears, we will hear freedom.

JOHN CAGE, COMPOSER (1912–1992)

John Cage (1912–1992) was born in Los Angeles, California. His father was an inventor. Cage was fascinated by the writings of James Joyce and Ezra Pound. He attended Pomona College in Claremont, California, but was disappointed with his studies and dropped out in his second year. Hoping to become a either a minister or a writer, Cage convinced his parents he needed to travel to Europe to experience more of life and culture. Cage first went to Paris, where he became interested in architecture, modern music, and painting. He then went to Spain and started painting and composing. He stayed in Europe for eighteen months; before he left, Cage destroyed the music he had composed there, since he had decided none of it was good.

Returning to California, the young Cage used the poetry of Gertrude Stein as the basis for his *Three Songs for Voice and Piano*. He met the pianist Richard Buhlig, who preferred the challenge of contemporary music; Buhlig agreed to work with Cage on his compositions. Cage then went to New York to study with the avant-garde composer, pianist, and theorist Henry Cowell, who suggested that the young man seek to work with Adolph Weiss, the first American student of Arnold Schoenberg. This led Cage, back in California, to approach Schoenberg for lessons. As Cage related in a lecture, when Schoenberg told Cage that he probably could not afford the master's fee, Cage replied that he had no money. Schoenberg then asked him if he was ready to devote himself to music, and when Cage responded that he was, Schoenberg offered to teach him for free. That was when Cage gave up painting and concentrated on music.

After studying with Schoenberg for two years, Cage found that Schoenberg's twelve-tone technique did not match his own views about composition. His works in the 1930s included *Inventions on the Subjects of the Solo* and *Composition for Three Voices*; these pieces reflected elements of Schoenberg's style. Eventually several disagreements arose between Schoenberg and Cage. Schoenberg was focused on harmony and twelve-tone methodology, while Cage viewed musical structure differently and thought that rhythm should be the focus.

Cage believed that music was to be found everywhere in everything. He started to write experimental pieces using common household objects. The score of his *Living Room Music* for percussion quartet suggested that any household objects or architectural elements could be used to produce the sounds for this piece. He recommended using magazines, newspapers, the furniture, or the floor, since the work is based entirely on the elements of pulse and rhythm.

In 1938 Cage accepted a position as a percussion teacher at the Cornish School of the Arts in Seattle, Washington, where he also worked as an accompanist for dancers. At the Cornish School he established a percussion ensemble that performed modern works and his compositions. The ensemble toured the West Coast and was certainly noticed. Cage was asked to write music for *Bacchanale*, a dance with an African theme created by Syvilla Fort, the first black student at the Cornish School. The stage was too small for his percussion ensemble, however, so Cage decided to adapt the piano to his needs. His teacher, Henry Cowell, had also treated the piano in a non-traditional manner. Cage decided to use what he called a "prepared piano," in which he placed a variety of objects on or between the piano strings or on the dampers for a percussive effect. These objects, such as coins, nuts and bolts, wood, and pieces of rubber, altered the tone and pitch of the piano keys and turned the piano into a percussion instrument. Almost all of his compositions that were composed between 1943 and 1945 were written for various types of prepared pianos.

The Wonderful Widow of Eighteen Springs, composed in 1942, is the earliest of Cage's songs for voice and closed piano. The accompaniment is created by tapping and knocking on the wooden cover over the piano keys. That year he also wrote *In the Name of the Holocaust* for prepared piano; his directions for this work include plucking the strings of the piano and playing note clusters with the arm or the flat hand.

Cage taught percussion at the Chicago School of Design, where his classes caused so much noise that the other professors complained. Cage had a great interest in rhythmic structure. He was a composer of chance music, which left some of the elements to be decided by the situation or occasion. In this type of music the composer's contribution to the end product is greatly reduced or possibly entirely removed. In 1943 Cage moved to New York City; there he reconnected with many of the artists he had gotten to know in Europe. His concert debut created a stir: it featured flowerpots and assorted gadgets as instruments. Cage experimented with oscillators, electronic devices, magnetic tape, and a variety of sounds to pursue his musical concepts. He was attracted to Zen Buddhism and Eastern philosophy.

Cage earned awards from the Guggenheim Foundation and National Academy of Arts and Letters for this work. In 1948 Cage joined the faculty of Black Mountain College in North Carolina, where his colleague Robert Rauschenberg had created a series of "white paintings": they contained no image but simply responded to the light in a room. Rauschenberg's paintings inspired Cage to allow the sounds of the room to be heard during each performance. Working with Cunningham and Rauschenberg at Black Mountain College, Cage produced sounds for performances and examined how music composed through chance could be developed into something extraordinary.

After spending a year traveling in Europe, Cage returned to New York and became involved with the work of the composer Morton Feldman, who was experimenting with different forms of notation that allowed the performer more freedom. Between 1950 and 1970 Cage became increasingly concerned with the creation of "open form" works, which limit the control the composer exercises over the work and are significantly different from performance to performance. Continuing to experiment, Cage used the concepts suggested by the *I Ching* (an ancient Chinese book whose title is translated as Book of Changes) as a method of selecting the components of his works by throwing dice or a coin and working out a chart to outline a composition. His 1951 *Music of Changes* was composed using the I Ching method; every pitch, interval, and combination of sounds, as well as its duration and volume, was determined by tossing coins onto the charts to decide how they would combine. It was up to the performer to navigate the score and reason it all out. *Music of Changes* was the first work to be fully composed using chance operations. The score contains eighty pages of instructions regarding the performance of the work, including closing the piano lid and knocking under the keyboard.

Cage was unhappy with the outcome of this approach and decided that his future works had to be more variable, more left to chance, meaning that they had to be indeterminate. His 1956 *Radio Music* calls for one to eight performers to tune radios to certain notated frequencies for six minutes. The mixture that results is dependent upon the time of day, the location of the performance, and the radio stations that are received in the area, as well as the number of performers.

Silence and stillness were qualities that Cage admired. His most talked-about piece is his work *4'33"*, which has the musician simply sit at a piano for four minutes and thirty-three seconds. Cage believed that the music came from people paying attention to the atmosphere and vibes of the room. He believed there was no such thing as complete silence and that the most important act of a musical performance was not making the music but listening. The piece was premiered on August 29, 1952, at Woodstock, New York, during a recital of contemporary piano music. The audience watched as a man sat down in front of the piano and lifted the lid. Without playing any notes, he closed the lid and continued to sit there. The performer held a stopwatch while turning the pages of the score; after a certain amount of time he lifted the lid before closing it once again and standing up. Cage's *4'33"* is still very controversial and challenges the commonly accepted definition of music.

Cage achieved an international reputation, and in 1968 he was elected to the National Institute of Arts and Letters. Cage staged many public concerts he called "Happenings," where he often asked the audience to participate in the piece. These were often unmusical programs that called for people to bang on walls or garbage cans that they would bring in from the street. Sometimes Happenings were complicated performances that were intended to remove the differences between the performer and the audience or the presentation and reality.

In 1967 the first *Musicircus* was presented at the University of Illinois. The Musicircus consisted of dancers, singers, jazz bands, pianists, slide shows, black lights, colorful balloons, and popcorn. Cage wanted to blend all of these into a single event so that the audience members could create their own experience of the piece. On May 16, 1969, Cage collaborated with Lejaren Hiller on a work called *HPSCHD*, which employed seven harpsichords playing music selected by chance of various composers, including variations by Mozart, fifty-one tapes of computer-generated sounds, swirling images, slides that NASA provided of outer space, and slides of abstract designs, as well as forty-one films. All of these were presented at the same time. Cage had created multidirectional music that offered forever-changing possibilities.

Between 1987 and 1990 Cage composed a major series of works entitled *Europeras*, which are numbered from 1 to 5 and consist of fragments of operas from the eighteenth and nineteenth centuries. Cage added props, light effects, pantomime, costumes selected by the performers, and, in *Europera 5*, masks of animals, a radio, and a television. The composer combined the fragments of existing libretti according to chance, so there is no actual plot, and the works do not develop dramatically. The music, text, and scenery change independently of each other, and a computer program randomly determines when the singers and/ or the instrumentalists should play.

Cage toured Europe and the United States as a lecturer and performer; he also wrote several books. One of his last works is entitled *One11*; it is a silent work composed entirely of random images of electric light in an empty space. *One11* was written several months before his death. Cage died in New York City a few weeks before a celebration of his eightieth birthday.

STEVE REICH

I discovered that the most interesting music of all was made by simply lining the loops in unison, and letting them slowly shift out of phase with other.

STEVE REICH, COMPOSER (BORN 1936)

Steve Reich (born 1936) is an American modernist composer. Although he dislikes being described as a minimalist, he will probably always be associated with that term. Reich was born in New York. His mother was a singer and songwriter and his father was a lawyer; they separated when Reich was a year old. The youngster therefore spent much of his time traveling between New York and California. As a child he took piano lessons but did not get really excited about music. In his teens, though, Reich was introduced to more modern composers and developed a great attraction for music.

Once he was exposed to the music that really interested him, Reich became more involved in learning about the composers and their styles. He started to listen seriously to the works of twentieth-century composers such as Igor Stravinsky, Béla Bartók, and Arnold Schoenberg. In 1957 Reich graduated from Cornell University with a degree in philosophy; he had minored in music. Accepted at Harvard for an advanced degree in philosophy, Reich suddenly changed his plans and decided to attend the Juilliard School, which he did from 1958 to 1961.

In 1961 Reich enrolled in Mills College in Oakland, California, for a master's degree in composition; there he studied with Darius Milhaud and Luciano Berio. After graduation he wrote music for the San Francisco Mime Troupe and the San Francisco Tape Music Center. In 1965 he returned to New York City, where he began to perform in concerts held at art galleries and various museums. He also established his own ensemble in 1966; the group started with three musicians and eventually grew to eighteen. The ensemble continues as a flexible group ranging from two to eighteen or more players.

After experimenting with twelve-tone techniques, Reich realized that he was more interested in the rhythmic than in the pitch elements of music. His first major work, *It's Gonna Rain*, was composed in 1965. This was the era of the American cold war with the Soviet Union and the Cuban Missile Crisis. Reich taped the voice Brother William, an African American Pentecostal preacher, speaking in San Francisco's Union Square. The minister was preaching about the end of the world and comparing it to the biblical account of Noah's flood. The various noises heard in the background during his discourse were included in the piece. The phrase "It's gonna rain" is repeated throughout the piece in a process called looping. Reich experimented with tape loops to create sounds that were somewhat suggestive of Gregorian chant. *It's Gonna Rain* is a prime example of minimalist and process music (music created by a process or a system).

Reich has also employed phasing that allows a rhythmic figure to move out of phase with itself. The 1966 work *Come Out* used two tape loops set to run at two slightly different speeds so that the tapes start together but gradually begin to shift out of rhythm with each other, causing them to move "out of phase." This generates another set of harmonies and rhythms, which then develop. In *Come Out*, the single phrase "Come out to show them" is recorded on two channels. The piece begins with the words being presented in unison, and then one voice begins to move ahead. As the phrase begins to shift, it slowly becomes a sort of canon or round until eventually the two voices divide into four and then eight. As the ability to understand the phrases diminishes, the listener hears a constantly changing polyphony of the rhythmic elements. *It's Gonna Rain* and *Come Out* were landmark events in tape/electronic music.

Reich's *Four Organs* was written in 1970. In this work, instead of using phase-shifting techniques, Reich focused on rhythmic augmentation (the lengthening or widening of rhythm or interval), which stretched the sound of a single chord from very short to very long. Reich has always been interested in how melody and rhythm interact; he played the drums in bands throughout high school and college. A grant from the Institute for International Education enabled Reich to go to Ghana for a summer to take courses in drumming at the Institute for African Studies at the University of Ghana in 1970. He came to the conclusion that percussion could be a dominant voice in a complex work.

On his return from Ghana, Reich composed *Drumming* for a nine-piece percussion ensemble with female voices and piccolo. *Drumming* was composed in four sections: part 1 for eight tuned bongo drums, part 2 for three marimbas and female voices, part 3 for glockenspiels and piccolo, and part 4 with all of the instruments combined. The work is an hourlong expansion of a single rhythmic cell containing a symmetrical twelve-beat phrase (eight notes and four rests) that is developed throughout the four parts, creating new melodic and harmonic patterns. His 1972 *Clapping Music* was written for two sets of hands. In this piece, one performer claps a steady pulse while the other moves ahead suddenly.

Reich further investigated non-Western musical concepts when he attended the American Society for Eastern Arts in Seattle and Berkeley, California, where he took classes in gamelan instruments and musical styles. Gamelan instruments come from the island of Bali and include an assortment of gongs, drums, flutes, and bronze metallophones (tuned metal bars that make sounds when they are struck with a mallet). Starting in 1973, the composer turned to writing for larger ensembles. His *Music for 18 Musicians* was based on a cycle of eleven chords, and the sections are appropriately named "Pulses." In this piece, written for a cello, violin, two clarinets, four pianos, three marimbas, two xylophones, maracas, a metallophone, and four women's voices, Reich presents the experience of gamelan style.

From 1976 to 1977 Reich turned to his own religious heritage when he studied the Bible and the traditional Hebrew chants used to read the Bible; he traveled to Jerusalem, Israel, to expand his education. His 1981 piece *Tehillim* (Psalms) is based on the Hebrew texts. In his composer's notes about this work Reich explained,

> There is no fixed meter or metric pattern in *Tehillim* as there is in my earlier music. The rhythm, of the music here comes directly from the rhythm of the Hebrew text and is consequently in flexible changing meters ... the overall sound of *Tehillim* and in particular the intricately interlocking percussion writing which, together with the text, forms the basis of the entire work, marks this music as unique by introducing a basic musical element that one does not find in earlier Western practice including the music of this century. *Tehillim* may thus be heard as traditional and new at the same time.

Different Trains, often considered to be Reich's masterpiece, is somewhat like his earlier works *It's Gonna Rain* and *Come Out* in the sense that the music is drawn from recorded speech. Composed in 1988, *Different Trains* contrasts the trains that during his childhood carried him back and forth between his parents' homes in New York and California with the trains of Europe that during the same time period carried the Jewish Holocaust victims to their deaths. Reich employs recorded voices, train whistles, sirens, and a string quartet in this haunting and disturbing piece. In the work the speech recordings produce the material for the musical instruments. *Different Trains* is a memorial to the Jews of Europe murdered during the Holocaust.

Daniel Variations, a choral work, was composed in tribute to the American journalist Daniel Pearl, who was kidnapped in 2002 and killed by his captors while reporting a story in Pakistan. Daniel Pearl's father had contacted Reich to explore the idea of having the composer commemorate his son's life in music. It seemed to Reich that this was just the theme he was seeking for his next project. Daniel Pearl had been an accomplished performer on the violin and mandolin, so Reich enlarged the string section of his ensemble to symbolize this detail. The composer wrote four contrasting movements using language from the biblical Book of Daniel for the first movement and Pearl's last words for the second. In the third movement Reich returned to the Book of Daniel, and in the fourth and final movement Reich selected another phrase of Pearl's. Reich has often used sensitive subject matter in his work. *Daniel Variations* became the focus of the celebration of Reich's seventieth birthday in 2006.

The *New Yorker* magazine called the composer "the most original musical thinker of our time." In 2007 Reich, along with Sonny Rollins, was awarded the Swedish Polar Music Prize, an international recognition of his achievements in music. On April 20, 2009, Reich was awarded the 2009 Pulitzer Prize for Music for his twenty-two-minute piece *Double Sextet*. The composer states in his notes, "The piece can be played in two ways; either with 12 musicians, or with six playing against a recording of themselves." His compositions have influenced many experimental and avant-garde musicians; Reich's aim has been to simplify music to pulse and tone. He has blazed his own path to create something new and distinctive.

PHILIP GLASS

I'm interested in all kinds of music, and sooner or later most of those musics find their way into my own compositions.

PHILIP GLASS, COMPOSER (BORN 1937)

Philip Glass (born 1937) comes from Baltimore, Maryland, and is the son of Jewish immigrants from Lithuania. His father owned a radio repair shop that also sold records. He brought home many records; the three Glass children listened to the recordings of the works of Beethoven and Schubert as well as contemporary music and jazz. At the age of six Glass began taking violin lessons, and at the age of eight he started studying the flute at the Peabody Conservatory of Music. During his sophomore year of high school he decided, with the approval of his parents, to apply for admission to the University of Chicago. He passed an early-entrance examination and was accepted.

The young man moved to Chicago to begin his college education, majoring in philosophy and mathematics. Glass worked in a restaurant waiting on tables to help support himself. He also began to compose music, having taught himself twelve-tone technique. He graduated from college at the age of nineteen. In 1959 he won a prize sponsored by the Broadcast Music Incorporated Foundation's BMI Student Composer Awards.

Having decided that he wished to become a composer, Glass went on to study composition at the Juilliard School in New York, where he also concentrated on keyboard instruments and earned his master's degree in 1962. After graduating from Juilliard, Glass received a grant from the Ford Foundation to be composer-in-residence for the Contemporary Music Project in Pittsburgh, writing music for the public school system. At this time he was composing serialist works.

Still searching for his own musical style and with a Fulbright Scholarship, Glass traveled to Europe; in 1965 he arranged to spend two years studying with Nadia Boulanger. During his second year with Boulanger the French filmmaker Conrad Roods hired Glass to transcribe, in Western musical notation, the music of the Indian sitar (a stringed instrument) player and composer Ravi Shankar and the tabla drum player Ustad Alla Rakha that was to be used in the score of a film. This allowed Glass to experience Indian music, and he became very attracted to its techniques and traditions.

In the United States, during the middle of the twentieth century, many young people began to seek new directions from other cultures. Glass joined this search; intending to further his education in Eastern music, he journeyed to India, North Africa, and the Himalayas. Upon his return to the United States, Glass rejected all of his earlier compositions, which had been composed in a style that had been influenced by the works of Aaron Copland, Charles Ives, Darius Milhaud, and Samuel Barber. His research had led him in a new direction, and his music now reflected the techniques he had gleaned from Eastern music: hypnotically repeating rhythmic components with stark textures. Glass continued to work with Shankar, who was a visiting professor at the City College of New York, when he returned to the United States in 1967.

Glass developed friendships with other young composers, including Steve Reich. In 1968 the Philip Glass Ensemble was born. It consisted of a small group of musicians performing on electronically amplified instruments, and the composer wrote many pieces for it. Now his music was released from the Western notions of rhythm and the ideas of clear musical divisions of time. His new works contained rhythmic cells, figures that would reappear with minor additions or subtractions of notes or some other type of transformation. Glass and his ensemble began presenting performances—mainly in art galleries, since minimalist music was still, at that point, outside the accepted repertoire of most concert halls. During this time he also worked as a taxicab driver and a plumber.

In 1974 Glass completed *Music in 12 Parts*, a work that stretches out over at least three hours. The composer wrote units of varying length that are repeated an indefinite number of times; changing to the next part is simply designated by the "conductor" with a gesture such as a nod of the head. The audience listens as the slight variations from unit to unit become more apparent, and they may try to predict when the next change will take place. Each of the twelve parts examines a single musical idea.

Glass sought to compose three operas about men who changed the world in which they lived through the influence of their ideas. Composed in 1975, his first large-scale opera, *Einstein on the Beach*, is in four acts and is written for ensemble, chorus, and soloists. Created with the playwright and director/designer Robert Wilson, it breaks all of the conventional rules about opera. The opera was first performed in Paris, Venice, Brussels, Hamburg, and New York. It takes about five hours to complete, and there are no intermissions; instead, the audience is expected to walk about during performances. *Einstein on the Beach* has no actual plot; rather, it revolves around reflections about the brilliant mathematician and scientist Albert Einstein. The opera is made up of nine connected twenty-minute-long scenes separated by what Wilson called "knee plays" that allow an interlude for scenery changes. The words in the opera consisted of numbers, nonsense phrases, solfège syllables, and some puzzling poetry. The work was extremely distinctive, and it met with a mixed response from the audience.

In 1980 Glass composed *Satyagraha* (Force for Truth); it was considered a more "traditional" operatic work. Satyagraha was a philosophy introduced by Mahatma Gandhi of India that was fundamental to his concept of non-violent resistance to political oppression. It is scored for strings, woodwinds, organ, six solo singers, and a chorus of forty. The libretto was written in Sanskrit, a very ancient Indian language, and is based on the *Bhagavad-Gita*, an ancient Sanskrit text. The opera focuses on Gandhi's years in South Africa and features Glass's repeated musical patterns.

Akhnaten, the third opera in Glass's series of portrait trilogies, which also includes *Einstein on the Beach* and *Satyagraha*, was written in 1983 in three acts for orchestra, chorus, and soloists. The libretto uses Egyptian, Arcadian, and Hebrew texts as well as the language of the audience; it was written by the composer in association with Shalom Goldman, Robert Israel, and Richard Riddell. The opera describes the rise, reign, and defeat of the ancient Egyptian pharaoh Akhnaten, the first monotheist in recorded history. A scribe presents translations in the language of the audience to bridge the scenes. In the unique final scene, set in the present time, tourists including Akhnaten and his family visit an ancient Egyptian site.

Glass wished to write a piece that would represent a broad spectrum of many of the world's great "wisdom" traditions. His Symphony No. 5 begins before the creation of the world and portrays life and paradise; it ends with a future dedication to enlightenment. The texts, in Hebrew, Chinese, Greek, Sanskrit, Arabic, Japanese, and other languages, are performed by a chorus, a children's choir, and soloists. His Symphony No. 8, which premiered in 2005 at the Brooklyn Academy of Music in New York City, is a purely instrumental piece, and each of its three movements is distinctive.

Today only a few minimalist composers remain familiar to audiences. Glass never speaks of himself as a minimalist composer; in an online biography he states that he prefers to be called a composer of "music with repetitive structures." His music consists of fascinating rhythms with extended repetitions of tonal and melodic fragments that interact and transform. He is often labeled a controversial composer, since minimalist music is viewed as unacceptable to the people who prefer a more traditional classical repertoire; in their view, Glass and other contemporary composers have violated the goals of classical music by bringing in the influences of non-Western cultures.

Glass has composed more than twenty operas, eight symphonies, works for solo piano, and two concertos for piano, as well as concertos for violin, piano, timpani, and saxophone quartet and orchestra. He has written soundtracks for films, including the original music for *The Truman Show*, which won a Golden Globe Award for Best Score in 1999. Glass's opera *Appomattox*, commissioned by the San Francisco Opera in honor of the composer's seventieth birthday, premiered in 2007. It is based on the surrender of the Confederate General Robert E. Lee to the Union General Ulysses S. Grant at Appomattox, Virginia, at the end of the American Civil War. In the November 5, 2007, edition of the *New Yorker* magazine, the music critic Alex Ross stated, "Philip Glass is without a doubt America's most famous living composer of classical music."

JOHN ADAMS

Also classified as a minimalist, John Adams (born 1947) developed his own personal musical language in his works, which range from operatic to symphonic. He was born in Massachusetts and raised in New England; the composer-conductor now lives in the San Francisco Bay area.

As a youngster Adams studied the clarinet. He composed his first piece of music when he was ten, and it was performed a few years later. Adams attended Harvard University; during his student days he conducted the Bach Society Orchestra and played the clarinet as a replacement instrumentalist for the Boston Symphony and the Boston Opera Company. The composer received both his bachelor's and master's degrees from Harvard.

Adams wrote his first opera, *Nixon in China*, in the mid-1980s. The opera had been commissioned by the Brooklyn Academy of Music, the Houston Grand Opera, and the John F. Kennedy Center for the Performing Arts. It premiered in 1987 in Houston, Texas. The work is based on President Richard M. Nixon's historic trip to China in 1972. The libretto, by Alice Goodman, draws attention to all of the diplomatic details that surrounded this groundbreaking voyage of an American president to communist China. The opera unfolds over the course of three acts with repetitive phrases that capture the nervousness of the participants in the event. The soaring arias, the tonal music, and the ballet in act 2 make this work seem more of a romantic work than the creation of a minimalist.

Adams received the 2003 Pulitzer Prize for music for his *On the Transmigration of Souls*, written as a remembrance of the people who lost their lives during the September 11, 2001, attacks on the World Trade Center. The piece features a chorus, a children's chorus, an orchestra, and pre-recorded sound. Premiered by the New York Philharmonic in 2002, the text uses parts of the words left on posters and memorials that were placed around Ground Zero. *On the Transmigration of Souls* employs voices and instruments plus recorded sounds. A choir and a youth choir chant the text while the orchestra and the background sounds rise and fall. The work is a powerful experience for the listeners.

A member of the American Academy of Arts and Letters, Adams also was presented with the Centennial Medal of Harvard University's Graduate School of Arts and Sciences and was the first-ever recipient of the Nemmers Prize in Music Composition. New York's Lincoln Center presented a program entitled "John Adams: An American Master" in 2003. Adams was the composer-in-residence at Carnegie Hall from 2003 until 2007. In 2009 Adams received the National Endowment for the Arts Opera Honors. His dramatic works have been performed by all of the major orchestras in the United States and many of the foremost orchestras throughout the world.

LUKAS FOSS

Lukas Foss (1922–2009) was a composer, conductor, and pianist born in Berlin, Germany. His father was an attorney, and his mother was an artist. In 1933 his family escaped Nazi Germany and moved to Paris, where he was able to further his musical education. Foss came to the United States in 1937 and became an American citizen in 1942. After graduating from the Curtis Institute of Music, Foss began conducting with Serge Koussevitzky at Tanglewood and took classes in composition with Paul Hindemith at Yale. In 1953 he took over Arnold Schoenberg's position as the head of

Lukas Foss

the music department at the University of California, Los Angeles. Foss urged his students to improvise and formed the Improvisation Chamber Ensemble in 1957.

Foss enjoyed experimenting with the avant-garde; his interests ranged from serialism to electronic music. *Baroque Variations*, composed in 1967, contains three movements, each based on a baroque composer. The work employs fragments of Bach, Scarlatti, and Handel combined with unusual and unexpected musical events. Foss conducted several orchestras: the Buffalo Philharmonic in the 1960s, the Jerusalem Symphony in the 1970s, and the Milwaukee Symphony in the 1980s. He died in New York in 2009.

Foss's polystylism (the use of two or more musical styles in a single composition), experiments with chance music, and improvisation prompted Aaron Copland to say that Foss had written "among the most original and stimulating compositions in American music." In 1983 he was elected to the American Academy and Institute of Arts and Letters; Foss also twice received the New York Music Critics' Circle Award, once for his oratorio *The Prairie* and once for *Time Cycle*, a work for soprano and orchestra that employs atonal and twelve-tone techniques.

A New Generation of Composers

Serialism was at one time considered to be the future of classical music, but now that trend has diminished and others have taken its place. New ideas attract contemporary composers who try to write music that reflects and expresses our current era and that sounds new and distinctive. There are many composers who blend together a unique sound.

CHEN YI

At present there is a generation of American composers born and brought up in Asia. Chen Yi (born 1952), originally from Guangzhou, China, was the recipient of the prestigious Charles Ives Living Award from the American Academy of Arts and Letters, a Grammy Award, and the Lili Boulanger Award, among others. She holds degrees from China's Beijing Central Conservatory, where she was the first Chinese woman to receive a master's degree in music, and from New York's Columbia University.

Her music combines Chinese and Western traditions and often includes Asian instruments in her pieces. A chamber work, *Chinese Fables*, incorporates a pipa (a four-stringed Chinese instrument), an erhu (a Chinese violin), cello, and percussion. The piece conveys her musical interpretations of three well-known Chinese fables. In 2006 Chen was appointed the three-year Changjiang Scholar Visiting Professor at the Beijing Central Conservatory of Music by the China Ministry of Education. She also serves on the boards of the National Endowment for the Arts and the International Alliance of Women in Music.

The minimalist movement, which includes Steve Reich and Philip Glass, has led to post-minimalism. Minimalist music (also known as systems music) began in the 1960s as a genre of experimental music that attempts to use a small (or minimal) amount of musical material to create an effect. Although the piece may seem simple to the listener, this system actually requires a great deal of planning on the part of the composer. Minimalists draw from many cultures, since they reject the idea of being limited by Western musical traditions. The musical traditions of India, Africa, and Asia have influenced composers of this genre. Minimalist music usually contains certain distinguishing elements: stripped-down musical patterns, constant repetition of short melodic, rhythmic, and harmonic patterns, and a slow variation of these patterns.

WILLIAM DUCKWORTH

William Duckworth (born 1943) is a leading composer who was the first to compose music using a post-minimalist approach. The first example of this style is Duckworth's *The Time Curve Preludes*, consisting of twenty-four pieces for solo piano. Composed in the late 1970s, each of the preludes develops from a single rhythmic figure; the modal patterns shift and unfold in a smooth melodic and rhythmic manner. The composer used a small quantity of thematic material to expand into a variety of patterns.

William Duckworth

The post-minimalist style evolved over time, and by the 1990s the repertoire was considerably different from the music that had employed the minimalist concepts. In post-minimalism, no rules guide the composer outside of the composition, which is guided solely by the logic of the piece and the thoughts of the composer. In this style one chord has the same value as another, and the sounds may be either consonant or dissonant. In 1997 Duckworth and the computer programmer Nora Farrell created *The Cathedral Project*, the first interactive, continuously evolving work of music and art for the Web.

JULIA WOLFE

Julia Wolfe (born 1958), the cofounder of New York's Bang on a Can Festival, is considered a post-minimalist composer. She is a member of the composition faculty of the Manhattan School of Music. Wolfe's music features new combinations that are bold, dissonant, and rhythmically complex; her focus is on creating artistic sounds. *My Beautiful Scream* was written in response to the attacks on September 11, 2001. It was composed for orchestra and amplified string quartet. Wolfe based the piece on a continual expansion of the emotions of the people who experienced the event, including the blare of police sirens and the screams of victims.

LEJAREN HILLER

Lejaren Hiller (1924–1994), a composer, chemist, and oboist, was the founder of the University of Illinois Experimental Music Studio. Hiller believed that a computer could also compose music. In 1957 Hiller and Leonard Isaacson, a graduate assistant, collaborated to create the *Illiac Suite for String Quartet*, the first piece of music to be written with the assistance of a computer. The men applied programming techniques to music, and the title was derived from the name of the computer: Illinois Automatic Computer. *Illiac Suite for String Quartet* was divided into four movements based on a specific musical experiment that had been applied to generate that movement. The composition caused an uproar in the musical world at the time; today the work is known as Hiller's String Quartet No. 4.

✲

Young composers of classical music today certainly have an expansive field of musical concepts and experiments to draw upon for inspiration. Many composers have examined the traditional views of music and have constructed unusual and interesting directions for their works. Various forms of media and electronic devices have been integrated into their music, adding to the appearance and texture of the composition. This allows stylistic freedom and variety as well as uncommon combinations in contemporary classical music.

As technology advances, there will be new intelligent musical systems that have the ability to develop their own rules for musical composition. They all must have the ability to interact with musicians in a more inventive and sophisticated manner as expectations rise among contemporary composers. Computers and synthesizers have changed and evolved dramatically from their simpler beginnings. Composers will continue to put them to use while trying out new sounds and musical concepts.

22 Music Appreciation

Appreciation is a wonderful thing: It makes what is excellent in others belong to us as well.

VOLTAIRE, FRENCH PHILOSOPHER (1694–1778)

In order to truly appreciate music, you must hear it. Each individual experiences a piece of music differently. Every time you hear the same work, you gain even more insight, which leads to greater enjoyment of the piece. Listening to music with information about its background helps us to understand the historical and technical ingredients that came together to create this composition and heightens our enjoyment of the work. Knowing how a piece of music was put together and why the composer chose to write it that way increases our pleasure.

Music has a definite effect on our emotions and frame of mind. Listening to music is an experience; depending on the mood of the work, it can promote a feeling of peace, or it can make you feel nervous and upset. Recent research has found that music can provide us with a mental and emotional workout, reduce stress, and increase our energy levels. Scientists have been studying the relationship between learning in general and exposure to music; many reports demonstrate a definite connection between music and academic achievement. The Chinese sage Confucius stated, "Music produces a kind of pleasure which human nature cannot do without."

The music of different cultures is often misunderstood and not valued by someone coming from another cultural background. Frequently, to Western ears, Asian music sounds hard to relate to, odd, and unfamiliar—until it is explained (although it is almost impossible to explain music in words), listened to more often, and finally understood. People generally have a preference for certain types of music that is most likely based on the types of music that they have been exposed to over the years. Today a vast variety of styles is readily available. Each person reacts differently to a musical encounter; it is a personal response that cannot be analyzed with complete success. Why does one person gravitate toward Beethoven while another is absolutely enthralled with Hindemith? The only answer can be experience and personal taste.

Some questions that are frequently asked: What actually constitutes classical music today? Are the works of the experimental composers a passing fad? Will the unique compositions written in the present era pass the test of time?

The only classical music that was truly a part of the popular culture in the past was Italian opera in Italy. All of the rest was composed to satisfy the needs of religious rituals or to please the whims and preferences of the patrons of music. The original object of non-religious music was to entertain the nobility and the upper classes; later, music was composed to satisfy the audiences who would attend a concert. Current circumstances have drastically changed the dynamics; the great breadth of musical choices offered today gives the listener an enormous number of possibilities for selection. Now music belongs to the global general public, and only the sale of concert tickets or recordings determines what will remain in demand or what will fade away.

The best way to experience music is to attend a concert, an opera, or a recital. Being present at a live performance adds to your enjoyment because you can see the musicians at work, and also because you get caught up in the enthusiasm radiating from the other people in the audience. Another way to increase your familiarity with music is to listen to a recording or a classical music radio station or to watch a DVD. Orchestras such as the New York Philharmonic and the Los Angeles Philharmonic are establishing direct-to-download recording deals for digital music players. Many great performances are available, and new ones are being issued all the time.

The following tables contain a suggested list of musical pieces from each period. It is important to practice perceptive listening when hearing the music. This means understanding the era in which the piece was composed and what the composer wanted to achieve, as well as how the composer accomplished his goal. Listening to a work in a perceptive manner requires practice, but with effort and some patience, it will lead to a deepening appreciation of music.

Suggested Works

RENAISSANCE

COMPOSER	WORK	WHAT TO HEAR
Roland de Lassus	*Tristis est anima mea*	This is a five-voice motet. Listen for the spiritual quality, the counterpoint, and the flexible rhythms that allow the words to flow.
Giovanni Pierluigi da Palestrina	*Mass for Pope Marcellus*	Written as a Catholic mass for six parts a cappella. It is polyphonic; notice how the voices move independently and still form a balanced harmony.
Claudio Monteverdi	"Tu se' morta" (Orfeo's Lament) from the opera *L'Orfeo*	A recitative in act 2 of the opera. Observe that the vocal line is accompanied by a basso continuo with no ornamentation and that the text is sung in a manner that resembles speech.

BAROQUE

COMPOSER	WORK	WHAT TO HEAR
Jean-Baptiste Lully	Overture to *Thésée*	The overture to this opera is a typical French overture. Notice the dotted rhythms in the opening section.
François Couperin	*Les nations*	A set of four suites in which the composer forged a fusion of the Italian and French musical styles.
Henry Purcell	"When I Am Laid in Earth" (Dido's Lament) from the opera *Dido and Aeneas*	This aria is the most famous one in this opera. The accompaniment is a constantly repeating bass figure.

Antonio Vivaldi	*The Four Seasons*	Vivaldi's well-known work represents the moods of the four seasons. These concertos are part of a larger collection of twelve titled *Il cimento dell'armonia e del'invenzione* (The Contest of Harmony and Invention). This is one of the earliest examples of program music, which was extraordinary for this era. Each of the four concertos contains three movements: fast--slow--fast. Listen for the contrasts.
Domenico Scarlatti	Sonata for Harpsichord in G Minor (Kirkpatrick No. 30)	This one-movement harpsichord sonata is the famous "Cat's Fugue," which contains an unusual motive.
Johann Sebastian Bach	Organ Fugue in G Minor	This fugue is nicknamed the "Little Fugue." Listen to the subject and its harmonic structure.
George Frideric Handel	Hallelujah Chorus from the oratorio *Messiah*	The radiant chorus from this oratorio is the climax of the second of the three parts. Note the driving drum beats and sounding of the trumpets. Listen for the upper voices against the "Hallelujah"s of the lower voices. Notice the entwining and sustaining of the voices and the harmonic effects.

CLASSICAL

COMPOSER	WORK	WHAT TO HEAR
Joseph Haydn	Symphony No. 88 in G Major	The first movement begins with an opening theme presented by strings, then repeated by the full orchestra. Two more themes appear in this movement. The second movement has the oboes and cellos introduce a melody; notice how the accompaniment changes. The third movement is a minuet with brass and timpani added, and the fourth movement is a rondo.

Wolfgang Amadeus Mozart	*Eine kleine Nachtmusik*, Serenade for String Orchestra, K. 525	This four-movement serenade is a compact and beautifully balanced work for chamber ensemble. Listen for the "rocket theme" in the first movement.
Ludwig van Beethoven	Symphony No. 9 in D Minor, Op. 125	This is Beethoven's great choral symphony. The first three movements lead to the finale, when the soloists and chorus join the orchestra to present Schiller's ode. Notice how the composer builds up to the climax of the piece; listen for the transition to the finale as the wind instruments and drums soar into a riotous fanfare.
Franz Schubert	*Die schöne Müllerin* (The Pretty Maid of the Mill), Op. 25	This song cycle contains twenty lieder. Observe how the piano imitates a variety of sounds and how musical motifs are employed.

ROMANTIC

COMPOSER	WORK	WHAT TO HEAR
Felix Mendelssohn	Overture to *A Midsummer Night's Dream*, Op. 21	Composed while Mendelssohn was a teenager, this concert overture is based on Shakespeare's play. The themes represent various characters in the play. The overture begins with four sustained chords in the wind instruments; the same chords also end the piece.
Frédéric Chopin	Polonaise in A flat major "Heroic" (Op. 53)	This solo piano piece, based on a Polish dance rhythm, contains two sections. Listen for the introduction with its fast ascending chromatic notes, the modulations, and the ornamentation.
Robert Schumann	*Carnaval* (Carnival), Op. 9	A collection of twenty-one brief pieces that describe a masked ball. All but two of the pieces are based on some sequence of the four notes A–E-flat–C–B with variations on these four notes.

Clara Schumann	Piano Sonata in G Minor	Written as a gift for the composer's husband, this sonata is a difficult and complex work that indicates her own virtuosity as a pianist.
Johannes Brahms	*Academic Festival Overture*, Op. 80	This tribute to student life contains various German student songs celebrating the amusing side of the academic experience. This concert overture is full of humor and excitement. It is one of a pair of contrasting orchestral overtures (the other being the *Tragic Overture*, Op. 81). Listen for the blend of orchestral colors.
Hector Berlioz	*Symphonie fantastique* (Fantastic Symphony)	In this work Berlioz uses an idée fixe (fixed idea), employing a motif to represent a certain character or mood. The composer's alternate title for the symphony was "Episode in the Life of an Artist." The opening movement introduces the musician in love with a "perfect" woman. The second movement brings us to a ball, where the melody representing the woman haunts the composer. The third movement is set in a pastoral scene that evokes the memory of the woman he loves. Listen also for innovative effects such as the timpani's suggestion of thunder. The fourth movement includes the tolling of bells and the roll of muted drums, signifying that his love is not reciprocated. This idea continues in the last movement, which portrays the musician among witches and demons.
Franz Liszt	Piano Concerto No. 1 in E-flat Major	This concerto is in a single movement with four contrasting sections performed without a break between them. The same basic themes reappear in each section, altered but still identifiable; this is called cyclic form.

Richard Wagner	"Liebestod" (Love-Death) from *Tristan und Isolde*	This aria at the end of act 3 is sung by Isolde over the lifeless body of Tristan. The words blend into the music as her emotional agony becomes the focus.
Giuseppe Verdi	Grand March from *Aida*, act 2, scene 2	This is often known as the "Triumphal March." The trumpet fanfares open the work, and the orchestra responds. Verdi wove a ballet scene into the march—something opera audiences of the time demanded. The music sets the background for the scene taking place on the stage; notice the mood changes as the procession moves by and creates a grand spectacle.
Georges Bizet	"Habanera" from *Carmen*	This aria was derived from a Spanish folk song, has a tango rhythm, and portrays Carmen's character. Bizet never saw Spain; Carmen is an example of the popularity of exotic locales for operas.
Modest Musorgsky	*Pictures at an Exhibition*	Written as a group of pieces for piano, this suite is a musical description of an exhibition of paintings. The returning "Promenade" movement represents the visitor walking through the gallery while viewing the exhibit.
Mikhail Glinka	*Kamarinskaya*	This orchestral fantasy is based on two very different Russian folk songs: a wedding song and a dance. The piece is a superb model of the art of combining melodies. It ends with a surprise.
Peter Ilyich Tchaikovsky	*The Nutcracker Suite*, Op. 71a	Tchaikovsky chose eight numbers from his ballet to form *The Nutcracker Suite* for concerts. The work is known for its orchestral colors and advanced harmonies.

| Nikolai Rimsky-Korsakov | *Shéhérazade,* Op. 35 | This symphonic suite in four movements was based on tales from the *Arabian Nights,* but the work is certainly Russian, and the orchestration is brilliant. The composer used several themes to unify the four separate stories illustrated in the different movements: the powerful theme that opens the work is the voice of the Sultan demanding his stories, and the sinuous theme played by the violin is Shéhérazade as she begins weaving her tales. |

POST-ROMANTIC

COMPOSER	WORK	WHAT TO HEAR
Giacomo Puccini	"Viene la sera" (Evening is falling) from *Madama Butterfly*	This is a love duet between an American sailor and his young Japanese bride. Puccini set this opera in exotic Japan, and the melodies, rhythms, harmonies, and instrumentation of the opera reflect its location.
Richard Strauss	*Till Eulenspiegel's Merry Pranks,* Op. 28	This tone poem in rondo form is about a German folk hero and his antics. It begins with "once upon a time" in the strings. The themes symbolize Till in numerous situations, and their development portrays his comical tricks. The first theme that represents Till is played first by the solo horn and then by the oboes. The second theme is introduced by the clarinets. Listen for the syncopated rhythm suggesting the mischief of the prankster. The warning tones played by the trombones and horns point out his approaching fate.

Jean Sibelius	*Aallottaret* (The Oceanides or Sea Nymphs), Op. 73	This tone poem depicts, in an almost impressionist style, all of the characteristics of the sea. Listen to how the timpani is used and to the development of the themes.
Gustav Mahler	*Das Lied von der Erde* (The Song of the Earth)	Mahler used a collection of Chinese poems as an inspiration for this symphonic song cycle. It consists of six pieces: two larger outer movements separated by a group of shorter pieces. Listen for the pentatonic motifs and instruments that suggest the Far East.
Claude Debussy	Nocturne from *Fêtes* (Festivals)	In this nocturne the composer wished to convey the "vibrating, dancing rhythm of the atmosphere with sudden flashes of light." Listen for the harp and cymbal effects.
Maurice Ravel	*Boléro*	This is the composer's most spectacular work. Hear how the tension rises as the piece gradually builds to a crescendo.

MODERN

COMPOSER	WORK	WHAT TO HEAR
Arnold Schoenberg	String Quartet No. 2 in F-sharp Minor, Op. 10	The composer begins this work in F-sharp minor but quickly moves into uncertain harmonies. The second movement contains the tune of a German folk tune ("Ach, du lieber Augustin"). In the next two movements a soprano voice is added, and the music floats into atonality. The fourth movement has no key signature, yet the coda provides tonal resolution.

Charles Ives	*Three Places in New England* (Orchestral Set No. 1)	This work contains all of the elements the composer is known for: layered textures, hymns and marching tunes, American images, and chord clusters. Listen for the two marching bands in the second movement.
Ernest Bloch	*Schelomo (Solomon)* for cello and orchestra	The solo cello represents the voice of Solomon. Bloch wrote, "The complex voice of the orchestra is the voice of his age...his world...his experience." Written in a free rhapsody form with three large sections. Notice how the climax creates tension.
Béla Bartók	*Concerto for Orchestra*	This is a five-movement concerto. Note how the focus moves from one section of the orchestra to the other. A taste of Hungarian folk tunes opens four of the movements, and the last movement ends with a stirring brass coda.
Igor Stravinsky	"Sacrificial Dance" from the ballet *Le sacre du printemps* (The Rite of Spring)	This is from the ballet that caused a riot. As the dance progresses, the music increases in intensity. Notice the dissonance, the constantly shifting meters, and the complex rhythms.
Sergei Prokofiev	*Alexander Nevsky, cantata for mezzo-soprano, chorus and orchestra,* Op. 78	This choral cantata is an independent concert work based on the composer's score for the film Alexander Nevsky. The cantata contains seven harmonic scenes that portray the Russian epic. The listener can sense the heroic spirit of Prince Alexander Nevsky.
Darius Milhaud	*Saudades do Brazil* (Souvenirs of Brazil), Op. 67	Consisting of an overture and twelve short pieces, this piano series is a composite portrait of the dances of Brazil divided by the twelve separate sections of the city of Rio de Janeiro. Listen for the polytonal harmonies and the South American rhythms.

Paul Hindemith	*Mathis der Maler* (Matthias the Painter) Symphony	This symphony was actually composed before the opera was completed, but themes taken from the opera make up this work. The piece begins in G major but shifts to D-flat; these dissonant keys are played against each other through the symphony. In the finale, note the introduction for the lower strings, which is interrupted by the percussion.
Virgil Thomson	Suite from *The River*	The score, written for a documentary about the need for flood-control projects on the Mississippi River, includes several traditional American hymns and songs. Notice the harsh chords that depict floods and soil erosion, and the throbbing rhythms. Aaron Copland stated that this composition is "a lesson in how to treat Americana."
Benjamin Britten	*Four Sea Interludes*, an orchestral suite from *Peter Grimes*	This suite was created from the orchestral pieces that introduce the acts of the opera. The *Interludes* are tone poems portraying the moods of the sea. Listen for the orchestral effects that evoke the waves and winds.
George Gershwin	*An American in Paris*	This symphonic poem reflects the composer's impressions of his visit to Paris. It is program music that tells a specific story. The listener strolls down the avenues with the composer and experiences the sights and sounds of the city. Listen for the jazz elements and for the blues passage in the trumpet.
Aaron Copland	"Hoedown" from the ballet *Rodeo*	These dance tunes are traditional American square dances. Notice the introduction and how the composer uses the tunes and the rhythms to capture the mood and sounds of the American West in the 1800s.

Elliot Carter	String Quartet No. 1	This piece is filled with rhythmic innovations; in the last movement, every time a theme returns, it is played more rapidly than before. This counterpoint of themes becomes a polyrhythm, with some getting faster at one rate and others getting faster at a different rate. This allows for various layers of rhythms to occur at the same time but at different speeds.
Samuel Barber	*Adagio for Strings*	The work is composed in an arch form: a single lyrical subject beginning in the violins that is repeated, reversed, extended, and embellished by the other voices, rising in the high strings to its fortissimo climax before it fades into stillness.
Leonard Bernstein	*Divertimento for Orchestra*	This piece, which was composed for and dedicated to the Boston Symphony Orchestra on the occasion of its centenary, expresses Bernstein's fond memories of that city. The work is filled with suggestions of the music he heard in his youth. It is unified by a two-note theme: the notes B and C represent Boston and Centennial. The piece also contains two twelve-tone rows, fanfares, and nostalgia for that time.
Ned Rorem	*Evidence of Things Not Seen*	A tonal and lyrical cycle of thirty-six songs set to the poetry of twenty-four poets. Scored for four voices and piano, the work portrays a person's life cycle. The composer divided the songs into three sections: "Beginnings," "Middles," and "Ends." Notice how the songs connect to each other and the complex rhythms.

CONTEMPORARY

COMPOSER	WORK	WHAT TO HEAR
John Cage	*HPSCHD*	This piece calls for seven harpsichordists, various other performers, and fifty-one tapes, as well as multiple films, slides, and light shows. It was composed using chance procedures.
Steve Reich	*Different Trains*	The three movements are labeled "America—Before the War," "Europe—During the War," and "After the War" and are played without pause. This work is for string quartet and prerecorded tape. As each theme in the piece is introduced, the spoken phrase from which it was derived is heard. Listen for the strings imitating the speech melody.
Philip Glass	Symphony No. 5	Using an orchestra, five singers, and multiple choruses, this choral symphony presents the scriptures of many religions in twelve movements. Each movement is a comment on a phase of life. Listen for the unusual combinations, modulations, and changes in rhythmic patterns.

Bibliography

Beethoven, Ludwig van. 1972. *Beethoven's Letters*. With explanatory notes by A. C. Kalischer. Selected and edited by A. Eaglefield-Hull. Translated by J. S. Shedlock. New York: Dover.

Bernstein, Leonard. 1959. *The Joy of Music*. New York: Simon and Schuster.

Burney, Charles. 1957. *A General History of Music*. New York: Dover.

Cole, Richard. 1996–2009. *Virginia Tech Multimedia Music Dictionary*. Virginia Tech Department of Music. http://www.music.vt.edu/musicdictionary/.

Copland, Aaron. 1957. *What to Listen For in Music*. New York: McGraw-Hill.

Erman, Adolf. 1971. *Life in Ancient Egypt*. Translated by H. M. Tirard. New York: Dover.

Ewen, David. 1961. *The New Book of Modern Composers*. 3rd ed. New York: Alfred A. Knopf.

Forney, Kristine, and Joseph Machlis. 2007. *The Enjoyment of Music: An Introduction to Perceptive Listening*. 10th ed. New York: W. W. Norton.

Del Mar, Norman. 1983. *Anatomy of the Orchestra*. Berkeley: University of California Press.

Grout, Donald Jay. 1973. *A History of Western Music*. New York: W. W. Norton.

———. 1988. *A Short History of Opera*. 3rd ed. New York: Columbia University Press.

Heyman, Barbara B. 1992. *Samuel Barber: The Composer and His Music*. New York: Oxford University Press.

Hindemith, Paul. 1961. *A Composer's World: Horizons and Limitations*. Garden City, NY: Doubleday.

Idelsohn, Abraham Zebi. 1992. *Jewish Music: Its Historical Development*. New York: Dover.

Kennedy, Michael, ed. 1996. *The Concise Oxford Dictionary of Music*. 4th ed. London: Oxford University Press.

Library of Congress. Prints and Photographs Online. http://www.loc.gov/rr/print/catalog.html.

Marcus, Scott. 2006. *Music in Egypt: Experiencing Music, Expressing Culture*. New York: Oxford University Press.

McGrain, Mark. 1990. *Music Notation: Theory and Technique for Music Notation*. Boston: Berklee Press.

Musgrave, Michael. 1996. *Brahms: A German Requiem*. Cambridge: Cambridge University Press.

Parker, Roger. 1996. *The Oxford History of Opera*. New York: Oxford University Press.

Peyser, Joan. 1971. *The New Music: The Sense behind the Sound*. New York: Delacorte Press.

Sachs, Curt. 2006. *The History of Musical Instruments*. New York: Dover.

Sadie, Stanley, ed. 2008–9. *Dolmetsch Online Music Dictionary*. Dolmetsch Musical Instruments. http://www.dolmetsch.com/musictheorydefs.htm.

Sadie, Stanley, ed. 1980. *The New Grove Dictionary of Music and Musicians*. London: Macmillan.

Sadie, Stanley, and Alison Latham. 1994. *The Grove Concise Dictionary of Music*. London: Macmillan.

Schmeling, Paul. 2005. *Berklee Music Theory Book 1*. Boston: Berklee Press.

Schoenberg, Arnold. 1975. *Style and Idea: Selected Writings of Arnold Schoenberg*. Edited by Leo Stein. Translated by Leo Black. New York: St. Martin's Press.

Schwartz, Elliot, Barney Childs, and James Fox. 1998. *Contemporary Composers on Contemporary Music*. New York: Da Capo Press.

Swafford, Jan. 1998. *Charles Ives: A Life with Music*. New York: W. W. Norton.

Thomson, Virgil. 1981. *A Virgil Thomson Reader*. Boston: Houghton Mifflin.

Wade-Mathews, Max. 2001. *The History of Musical Instruments and Music-Making: A Complete History of Musical Forms and the Orchestra*. London: Southwater.

Whittall, Arnold. 1999. *Musical Composition in the Twentieth Century*. New York: Oxford University Press.

Wigoder, Geoffrey. 1989. *The Encyclopedia of Judaism*. New York: Macmillan.

Index

Illustration Credits

P. 3: Photo by Marie-Lan Nguyen; p. 5: © Sybille Yates/Dreamstime.com; p. 7: © Noah Armonn/Dreamstime.com; p. 10: © Nikolaev/Dreamstime.com; p. 11: © Ben Green/Dreamstime.com; p. 55: © James Steidl/Dreamstime.com; p. 56: IMSLP/Petrucci Music Library; p. 57: © James Steidl/Dreamstime.com; p. 61: Graphic by Susan Silberman using Inspiration software; p. 65: © James Steidl/Dreamstime.com; p. 66 (top): © Jessica Tugas/Dreamstime.com; p. 66 (bottom): Photo by Nick Michael; p. 67: © James Steidl/Dreamstime.com; p. 68: United States Naval Academy; p. 69: © Orlando Florin Rosu/Dreamstime.com; p. 72: © Isabel Poulin/Dreamstime.com; p. 74: Library of Congress, Work Projects Administration Poster Collection; p. 79: © Dario Rota/Dreamstime.com; p. 85: Photo by Håkan Svensson; p. 104: Painting (1910) by Georges Braque; p. 111: Anonymous copy of painting (ca. 1640) by Bernardo Strozzi; p. 113: © Matteo Malavasi/Dreamstime.com; p. 114 (top): Engraving by Jean-Louis Roullet; p. 114 (bottom): Painting after John Closterman; p. 115: Engraving (1725) by François Morellon de la Cave; p. 117: Painting (1748) by Elias Gottlob Haussmann, courtesy of William H. Scheide (Princeton, New Jersey); p. 118: Engraving after painting (ca. 1729) by Balthasar Denner, from *The Musical Times*, December 14, 1893; p. 123: Painting (1792) by Thomas Hardy; p. 125: Painting (1819) by Barbara Krafft; p. 128: Painting (1820) by Joseph Karl Stieler; p. 132: Painting (1875) by Wilhelm August Rieder; p. 136: Project Gutenberg; p. 137: Engraving (1845) by August Prinzhofer; p. 138: Painting (1839) by James Warren Childe; p. 144: Photo (1849) attributed to Louis-Auguste Bisson; p. 146: Photo (1858) by Franz Hanfstaengl; p. 148: Photo (1871) by Franz Hanfstaengl; p. 153: Painting (1886) by Giovanni Boldini; p. 157: Photo (1889) by C. Brasch; p. 163 (right): Painting (1891) by Eilif Peterssen; p. 167: Painting (1893) by Nikolai Kuznetsov; p. 174: Photo from *Modern Music and Musicians*, Louis C. Elson, ed. (New York: University Society, 1918); p. 176: Photo (1892) by Leonhard Berlin-Bieber; p. 178: Photo from *What We Hear in Music*, Anne S. Faulkner (Camden, NJ: Victor Talking Machine Co., 1913); p. 180: Photo (ca. 1908) by Félix Nadar; p. 186: Photo (ca. 1948) by Florence Homolka; p. 194: Library of Congress Prints and Photographs Division, George Grantham Bain Collection; p. 203: Photo courtesy of Don Campbell, nadiaboulanger.org; p. 204: Photo courtesy of Don Campbell, nadiaboulanger.org; p. 205: Library of Congress Prints and Photographs Division, George Grantham Bain Collection; p. 206: Library of Congress, Office of War Information Collection; p. 212: Photo by Carl Van Vechten, Library of Congress Prints and Photographs Division, Carl Van Vechten Collection; p. 215: Library of Congress; p. 217: Photo from *The Musical Languages of Elliott Carter*, Charles Rosen (Washington, DC: Music Division, Research Services, Library of Congress, 1984); p. 219: Photo by Carl Van Vechten, Library of Congress Prints and Photographs Division, Carl Van Vechten Collection; p. 221: Photo by Al Ravenna, Library of Congress, New York World-Telegram & Sun Collection; p. 239: Photo by Victor Kraft, Library of Congress, Music Division, Aaron Copland Collection; p. 241: Photo by Nora Farrell, courtesy of William Duckworth.